Alain Robbe-Grillet

the film career of Alain ROBBE-GRILLET

A
Reference
Publication
in
Film

Ronald Gottesman
Editor

the film career of Alain ROBBE-GRILLET

WILLIAM F. VAN WERT

G.K.HALL &CO.
70 LINCOLN STREET, BOSTON, MASS.

Library of Congress Cataloging in Publication Data
Van Wert, William F
The film career of Alain Robbe-Grillet.

(A Reference publication in film)
Bibliography: p.
Includes index.
1. Robbe-Grillet, Alain, 1922- I. Title.
II. Series.
PN1998.A3R5928 791.43'0924 [B] 77-21656
ISBN 0-8161-7992-1

This publication is printed on permanent/durable acid-free paper
MANUFACTURED IN THE UNITED STATES OF AMERICA

Contents

Introduction

Alain Robbe-Grillet became a novelist in 1953 (Les Gommes/The Erasers), a filmmaker in 1963 (L'Immortelle/The Immortal One) and a painter in 1973. Despite the cyclical coincidence in those conversions, he is not a "dabbler" in the arts. He approaches his art, whatever the form it takes, with a kind of medieval, monastic intensity uncommon in today's jet-age marketplace of fads, "isms," and schisms; yet, he has found resistance to everything he has done. He notes that critics dismissed his novels when they first appeared as the inane, awkward and endless descriptions of an agricultural engineer, just as they dismissed his early films as the ignorant attempts of a novelist gone astray. And when he decides to exhibit his paintings, these same critics will perhaps look back with nostalgia upon his films. Robbe-Grillet persists. He keeps exploring new forms, both within a given medium and across media, confident that critical and public acceptance will catch up to him.

The jet-age complies in strange ways. Acknowledgment comes from French President Giscard d'Estaing: he announces that he will call his book L'Eden et après (Eden and After), the title of a Robbe-Grillet film. Acknowledgment comes from Saul Bellow, who singles out Robbe-Grillet for attack in his acceptance speech (December 12, 1976) for the Nobel Prize. Acknowledgment comes from Alain Resnais and Jean-Luc Godard, his two film mentors, who speak of the films he has directed. But for Robbe-Grillet, the most rewarding acknowledgment comes from the new generation of film critics like François Jost and Dominique Chateau, a generation that knew Robbe-Grillet first by his films, not his novels.

This last distinction is crucial, for Robbe-Grillet wants to be considered as a complete artist within a medium. He is known internationally as a novelist. He wants to be considered as a filmmaker as well, not as a hybrid engineer-novelist-filmmaker-editor-painter. There are only two book-length studies of Robbe-Grillet as a filmmaker: André Gardies' Alain Robbe-Grillet (Paris: Seghers, 1972) and Fernando Trebbi's La Trasparenza Cinematografica: Saggio su Alain Robbe-Grillet (Bologna: Casa Patron, 1973). The present work will be the third, the first in English.

Thus, the scope of my study is pre-defined. I am dealing with Robbe-Grillet as a filmmaker, not as a novelist. There are three exceptions. First, I have chosen to treat L'Année dernière à Marienbad/Last Year at Marienbad (1961), which was scripted by Robbe-Grillet and directed by Resnais, as though it were Robbe-Grillet's film as much as Resnais', which is entirely in keeping with their original intention to co-sign the film equally, thus obliterating the traditional distinctions between director and screenwriter. The rationale behind this decision is fully explained in Section II. Second, I have included materials by and about Robbe-Grillet which deal with the ciné-roman (film-novel), which is essentially a writing/publishing activity, but which is essential to understanding Robbe-Grillet's film activity. Finally, I have included a few articles in Section IV which deal with the cinematographic techniques in Robbe-Grillet's novels or which compare one or more of his novels with one or more of his films. My reasons for including them were again that they illuminated Robbe-Grillet's film activity in some way.

I would like to discuss briefly the various sections of my book, beginning with Section III, in order to explain to the reader my approach to each section, my research and organization methods, the limitations of the research and organization, and any instructions for using each section in the most fruitful manner.

Section III (The Films: Synopsis, Credits and Notes) was an immediate problem. For almost any other director, a synopsis is both feasible and instructive; with Robbe-Grillet, the traditional synopsis is less than helpful. It may even be engimatic or misleading. Robbe-Grillet does not conceive of film in terms of plot or story or "what happens"; instead, he thinks in terms of "how" it happens. He thinks in terms of themes which generate story and structures interacting with themes. When I discussed this section with him, he pointed out that the synopsis was only one of many possible approaches to his films. He suggested that I include a list of the basic themes/myths and basic structures which would help the prospective reader of my study and viewer of his films. I have done so. Furthermore, wherever possible, I have paraphrased Robbe-Grillet's personal synopsis of a given film. Thus, the reader will note that with the more recent films there is less emphasis on the anecdotal quality of a film and more reliance on the theme/structure interplay.

Section IV (Writings about Robbe-Grillet) represents a thorough search of texts in English, French and Italian both by and about Robbe-Grillet, gathered from the Lincoln Center Library for the Performing Arts in New York, the Paley Library at Temple University and the Annenberg School of Communications Library at the University of Pennsylvania. I found the following bibliographies especially helpful: Ona D. Besses' "A Bibliographic Essay on Alain Robbe-Grillet" (Bulletin of Bibliography and Magazine Notes, 26, 2:52-59 (April-June 1969); 26, 3:87-88 (July-September 1969)); Michel Rybalka's "Alain Robbe-Grillet: A Bibliography" (West Coast Review, 3, 2:31-38

(Fall 1968)); Dale Watson Fraizer's Alain Robbe-Grillet: An Annotated Bibliography of Critical Studies, 1953-1972 (Metuchen: The Scarecrow Press, 1973); the French VII and French XX bibliographies; Fred Silva's Film/Literature Index; and secondary bibliographies compiled by Bernard Pingaud and René Prédal. As much as from these, I received assistance from Robbe-Grillet, especially on articles too recent to have appeared in any bibliography.

I have appended a list of major sources to the end of this discussion, which should prove useful to the reader, for, when I was unable to gather complete bibliographical data, I listed the source of the item in parentheses at the end of the entry.

These entries in Section IV cover the period from 1958 to 1976, beginning with a special issue of La Revue des Lettres Modernes devoted to the inter-relationships between film and the novel and ending with the most recent articles devoted to Robbe-Grillet's Le Jeu avec le feu/Playing With Fire (1975). My guiding principle throughout this section was completeness, even at the expense of admitting my limitations; thus, ironically, I have included entries with incomplete bibliographical data for the sake of completeness. The length of the annotations was also governed by completeness. I have minimized evaluative judgments, except in the most blatant cases (whether good or bad), in order to provide the reader with something more than just an annotation. My assumptions were the following: my audience would be a predominantly English-speaking audience, so I have paraphrased a French author's arguments rather than reproduce them in quotes; and my audience would have great difficulty obtaining some of these items (I did), so I have annotated as though my annotations were the only means for my reader of knowing a particular author's style, theories and opinions. Admitting this, I am aware that the length of an annotation is in itself a value judgment.

I should forewarn the reader that there is no place within a given annotation to define or fully explain difficult concepts like ciné-roman, film punctuation, generative topology and game structures. If the reader is confused by such terms within an annotation, I would urge that he/she read or re-read Section II (Critical Survey of Oeuvre), in which, hopefully, all such confusion will be cleared up.

In Section V (Performances and Other Film-related Activity), I have listed Robbe-Grillet's fiction, his book-length critical writings and his published ciné-romans. I have not listed his many short articles on film nor his many interviews; the reader will find these in Section IV. I have, however, listed his unfinished books on film and his uncompleted screenplays in this section. I have also listed and annotated the film adaptations of Robbe-Grillet's novels in this section and not elsewhere.

Section VI (Archival Sources) is understandably short and perhaps the least useful section of the book. It was somewhat frustrating for me to uncover private collections, for example, only to find that the owners were not willing to have their names in print. I can only say that the ultimate source for anyone wishing to do research on Robbe-Grillet is Robbe-Grillet himself. He has been extremely prompt and thorough in answering all my letters and questionnaires. Others who have written him with a serious study in mind have reported the same willingness to cooperate on his part. I have given his address in Section VI.

Section VII (Film Distributors) is arranged by film, chronologically, and not by alphabetical listing of the various distributors, so that the reader can find all of the distributors of a given film in one place. I have given the most current rental rates for these films in this country. Rates, as well as the availability of the films, are of course, flexible and subject to change. These rates are for 16-millimeter prints for unpublicized educational use with no admission charged and for no more than a single screening. Thus, if one wishes to rent these films with any deviations from the above conditions, he/she should write well in advance of the desired screening date or, better still, apply and confirm booking by telephone.

I should also note that the cooperation of the distributors in terms of sharing distribution information or allowing on-the-spot previews of the films for study purposes is both seasonal and whimsical. A detailed outline of one's study project, a letter from one's publisher (for a book or an article) or a letter from Robbe-Grillet himself would be helpful. Even with all three, there are no guarantees. This point is perhaps more important than any other made in this book. All of Robbe-Grillet's color films have very precarious distribution circumstances, so that even knowing who the distributor is may not guarantee one's being able to rent one of those films. As for the earlier black-and-white films, the distributors are more reliable, but the circumstances are not. A spokesperson for Grove Press (who formerly distributed *L'Immortelle* and *L'Homme qui ment*) told me confidentially by telephone that they made no money on Robbe-Grillet's films, that I was one of the few people in the country to rent them with any frequency, and that they would not be seeking distribution of any other Robbe-Grillet films. Recently, the entire Grove Press film collection became the property of Films Incorporated.

Section VIII (Index) provides the reader with a film title index for Sections III-VII and an author index to Section IV. The numbers in the index correspond to the numbers assigned consecutively throughout the work. I have used my own judgment in determining whether or not a number should be assigned in the index. For example, if the author of an article on *L'Eden et après* has simply mentioned *L'Immortelle* in passing, I have not listed the entry number for that article in the index under L'Immortelle. I have, however, mentioned the reference to L'Immortelle in my annotation of the article in Section IV. Finally, the entry numbers in the index under Robbe-Grillet's name refer only to books, parts of books or articles authored wholly or in part by Robbe-Grillet and to published interviews with him, in which case the same entry number is cross-listed under the interviewer's name, since the interview in question is listed in Section IV under the interviewer's name and not under Robbe-Grillet's name.

Finally, I would like to acknowledge the many people who assisted and participated in this book. I can single out only a few, and I beg forgiveness of the rest. Deep thanks, then, to the following: Ron Gottesman, the Editor of the series, for giving me the chance to do the book in the first place and for his patience throughout several deadline extensions; Dale Watson Fraizer, for having done the annotated bibliography of Robbe-Grillet's fiction and for her helpful suggestions concerning library sources; Angela Martin at the British Film Institute, for her assistance; Claudine Guilmain, for sending me articles, despite her objections to Robbe-Grillet on feminist grounds; Bruce Morrissette, for sending me articles and offering helpful suggestions; Fred Silva, for sending me listings of recent Robbe-Grillet criticism; Jayne Kribbs, for editorial and technical assistance; all of the people who work on the third floor at the Lincoln Center Library for the Performing Arts, for their efficiency and patience throughout my many merciless raids on their book, journal, clippings, review, microfilm and xerox facilities; Alain Robbe-Grillet, who had been an acquaintance since my doctoral dissertation begun in 1973 and who has become a personal friend in the process of this book, for his encouragement, his assistance and, most of all, his trust; Johanna, my wife, for her love and support, her patience in allowing me to complete the book and her impatience during those moments when it seemed that the book would never get finished; and Ian, our infant son, for providing me with distractions from the book and a necessary perspective on the book; throwing my neatly arranged stacks of index cards on the floor was just as much fun for him as throwing toys, and eating my cards was apparently as enjoyable for him as eating bananas and yogurt.

SOURCES

The following is a source list for unconsulted works. Where applicable, years consulted are noted as well as the entry number, if the work appears in the Annotated Guide. The sources are arranged alphabetically.

Besses, Ona D. "A Bibliographic Essay on Alain Robbe-Grillet." Bulletin of Bibliography and Magazine Notes, 26, No. 2 (April-June 1969), 52-59; 26, No. 3 (July-September 1969), 87-88. (#377)

British Film Institute (BFI) Library References. London: 81 Dean Street.

Film/Literature Index (1973-1975). Editors: Vincent Aceto, Jane Graves, Fred Silva. (Self-published?) Box 532DD SUNY-A, 1400 Washington Avenue, Albany, New York, 12222.

Fraizer, Dale Watson. Alain Robbe-Grillet: An Annotated Bibliography of Critical Studies, 1953-1972. Metuchen, New Jersey: The Scarecrow Press, 1973. (#475)

French VII (later French XX) Bibliography: Critical and Biographical References for the Study of Contemporary French Literature (1962-1976).

Gardies, André. Alain Robbe-Grillet. Paris: Seghers (Cinéastes d'aujourd'hui), 1971. (#440)

Heath, Stephen. "Alain Robbe-Grillet," in his The Nouveau Roman: A Study in the Practice of Writing. London: Elek; Philadelphia: Temple University Press, 1972. (#454)

Klapp, Otto. Bibliographie der Französischen Literatur-Wissenschaft (1962-1971).

Morrissette, Bruce. Personal correspondence.

Pingaud, Bernard. Alain Resnais, special issue of Premier Plan, No. 18 (Autumn 1961), p. 93. (#65)

Prédal, René. Alain Resnais, special issue of Etudes Cinématographiques, Nos. 64-68 (1968). (#362)

Robbe-Grillet, Alain. Personal correspondence.

Rybalka, Michel. "Alain Robbe-Grillet: A Bibliography." West Coast Review, 3, No. 2 (Fall 1968), 31-38. (#365)

Schuster, Mel. Motion Picture Directors: A Bibliography of Magazine and Periodical Articles, 1900-1972. Metuchen, New Jersey: The Scarecrow Press, 1973, p. 324.

Sturdza, Paltin. "The Structure of Actants in Robbe-Grillet's L'Immortelle." Language Quarterly, 12, Nos. 3-4 (Spring-Summer 1974), 26-28. (#534)

Zeitschrift für Romanische Philologie Bibliographie (later Romanische Bibliographie) (1961-1964).

Biographical Background

Alain Robbe-Grillet was born in Brest on August 18, 1922. He studied in Paris and became an agricultural engineer. He was placed in charge of the "mission" at the Institut National des Statistiques (National Bureau of Statistics) in 1949 where he devoted himself to biological research. In 1950 and 1951 he worked at the Institut des Fruits et Agrumes Coloniaux, through which he made several business trips to Morocco, Guinea, Martinique and Guadeloupe, as well as various study trips to Turkey, Roumania, Latin America and Yugoslavia.

This "first career" was important for several reasons. It gave him the technical expertise and the "scientific" style for the very detailed, "objective" descriptions of objects and locales, which would become a trademark of his fiction (the elaborate descriptions of the banana plantations in La Jalousie, for example). It set the pattern for incessant world travel, which has continued ever since. The travel experience is important for two reasons: first, it provided Robbe-Grillet with the foreign, often exotic settings of both his novels and films (the Hong Kong of La Maison de Rendez-vous, the New York of Projet pour une révolution à New York, the Djerba of L'Eden et après), although those settings are manifestly the product of Robbe-Grillet's fictive and fertile imagination and not of his memories of the actual places. Robbe-Grillet is a voyager in the manner of Roussel: his trips involve parallel universes. For every object perceived in a real Hong Kong, there is a parallel object conceived in Robbe-Grillet's imagination. Second, this travel experience would determine Robbe-Grillet's unique form of financing his films through co-productions. None of his films have been Franco-American co-productions, for example. He has filmed on location in Turkey, Belgium, Czechoslovakia and Tunisia and gotten production financing from concerns in those various countries by using film crews from those countries.

Finally, this first career had a profound impact on his personal life. He met his wife Catherine in Turkey. She has since had roles in almost all of his films as well as producing the still photographs for press release for all of his films.

In 1953, his first novel Les Gommes (The Erasers) was published by the Editions de Minuit, which began a long relationship with Minuit, culminating in Robbe-Grillet's becoming literary editor for them. It also began a long-standing friendship between Robbe-Grillet and Jerome Lindon, who would act in some of Robbe-Grillet's films. Editions de Minuit not only enabled Robbe-Grillet to publish his original film outlines/descriptions in Minuit, the journal of the firm; it also allowed him to publish his finished ciné-romans (film-novels). In addition, Editions de Minuit became the eventual "home" of the nouveau roman (new novel) in France by publishing Robbe-Grillet, Nathalie Sarraute, Claude Simon, Robert Pinget and Samuel Beckett, among others. In fact, these novelists have sometimes been referred to as the "midnight" (translation of "minuit") novelists.

Critical reaction to Robbe-Grillet's first novel was immediate and heated. There were those who accused Robbe-Grillet of chosisme or object-mania, of reifying the universe, a fictional universe devoid of character, feelings and emotions. There were others who maintained that Robbe-Grillet was more subjective than objective, since his elaborate descriptions of things could ultimately be traced to the observations and imaginations of deranged narrators with sexual obsessions and violent urges. Whatever the critical camp, Robbe-Grillet benefitted from the analyses of the most fertile group of critics France has ever known: Roland Barthes, Philippe Sollers, Gérard Genette, Bernard Pingaud, Robert Benayoun, Jacques Brunius, Claude Ollier.

Robbe-Grillet was prolific in the second half-decade of the 1950's, producing Le Voyeur (The Voyeur) in 1955, La Jalousie (Jealousy) in 1957 and Dans le labyrinthe (In the Labyrinth) in 1959. Each of these novels was greeted with a flurry of critical articles, pro and con, which helped to establish Robbe-Grillet as the leading practitioner of the nouveau roman or new novel. In 1958, while sick in a hospital bed in Martinique, Robbe-Grillet decided to break completely with agriculture and devote himself to literature.

In 1960 Pierre Corau and Raymond Froment suggested that Robbe-Grillet and Alain Resnais collaborate on a film. Robbe-Grillet had seen in Resnais' Hiroshima mon amour (1959) the same concerns he had in his fiction: the exaggerated acting, gestures and dialogue, more theatrical than realistic; a firm and studied composition, with a certain rigid quality about it; a sense of ritual; and an attempt to construct time and space in purely mental terms (dreams, memories, affective life), without the usual concerns for causality or chronology in the narrative. For his part, Resnais, upon reading some of Robbe-Grillet's novels, remarked that the universe within them was already very familiar to him. The two also shared similar beliefs about what constituted a literary cinema, which involved a collaboration between novelist and filmmaker in transposing literary techniques, not plots, to the screen.

The two met. There was some discussion about adapting Robbe-Grillet's La Jalousie. The idea was rejected, because neither of them wanted to "re-do" an already published novel. Robbe-Grillet's script for what would eventually become L'Immortelle was also discussed but eventually rejected. They decided upon L'Année dernière à Marienbad (Last Year at Marienbad), and the 1961 film was an immediate and scandalous success both in France and abroad and has since become regarded as the definitive example of so-called "left-bank" filmmaking. The film received various prizes, including the Gold Lion of St. Mark at the Venice Film Festival and the Méliès Prize in France.

If Dans le labyrinthe represents a kind of endgame or limit to the cinematographic novel and L'Année dernière à Marienbad represents a logical extension of Robbe-Grillet's fictional concerns as well as Resnais' preoccupation with a literary cinema begun with his collaboration with Marguerite Duras on Hiroshima mon amour, then Instantanés (Snapshots), a collection of short stories published in 1962, represents a kind of reversal of Dans le labyrinthe as well as a reconciliation between Robbe-Grillet's last novel and first film. Ironically, less has been written about Instantanés than about anything else Robbe-Grillet has written.

Ten years after the publication of his first novel, Robbe-Grillet completed his first film, L'Immortelle (The Immortal One) (1963). The film had been scripted prior to his writing L'Année dernière à Marienbad for Resnais, and, while Resnais was shooting his film in and around Munich, Robbe-Grillet was already in Turkey at work on L'Immortelle. Critical reaction to the film was mixed but predominantly negative. Jacques Doniol-Valcroze, who played the male lead in the film and who was one of the editors at Cahiers du Cinéma, was one of the few to praise the film. Noel Burch dismissed the film, only to recant some years later, calling the film a masterpiece. Most critics compared the film with Marienbad, to the credit of Resnais and to the detriment of Robbe-Grillet. Nevertheless, the film won the Louis Delluc Prize for 1963.

Just as he had done for Marienbad in 1961, Robbe-Grillet published the ciné-roman for L'Immortelle, with a theoretical introduction, a detailed script and selected illustrations, in 1963.

Robbe-Grillet also published in 1963 his first book-length collection of critical essays, entitled Pour un nouveau roman (Essays for a New Novel), in which he attacked nineteenth-century notions about the novel, as exemplified by Balzac. He also attacked the Existentialists, most notably the use made of fiction by Sartre and Camus. In terms of style, he attacked the omniscient narrator, anthropomorphic metaphors and figurative language that produced a false subjectivity, since it could not be visualized. He praised such writers as Raymond Roussel, Joe Bousquet, Samuel Beckett and Robert Pinget. In the chapter entitled "Temps et description dans le récit d'aujourd'hui," he discussed his film activity.

At this point (1963) there is a complete break with both his earlier fiction and his previous films. His novel La Maison de Rendez-vous (1965) has the same circular patterns, geometric composition, doubling of character, fixed poses of animate beings and animation of inanimate objects and beings found in his earlier fiction, but, for the first time, the locale (Hong Kong) has a real-life referent. For the first time, the sexuality is overt. And, for the first time, the mad king figure (Boris) and the anarchist artist figure (Manneret--Manet? Man Ray?) appear.

Robbe-Grillet made Trans-Europ-Express in 1966. The film reflected a shift in influence, from that of Resnais, which had carried over to L'Immortelle, to that of Jean-Luc Godard. The film was a parody of the detective thriller, deliberately banalized by exaggerated action, contradictory plot shifts, illogical jumps from the "story" to the filmmakers fabricating the story on the same train that the "story" takes for its vehicle. Like Godard, Robbe-Grillet employed numerous endistancing effects, so that the audience could not identify with either the characters or the story. The film was more explicitly graphic than L'Immortelle, and a pornography trial was instigated against Robbe-Grillet and the film in Italy. That trial and a second trial against Glissements progressifs du plaisir, also in Italy, confirmed Robbe-Grillet in his attack on societal discourse and the pop-art presentation of sexuality.

In 1968 Robbe-Grillet made what was to be his last black-and-white film, L'Homme qui ment (The Man Who Lies). Already complex in the visualization of mental images, dreams, lies and imagined scenes, the film was also one of the most sophisticated films ever made in terms of its figurative use of natural and found sounds. It also established Robbe-Grillet and his collaborators: Bob Wade, his editor; Michel Fano, his musical composer and sound designer.

After one of many trips to New York City, a mythical city for Robbe-Grillet, he published Projet pour une révolution à New York (Project for a Revolution in New York) in 1970. Even more so than La Maison de rendez-vous, Project revealed Robbe-Grillet's commitment to a fictional universe, to generative structures and to a use of language more Rousselian than he had ever done before.

In 1970 he also wrote the Preface for La Nouvelle Justine in the Complete Works edition of the Marquis de Sade (J. J. Pauvert), whom Robbe-Grillet had always greatly admired.

In 1971 he made L'Eden et après (Eden and After), his first color film and the first in which the protagonist is a woman. Commissioned by L'O.R.T.F. (French Television), he also made N a pris les Des (N Took the Dice) from the out-takes of L'Eden et après. The film was never shown.

In 1971 he began his collaboration with David Hamilton, the photographer. This collaboration produced Rêves de jeunes filles (1971), Autres rêves de jeunes filles (1972), to become Les Demoiselles (1973). This collaboration produced a heightened eroticism/parody of eroticism in Robbe-Grillet's own fiction and films and, specifically, a fascination with nubile young women in lesbian relationships, a theme he had first explored in L'Homme qui ment. Even with his collaborators, there is a parallel universe. David Hamilton was to become a fictional character in Robbe-Grillet's novel Topologie d'une cité fantôme (1976).

The period from 1974 to the present has been very fertile for Robbe-Grillet. He published Glissements progressifs du plaisir (1974), his first ciné-roman since L'Immortelle, to coincide with the film of the same title. The ciné-roman for the film revealed a theoretical opposition to Lévi-Strauss, a knowledge of Saussure and an interest in structuralist principles. The film Glissements was Robbe-Grillet's most explicitly sexual (which explains the pornography trial instigated against the film in Italy) and his most complex structurally (which explains the commercial failure of the film).

In 1975 he taught a course on film at New York University. His intention was to make a film communally with his students. The film was never made. He also wanted to finish writing Avant L'Eden: Théorie des images génératrices, which was intended to explore the structural complexities of generative images in film that Robbe-Grillet had begun in L'Eden et après and which also would do for film what Pour un nouveau roman had done for literature. The book was never completed.

Nevertheless, he was extremely prolific during this time. He made Le Jeu avec le feu (Playing With Fire) in 1975, a film which was at least as graphic as Glissements. It was also the most edited of all his films and the first of his color films to achieve the complexity of sound that he and Michel Fano had accomplished with The Man Who Lies. At the same time, he collaborated with Robert Rauschenberg on a book entitled Traces suspectes en surfaces (to go on exhibit at selected American museums in 1977), with original lithographs by Rauschenberg. This collaborative text was the outgrowth of Robbe-Grillet's admiration of Rauschenberg's work as well as his having taken up painting as a serious "hobby" in 1973.

In 1976 he also published two novels: Topologie d'une cité fantôme and La Belle Captive, with illustrations by René Magritte. He intends another collaborative work with Paul Delvaux for sometime in the near future.

In the fall of 1976 Robbe-Grillet toured several major American cities with L'Eden et après, the only one of his films without an American distributor.

He is currently back in France, at work on a new film entitled Piège à fourrure (Fur Trap) in which he intends to explore serialism in the cinema more fully than it has ever been treated before.

He currently writes his fiction and screenplays in a Paris apartment or at his Louis XIV chateau of Le Mesnil-au-Grain near Caen, from where he commutes to Paris to continue his duties at Editions de Minuit.

Critical Survey of Oeuvre

Alain Robbe-Grillet's first contribution to the cinema was in his development of a cinematographic novel. The use of cinematic devices was not invented by Robbe-Grillet for the novel. One can find examples of close-ups and dissolves in medieval romances. What was new with Robbe-Grillet was the use of such devices to formulate the *je-néant* or "absent I" point of view in novels like *La Jalousie* or *Dans le labyrinthe*. The absent I in Robbe-Grillet's fiction should not be confused with the so-called "camera eye" of European and American writers between the wars. As with Kafka's novels, Robbe-Grillet's fictional universe is built upon the denotative level of his imagery; his images never evaporate or give way to figurative language, to the quick turn of phrase, to words alone. They retain the solidity (the present-ness) of the film image, somewhat independently of the obsessive narrators from whose imaginations they spring. Thus, Robbe-Grillet's use of cinematic devices (close-up, pans, freeze-frames, lap dissolves, rack focus, match cutting, jump cutting) in his novels does not validate the "fiction" so much as it calls into question the creative vision behind that fiction. Whereas a writer like Dos Passos could use the "camera eye" to give the feeling of reportage or authenticity to his descriptions, Robbe-Grillet's cinematic devices, such as immobilizing a character or animating a tableau, reinforce the "artifice" of his fiction, driving the reader out from the work and toward the narration of the work: in other words, away from meaning in a functional sense and toward structures in a plastic sense.

Whereas with other writers such a rapprochement between film and literature would naturally lead to film adaptations of the literary work, a literary work that many critics now see as "film scripts in disguise," with Robbe-Grillet such a rapprochement means not only the possibility of cinematographic novels but of a "literary" cinema as well. Using one medium as an adjective for the other is not to deny the specificity of each. Robbe-Grillet could never adapt one of his novels to film, for what interests him is not the transposition of works (plots) from one medium to the other, but rather the transposition of structures. Again, the emphasis is upon point of view, not upon the fiction itself. Robbe-Grillet has stated that he is more interested in the movement of his description than in the thing described, and sometimes the movement of the description obliterates the thing described. As René Magritte noted, an image is more like another image than it is like the object or person represented in the image.

With this interest in structures, Robbe-Grillet has revived and refined the ciné-roman (film-novel), from the abstract justifications of the cinema as an art form for which Louis Delluc first used the term and the popular serials in film-stills which accompanied many of the silent films to the unique place the ciné-roman has come to occupy in France today. In this latter application, the ciné-roman serves many functions. Robbe-Grillet emphasizes that the ciné-roman, the publication of the script in conjunction with the making of the film, is to the resultant film what the libretto is to the opera: it serves (1) as a memory-aid for those who have seen the film or (2) as a form of meditation, reflection or close analysis for those for whom the images and sounds of the film have gone by too quickly to assimilate. Practically speaking, the ciné-roman gave the film experience a solidity comparable to that of the novel. The viewer no longer was at the mercy of the film distributor. It was possible to "preserve" the film in one's experience, to study the organization of the film in this inexpensive, portable book-format. The ciné-roman allowed critics the opportunity to abandon their notes taken hastily in the dark for working conditions comparable to those of their colleagues in literature or the social sciences.

The ciné-roman offered a means of approaching the film as well for those who had not seen the film and wanted to "prepare" themselves before seeing it. It afforded a means of approaching the film for those who would have no reasonable chance to see the film. Thus, someone in Aix-en-Provence could profitably "read" the film that would only play in Paris. Thus, someone in 1977 would not have to wait for a "retrospective" to be able to appreciate Last Year at Marienbad or L'Immortelle.

Ordinarily, the screenwriter has little control over the script once the director has begun filming; likewise, the director has little control (final cut privileges, distribution) over the film once it is finished. What is given to the public is dependent upon the economic necessities and moral whims of the producer and the distributor. The ciné-roman was a means of compensation for the irregularities in distribution, a means of retaining some degree of control over the work: control for the screenwriter from the director, control for both from the distributor. If Hiroshima mon amour (1959) was the film of Alain Resnais, the script still belonged to Marguerite Duras, with the publication of the ciné-roman. Resnais arbitrarily removed the rape scene from Last Year at Marienbad. It remains in the script. Robbe-Grillet, thus, retained "control" over the script, regardless of what Resnais chose to do with the film. And, had the producers or distributors decided to eliminate or re-cut some scenes in Hiroshima or Marienbad, the screenwriters and director of those films would still have been "protected" with the publication of the ciné-roman.

Resnais and Robbe-Grillet had originally intended to co-sign Last Year at Marienbad equally, thus obliterating the traditional hierarchical distinctions between scenarist and director. Yet, once filming began, Robbe-Grillet was already in Istanbul at work on L'Immortelle. Nevertheless, if their original intention could not be realized in the actual process of filming, it could be realized for the public, which now had the choice of buying the book or seeing the film or both. In addition, Robbe-Grillet used the introductions to the published ciné-romans for Marienbad and L'Immortelle to approach the public directly and in print, as opposed to the more indirect approach of the film in images, especially when that film was directed by someone else. Further, Robbe-Grillet used those ciné-romans as a critic as well as in the guise of creator, in terms of directing critics and audiences alike toward possible interpretations and authorial intentionality.

Is the ciné-roman, then, a mere memory-aid or subsidiary form, like the libretto for an opera? More than all the reasons exposed above, the ciné-roman was an invitation to the public to co-create the work, to begin to "read" films with the intensity of purpose and pluridimensionality of meaning that had previously separated literature from film. Still a mass art, film could be approached critically as well as emotionally. The audience was invited by Robbe-Grillet to perceive structures as well as meanings. The ciné-roman, then, was a necessary step toward initiating an "intellectual" cinema in France. Just as the directors of the New Wave proper (Godard, Truffaut, Rivette, Rohmer, Chabrol) drew upon their previous experiences as critics for Cahiers du Cinéma in their films, creating an encyclopedia of accolades to their favorite film directors of the past, so too the collaborators of Resnais (Robbe-Grillet, Duras, Jean Cayrol, Jorge Semprun) drew upon their literary and publishing activities in moving from their apprenticeship with Resnais to making films themselves. If Godard is right in affirming that allusions to Hitchcock or Howard Hawks or Samuel Fuller in his earlier films is a kind of re-education process (film history lessons) prior to his political films of the late 1960's and 1970's, then the ciné-romans of Robbe-Grillet can be seen equally as an education process, both allowing films like Marienbad and L'Immortelle to retain their structural complexities without the usual dilutions toward the common denominator of public taste and bridging the gap between such "intellectual" films and an otherwise baffled public.

A hybrid form, the ciné-roman risked becoming a form of literature, somewhat antagonistic to the film itself, as long as dialogue continuity was preserved intact, while the camera indications were given in short-hand. Bruce Morrissette pointed out the discrepancies between Robbe-Grillet's "neutral" style in the early ciné-romans, a style perhaps necessitated by the book-format, but a style which was absent in the films. As a result of this realization and because Robbe-Grillet found the actual filmmaking experience more effective with less scripting prior to the film and more improvisation during the shooting, he ceased publication of any of his films in *ciné-roman* form until *Glissements progressifs du plaisir* (1974), by which time it was clear that the form had undergone a radical facelift. In this latter *ciné-roman*, the synopsis for the film is noted as only one of many possible approaches to the film, perhaps the least fruitful. Robbe-Grillet's published *Glissements* also contained a detailed dialogue continuity and a montage record, both of which revealed Robbe-Grillet's structures, where the synopsis might only reveal meanings (or lack of meanings). Robbe-Grillet the critic is in equal evidence with the creator in *Glissements*. The margin notes added after filming and for the book "illuminate" the structures, as do the many references to "punctuations" and object-cuts. The more his films have abandoned traditional narrative devices or have relegated the anecdotal subject to the status of a pretext for structural operations, the more the *ciné-roman* has had to abandon prose for short-hand. The time it takes to read (study) a page of Robbe-Grillet's montage record is more similar to reading a page of mathematical theorems than it is to reading a page from a novel.

A hybrid form, the *ciné-roman* in its application by Marguerite Duras has come to signify the variable-work-of-art, a kind of *Gesamtkunstwerk* activity. The *ciné-roman* for *Destroy She Said* (1969) or *India Song* (1975) is simultaneously a novel, a play, a film. We might add: a poem, a libretto-opera, a sculpture. The variable-work-of-art in Duras has found its parallel in Robbe-Grillet with the notions of generative images and intertextuality. Robbe-Grillet's recent film and novelistic images do not send the reader or viewer referentially to their counterparts in everyday reality, but rather cross-referentially to other images within the works or, perhaps more importantly, across works. Thus, portions of the text for the novel *Topologie d'une cité fantôme* (1976) reappear in Robbe-Grillet's film *Le Jeu avec le feu* (1975) and his collaborative text involving Robert Rauschenberg's lithographs in *Traces suspectes en surfaces* (1976). The latter work retains its specificity in the original conjunctions of text next to lithographs or text partially or wholly covered by lithographs. *Le Jeu avec le feu* retains its specificity as a film, whether the text was ever written elsewhere or not. And *Topologie d'une cité fantôme* is still a novel and nothing but a novel, in the full sense of that word. Just as point of view generated (while remaining independent of) the fictions in Robbe-Grillet's earlier novels and films, so too the text now generates topologies whose many manifestations can take the form of a novel, a film or an "art" book. And just as Eisenstein expanded film form so vastly by drawing his comparisons and influences from art forms other than film, so too Robbe-Grillet's collaborative works with Rauschenberg, Magritte, David Hamilton and Paul Delvaux, as well as his use of structures from Mondrian and Paul Klee in *L'Eden et après* (1971) and Yves Klein in *Glissements* signify new directions for the cinema as a repository art form for all the other arts.

Critical Survey of Oeuvre

Alain Robbe-Grillet has had few champions among the critics in his fourteen years of filmmaking: Bruce Morrissette in this country; Roy Armes in England; Jacques Doniol-Valcroze, André Gardies and François Jost in France. His stature as a novelist has often been more a hindrance than a help. His novels and films are of difficult access for most critics and audiences alike to begin with, and those critics who hailed Robbe-Grillet's stylistic innovations in the novel while ignoring or sidestepping the erotic motifs and "pop" violence have been the same critics to cringe or shrug shoulders uncomprehendingly before the spectacle of Robbe-Grillet's cinematic innovations, before his filmic use of those same erotic motifs and that same "pop" violence.

Yet, it is encouraging to trace the development of a Bruce Morrissette, for example, from his early writings, which "reviewed" the literature ("Roman et cinéma: le cas de Robbe-Grillet," 1961) or which analyzed the films of Robbe-Grillet from a thematic, specifically psychoanalytical perspective ("Une voie pour le nouveau cinéma," 1964) to a speculative, "ground-breaking" structural analysis of the recent Robbe-Grillet ("Post-Modern Generative Fiction: Novel and Film," 1975). Robbe-Grillet challenges the most faithful among his followers; critics like Morrissette, Armes and Gardies have grown up with Robbe-Grillet and have expanded their critical horizons considerably because of him. Other critics, most notably Noel Burch and Peter Wollen, have reassessed their original positions on Robbe-Grillet and have come to put him in a class with Alain Resnais and Jean-Luc Godard in the first rank of French film. Yet Robbe-Grillet, anonymous for the most part, remains anonymously or barely tolerated, an eccentric outside the mainstream.

His films will always be "uneven," if that implies a smooth reconciliation between form and content. The "stories" and themes of his films remain largely the same as those of his first novels: the quest and its variations, from detective and pulp fiction; the reworking of old myths (the siren, Oedipus, Don Juan, the mad king, etc.), derived from literature, legend or popular culture, which are often chosen for their sexual content and which are usually treated in deliberately hackneyed or comic ways; triangular or geometrically multiple relationships, involving character doubling in a simply circular or complex, serial progression, which begin with sexual repression and which end in sado-masochism, torture and murder, often with ensuing rebirth; stock characters (characters with letters for names, Franck/Frantz, Boris) and stock objects (broken glass, womens' shoes, bells, eggs, knives, instruments of torture); and a restructuring of the myths and visions of the Surrealist writers, painters and filmmakers (Man Ray, Chirico, Breton, Cocteau, Duchamp and Magritte).

In his novels the themes and "stories" can be seen to function as a pretext for the style, the narrative voice, the elaborately "objective" descriptions of the obsessively "subjective" I-void narrators. In the films, the themes and plots insist upon themselves, even when they are serialized, contradicted, undercut or dealt with in comic ways. The result is that the viewer seems caught between the seemingly facile or offensive content and the mind-boggling arabesque of innovative forms. Like Duchamp, Robbe-Grillet proposes elaborate explanations for commonplace and often silly objects. In his films the content of comic books merges with the structures of modern painting and music. The result will always be "uneven." Robbe-Grillet's films are experimental, in the root sense of that word: they experiment and often fail; they communicate less than they express. Robbe-Grillet is outrageous and incredibly accomplished in his failures.

Robbe-Grillet has shifted emphases, from that of the camera as a recorder of reality and as a mover of an anecdotal subject in the traditional cinema to that of an artist's tool, as malleable as paints and oils. With Robbe-Grillet film becomes a mode of construction. Meaning gives way to structures, those structures which have been his unique contribution to the cinema.

Primary among those structures from the outset in _L'Immortelle_, his first directorial effort (1963), have been the structures of mobility and immobility. Both of these structures derive from an idiosyncratic, highly subjective camera, and both emphasize point of view and temporality in film. The principle protagonist in any Robbe-Grillet film is the camera itself: a camera which emphasizes its own presence in the composition of every shot and in the movement from one shot to the next: a camera that purposefully emphasizes itself and, in so doing, it emphasizes its own subjectivity, its own fiction.

Immobility and mobility are accomplished primarily through the use of freeze-frames and a mobile camera, techniques which do not originate with Robbe-Grillet. It is the application of those techniques, running counter to the usual connotation given them in the traditional narrative cinema, that originates with Robbe-Grillet. Thus, freeze-frames in his films emphasize point of view: characters are deliberately and even artificially caught in mid-action, frozen in geometrical or architectural poses, immobilized, as it were, in the "mind's eye" of the camera-protagonist in Robbe-Grillet's black-and-white films (X in _L'Année dernière à Marienbad_, N or André Varais in _L'Immortelle_, Robbe-Grillet the actor and Elias/Trintignant in _Trans-Europ-Express_ and Boris Varissa in _L'Homme qui ment_). By calling attention to itself through the freeze-frames, the camera-mind accomplishes several objectives: the presentation of obsessional images that stem from reality but that transform reality into mental ritual by destroying the structural indicators of exterior reality, dream, imagination and lie; the total breakdown of traditional narrative into fictional description, in which certain images take psychic priority over others and, thus, solidify, traumatize, become frozen in the camera-protagonist's mind; the transformation of traditional narrative continuity through editing from an exterior function (with the express purpose of "telling," of providing the spectator with links between images) to an interiorized editing, an editing that functions as the mind of the protagonist and that calls the credibility of that mind into question.

In the experimental cinema, the films, for example, of Andy Warhol or Michael Snow, the use of immobility is common. But Robbe-Grillet appears to be the first commercial filmmaker to explore the possibilities of immobility, both objectively and subjectively, in film. It is ironic that film's greatest advantage over photography is also its greatest disadvantage: motion. Motion by definition implies sequential and spatial relationships. It is in terms of motion that film has been constrained with the responsibility of capturing "reality," that hobby-horse of literal and literary critics. It is because of film's ability to record motion that film's point of view has most often been objective and omniscient, that subjective point-of-view has often gone unnoticed, most spectators continuing to read the image as denotative and objective (physically real) and not as connotative and subjective (mental projection of the protagonist), unless the image itself is tampered with (thus destroying its denotative capacity) by using such subjectivity indicators as gradual fades and dissolves, blurred images, superimpositions and multiple exposures, the use of extreme angles or unusual lenses.

Robbe-Grillet asserts that to see (for the camera-protagonist) is to immobilize, to fixate, to desire a cessation of movement: "He is there, he looks at it, and I have the impression that one feels in him the desire to stop it.... This man that one sees in my novels and in my films is someone who needs to see and to immobilize, the two things being constantly linked."[1] Those structures of immobility are related to the unique style of acting required by Robbe-Grillet for his protagonists in the early films. The stiff and awkward gestures of Jacques Doniol-Valcroze in *L'Immortelle* are determined by the unseen camera-narrator, the real N watching the Doniol-Valcroze N in a projection. At the same time, these deliberately falsified gestures send the viewer outward, from Doniol-Valcroze (no interest inherent in his acting itself) to the people and things he perceives. Part of his perception as a voyeur is to fix people, objects and scenes, to immobilize them. In the same vein, when such immobilization does not take place and L or some other character in the film is about to turn and face the camera, the camera-protagonist "cuts" rather than face the prospect of being a voyeur who is looked upon. Time after time in the *ciné-roman*, Robbe-Grillet indicates such cuts when characters are about to face the camera frontally. The special acting indicated for Doniol-Valcroze was Robbe-Grillet's way of approximating the "absent I" narrators of his novels. "Why an N? No doubt it's to indicate his peculiar position in the narrative, somewhat comparable to the narrator in a modern novel: a narrator who doesn't 'tell' anything, but through whose eyes everything is imagined. It's this function, when he's present on-screen, that gives his acting this empty or awkward aspect, not at all in keeping with a 'hero' of the cinema. Likewise, in terms of framing or editing he is often found to be in a state of technical error or of awkwardness."[2] Thus, Doniol-Valcroze is often shown off to one corner of the frame and not "foregrounded" in the way we are accustomed to seeing a film protagonist.

This unique "absent I" narrator also explains the apparent contradictions between subjective and objective camera displacements in Last Year at Marienbad and L'Immortelle. In Marienbad the camera reveals X (who is also the unseen narrator on the sound-track). The camera then pans along the walls, along the guests at the chateau, apparently from X's point of view, an apparent use of subjective camera in its traditional sense. When the camera completes its half-circle pan, it comes to rest on X himself, which seems to return the camera to an objective recording instrument, which suggests that X may be "creating" a projection of himself, which calls into question any continuity in time-space relationships as well as point of view. Similarly, L in L'Immortelle stands near the window at N's Sunday party, and the camera begins to pan along the guests, as though from L's subjective point of view. The guests all turn, one after the other, away from conversations with other people and toward the direction of the camera's movement. Finally, the camera stops on L talking with N, then L talking with Catherine Carayoun in another room with N looking on, the switch having been possible through a "cut" within the frame: guests walking in front of the camera and filling the frame with their black silhouettes. In the same film, the camera pans left to right along a bridge in the woods, revealing N and L in three different poses at three different places on the bridge. Again, the technique does not originate with Robbe-Grillet. In the American experimental cinema, Maya Deren used the camera similarly as a co-participant, and her lateral pan at the beginning of A Study in Choreography for Camera (1950) reveals a dancer in several different stages of a pirouette in different areas of the woods and in different degrees of long shot moving to close-up. What originates with Robbe-Grillet is the use of such techniques in the commercial, feature-length, narrative cinema.

The characters in Marienbad and L'Immortelle are nameless, except for letter indications, as in Robbe-Grillet's novels. They are doubled, as in the novels, which makes a "synopsis" of the films extremely difficult for critic and general audience alike. In addition, their acting is not only deliberately stylized, as in the case of Doniol-Valcroze in L'Immortelle, but their typecasting runs totally counter to the traditional use of typage in film. Giorgio Albertazzi in Marienbad, Doniol-Valcroze in L'Immortelle and Jean-Louis Trintignant in Trans-Europ-Express (1966) and The Man Who Lies (1968) are stiff, cold and intellectual. There is nothing believable about their parts: the passions of Doniol-Valcroze, the possibility that Trintignant could be a drug-runner in Trans-Europ-Express or a hero of the Resistance in The Man Who Lies. Likewise, the women seem counter-cast. Delphine Seyrig in Marienbad is more a statue than a woman, Françoise Brion is hardly believable as a siren or belly-dancer in L'Immortelle, Marie-France Pisier is too intellectual in real life to have been type-cast for the part of the prostitute in Trans-Europ-Express. Such acting reinforces the artifice of acting, sending the film inward upon itself rather than outward. Audience identification with characters on any emotional level is replaced by games between character and creator, games in which the audience is invited to participate.

If the formal structure of a film like L'Immortelle holds up because of the authenticity of Istanbul and the Turkish music and language, such authenticity is abandoned in Trans-Europ-Express for the sake of the filmmakers within the film creating as they go along a work which, in the end, escapes them. Similarly, game structures take over in the Flaubert-like The Man Who Lies, in which the Trintignant character, contrary to any sacred notions in the traditional cinema, has absolutely nothing to say, but is compelled to keep on talking, because his existence depends upon his words. As well as the technical questions with which Robbe-Grillet's black-and-white films assault conventional notions of how to use the camera, how to frame, how to edit, there are thematic questions as well. Robbe-Grillet's films are puzzle-films in a sense far beyond that of Citizen Kane or Rashomon or The Third Man, in which there is ultimately a narrative truth grasped by the audience, even if the characters within the film don't grasp it. More than any other filmmaker, Robbe-Grillet has advanced the false and the make-believe as co-equals of the truth. There is no resolution to the double accident in L'Immortelle, the contradictions between real Trintignant and Trintignant as Elias in Trans-Europ-Express, no sorting out of the lies of Boris Varissa in The Man Who Lies. The spectator knows as much about the "truth" of such films as Robbe-Grillet does. There are "rosebud" endings to Robbe-Grillet's films, but without any real resolution behind them.

Robbe-Grillet has attacked the notion of "depth" on two fronts in his films. Depth as physical deep surfaces is replaced by flattening devices: cardboard sets, stereotyped characters, paint for blood. Robbe-Grillet praises Lichtenstein for replacing lyrical abstraction with the flat surfaces of cartoon strips, then faults him for finding in that flattening out a significance having to do with our American psychic deflation after the Vietnam war. Attaching a moral implication or a meaning to the technical innovation dates the innovation, destroying its future possibilities. Robbe-Grillet praises Godard for using paint instead of blood in his films for the reason that blood has depth while paint is flat. Robbe-Grillet faults Godard for attaching political reasons to his technical experiments. The attack on depth as a physical surface for Robbe-Grillet is at the same time a restoration of the artist's technical means in and for themselves as well as a way to bypass anthropomorphic metaphors, the falsification of figurative language, toward a new form of metaphor, a revolutionary art, in what he feels is the true sense of the word.

On a second level, Robbe-Grillet attacks depth as profundity, replacing meanings with structures. For Robbe-Grillet, profundity is a 19th-century notion, formulated at a time when the artist served a functional purpose as implicit "translator" of society's hidden truths. If there is no God, there can be no truth. Man makes up his "truth" (his existence) as he goes along. Instead of meaning, Robbe-Grillet offers games, a return to the _homo ludens_ of pre-technological society, a return to the work of art as fun or pleasure in and of itself. In an aesthetic sense, the game structures "orient" the film texts where no reference to external reality and its "rules" or "codes" is possible, restoring the notion of play to film. Thus, Robbe-Grillet continues with his stock characters, his object-fetishes, his "pop" sexuality and violence: nothing new under the sun and all new ways to say it or play it. On a more serious and critical level, the games are a critique of a society in which the sacred symbols have been replaced with commonplace objects, in which the unaided search for knowledge is made impossible by all the media bombardment, in which eroticism has become as much a billboard as a feeling. Whereas a Godard feels righteous indignation at this desacralization, Robbe-Grillet assimilates it, pokes fun at it, incorporates it as part of the game.

Robbe-Grillet's approach to the cinema has changed in the passage from black-and-white to color, yet he has been no less daring in these color films. He told me that he was ready to give up filmmaking after _The Man Who Lies_, because it was no longer possible to make films in black and white. His switch to color was a significant one. It corresponded with a loosening of censorship laws in France. Robbe-Grillet began to conceive his films in a more painterly sense, using colors formally as well as functionally. The blue and white of Djerba in _L'Eden et après_ clash in a formal construct with the red of the Cafe Eden: the colors of Paul Klee clashing with those of Mondrian. In addition, Robbe-Grillet notes that new themes became possible with color. Blood, for example, never appeared in his black-and-white films. In the color films it becomes a leitmotif for the protagonists: the blood of wounds, the blood of the feminine cycle, the blood of lost virginity, the drinking of blood for Alice in _Glissements progressifs du plaisir_. The sexual scenes that were ritualized in _L'Immortelle_, simulated in _Trans-Europ-Express_, and explored in partial nudity in _The Man Who Lies_, become full-blown in _L'Eden et après_, with the important shift from male narrator-protagonists to female protagonists. The cold and formal women of the black-and-white films are replaced by Catherine Jourdan in _L'Eden et après_ and Anicée Alvina in _Glissements_ and _Le Jeu avec le feu_: young, nubile women, prototypes of Nabokov's Lolita, Sade's Justine, Carroll's Alice and Queneau's Zazie. By way of analogy, Robbe-Grillet has gone full-circle, from the Emanuelle Riva of Resnais' _Hiroshima mon amour_ to the Jean Seberg of Godard's _Breathless_.

The mythical imaginary of time and place in the black-and-white films is replaced with a no less mythical but more contemporary society, especially in its sexual fantasies and fears. The always tenuous causality of the earlier films is replaced with serial arrangements of scenes and themes, characters being "moved" as pieces in the scenes, according to the structuring of generative images. Objects have changed roles. In Marienbad or L'Immortelle Robbe-Grillet restored what Maya Deren called "the malevolent vitality of inanimate objects": objects existed as a being-there, having as much present-ness as the characters. In the color films Robbe-Grillet has replaced his former associative editing with jump-cutting, specifically jump-cutting with the use of objects as "punctuation" points. Interrogation scenes in Glissements are intercut or "sabotaged" by quick cuts to objects in unfamiliar settings: a brass bed on the beach, a gravedigger's spade, three eggs in a bowl. In L'Immortelle the music of a Turkish belly-dance provided the continuity for several visual shifts from N and L watching the Turkish dance to N and L outside on a bench to N up in his window turning to see L do the Turkish dance in his room. In The Man Who Lies sound similarly signaled "real" or "imagined" scenes: Boris dropping a real glass with no sound of glass shattering, Boris throwing an imaginary (invisible) glass with the sounds of glass shattering. In the color films, sound becomes tied up structurally with these object-cuts in contrapuntal relationships never before explored in the cinema.

With the color films there has been a foregrounding of Robbe-Grillet's collaborators: Michel Fano's sound, Yves Lafaye's cinematography, Bob Wade's editing. Robbe-Grillet considers them co-creators of his films, a fruitful extension perhaps of his early collaboration with Resnais on Marienbad.

More now than ever before, Robbe-Grillet labors in unexplored territory. More than ever before, an "intellectual" audience is being called upon. Robbe-Grillet's notion has always been that one should not seek out works for a certain public, but rather that one should seek out a public for already existent works. More than ever before, a ciné-roman or some "memory aid" is necessary for the full comprehension of Robbe-Grillet's films. He notes that Hollis Frampton and other American experimental filmmakers have played with serialism in the cinema. He adds that L'Eden et après is the first feature-length commercial film to be based totally on a serial arrangement. Undaunted by voices of protest about the sexism of his images of women, the anarchy of his politics or his use of pop art and soft porn, he continues. Undaunted by the commercial failures of his films and the resultant distribution difficulties he has had to face, he continues. Willing to merge the most blatant elements of popular culture with the most formal elements of modern music or modern painting, he persists. Piège à fourrure (Fur Trap), the film he is currently working on, will present his most shopworn plot in a serial arrangement more advanced than that for L'Eden et après. One is tempted to object at every stage of his evolution: that's too facile, that's too abstract. One resists, knowing that Robbe-Grillet is closer than any other filmmaker working today to making film the total work of art.

NOTES

[1]Gardies, André. Alain Robbe-Grillet (Paris: Seghers, 1972), p. 74.

[2]Robbe-Grillet, Alain. L'Immortelle (Paris: Minuit, 1963), p. 9.

The Films: Synopsis, Credits and Notes

1 L'ANNÉE DERNIÈRE A MARIENBAD (Last Year at Marienbad) (1961)

In a baroque chateau in Bavaria, the camera pans the walls and ceilings, accompanied by eerie organ music and the voice of the unseen narrator: "Once again - I walk on, once again, down these corridors, through these halls, these gallaries, in this structure - from another century, this enormous luxurious, baroque - lugubrious hotel, where endless corridors succeed silent-deserted corridors overloaded with a dim, cold ornamentation of woodwork, stucco, mouldings, marbles, dark mirrors, dim paintings, columns, heavy hangings...." These words will be repeated several times during the film, with slight variations in the order but none in tone. Gradually, the voice mingles with that of a play going on. The woman in the play waits for the clock to strike, then yields to the man, which, in microcosm, is the story of the film as well. The play also contains a balcony, a statue and geometrically rigid gardens, all of which find their counterparts in the film. The camera moves among the guests, and fragments of conversations are overheard, suggesting mysteries, little intrigues, a story about someone named Franck. X meets the beautiful and statuesque A (Delphine Seyrig) and notes that she hardly seems to remember him. He begins the memory of their first meeting in the gardens of Frederiksbad (or maybe it was elsewhere), at which time they discussed a statue in the gardens. As with the play within the film, once the statue is evoked in a "memory," it comes repeatedly into play, actualized within the film, as though X's accounts created the physical spaces around him and A. Mixed with these "meetings" between X and A are "confrontations" between X and M, who may be A's husband or lover or guardian. X and M play games which X usually initiates and at which he usually loses: the Nim game, card games, match games, dominoes. X suggests further memories to A: a walk in the gardens and a story of a broken heel. When he suggests that he went up to her room one night, she seems horrified and drops her glass. The broken glass becomes tied figuratively with the memory of the broken heel and later with the broken balcony. Succeeding shots detail the various possibilities of A's room, from an exaggerated whiteness to a more realistic look, from elaborate ornamentation about her bed to a more simple (more realistic?) bed. X states that it is really M that A is afraid of, not the acceptance of a shared past. Gradually, A seems to accept X's verbalized past but not his invitation to go away with him. With the possibility that A might be persuaded, X seems to lose grasp of his accounts; his tales have been of the past, of last year, toward convincing A. Their going away together points now toward the present and future, which leaves X confused and struggling between possible "endings" to the story. In one possible ending, a jealous M kills A. X rejects this, saying that he must have A alive. Another ending involves a rape, also rejected by X and visualized in the film by the repeated overexposed shots of A coming to meet X with feathered arms outstretched. After a meeting in the garden, X hurdles the balustrade of the balcony and it breaks. A screams, and her screams are identical with those of an earlier scene, the visuals returning to that earlier scene in the bar when A dropped her glass. M and A meet in her bedroom, and it is clear that M knows she will leave him, despite her protestations that he keep her. While everyone else at the chateau is attending the play that began the film, X and A leave at midnight, as they had previously agreed. The voice of X reveals that the gardens outside present a new labyrinth, a new closed world to succeed the closed world of the chateau, which, for the first time, appears well-lit, friendly and even somewhat inviting. "It seemed, at first glance, impossible to get lost here...at first glance...down straight paths, between the statues with frozen gestures and the granite slabs, where you were now already getting lost forever, in the calm night, alone with me." A has been persuaded, then, to leave one imaginary world for another.

Robbe-Grillet notes that the theme of the film is that of persuasion, that it doesn't matter whether or not they really met "last year" at Marienbad or elsewhere (he thinks they didn't), that the only "time" in the film is the time of projection. He notes that the film could be taken, in fact, as a documentary about a statue, with all the various and contradictory interpretations given to the statue. The overall structure of the film is that of the labyrinth, in which linearity and causality are broken and by which any "restructuring" of the film's events in any order other than that given within the film is doomed to fail. The film merges several myths and legends: Death's reprieve of a year and a day to a beautiful maiden; Sleeping Beauty; Cinderella; the Arabian Nights; Orpheus and Eurydice in the underworld; Don Juan. The film also suggests the literary influence of Kafka, Borges and Bioy Casares, as well as the filmic influence of L'Herbier, Delluc, Epstein and Jean Cocteau.

Credits:

Producers:	Pierre Corau (Précitel), Raymond Froment (Terrafilm)
Production:	Précitel, Terrafilm, Société Nouvelle des Films Comoran, Como Films, Argos Films, Les Films Tamara, Cinétel, Silver Films (Paris); Cineriz (Rome)
Director:	Alain Resnais
Screenplay:	Alain Robbe-Grillet
Adaptation:	Alain Robbe-Grillet
Photography:	Sacha Vierny (black and white, Dyaliscope)
Camera Operation:	Philippe Brun
Art Decoration:	Jacques Saulnier
Set Decoration:	Georges Glon, André Piltant, Jean-Jacques Fabre
Music:	Francis Seyrig
Conducted By:	André Girard
Organist:	Marie-Luise Girod
Sound:	Guy Villette, Marchetti, Renault, Neny
Costumes:	Bernard Evein
Mme. Seyrig's Gowns:	Chanel
Editors:	Henry Colpi, Jasmine Chasney
Assistant Director:	Jean Léon
Production Manager:	Léon Sanz
Script:	Sylvette Baudrot
English Subtitles:	Noelle Gillmor
Cast:	Delphine Seyrig (A), Giorgio Albertazzi (X), Sacha Pitoeff (M). Guests: Pierre Barbaud, Françoise Bertin, Luce Garcia-Ville, Helena Kornel, Jean Lanier, Gérard Lorin, Davide Montemuri, Gilles Quéant, Françoise Spira, Karin Toeche-Mittlet, Wilhelm von Deek, Gabriel Werner.

Filmed on location for exteriors in Munich in baroque castles built by Ludwig II of Bavaria at Nymphenburg, Schleissheim and Amalienburg. Interiors filmed in Paris at Photosonor Studios in 1961.

Completed:	1961
First American Showing:	March 7, 1962 at the Carnegie Hall Cinema in New York
Prizes:	Gold Lion of St. Mark (Venice Film

	Festival, 1961); Méliès Prize (France, 1961)
Distribution:	Cocinor (France), Astor (USA, first rights), Macmillan (USA, current rights)
Running Time:	93 minutes
Note:	Resnais and Robbe-Grillet had originally an enormous struggle just to get the film shown. Both the producers and the distributor were disenchanted with the film, thinking that the film would only confuse and frustrate spectators. Resnais and Robbe-Grillet arranged private screenings for André Breton, Jean-Paul Sartre and Michelangelo Antonioni, with only varying degrees of encouragement from those three as a result. Somewhat surreptitiously, Resnais and Robbe-Grillet had the film entered in the Venice Film Festival. By winning a prize at that festival, the film's survival was assured. Resnais and Robbe-Grillet had intended to show in the credits that there was no separation between director and scenarist: they would co-sign the film equally. Yet, once the script was completed, Robbe-Grillet never appeared on the set. During the shooting of the film, he was already in Turkey, shooting L'Immortelle, which he had scripted prior to writing Last Year at Marienbad. There were ultimately several discrepancies between the shooting script and the final film. Robbe-Grillet's script called for a man much older than Pitoeff to play the part of M, and his scenes of a "realistic" rape, with exaggerated screams and theatrical gestures, were replaced by the "white angel" shots of Resnais. Robbe-Grillet notes that the continuity established by the organ music was Resnais' idea. Robbe-Grillet would have liked a sound-track of "natural" sounds (the elevator doors, the various bells) mixed with sounds of footsteps, single musical notes and

human screams, all in a serial arrangement. Finally, they disagreed on the basic premise of the film: Resnais still believes that X and A had met previously, while Robbe-Grillet contends that any meeting between them can only take place in the present-tense of the film itself.

2 L'IMMORTELLE (The Immortal One) (1963)

The title of the film is ambiguous, since it refers to the woman within the film as well as to the mythical city of Byzantium underneath the real and post-card city of Istanbul. The film opens on a long pan of the ruins along the water's edge, punctuated by Turkish music and sounds of a car crash: screeching of brakes, smashing of glass. N looks out of his window, and what follows are various capsule vignettes of L or Lâle or Leila (Françoise Brion) in different rigid poses, and in different spatial locales, suggesting that N looking out of the window could not possibly be seeing all of this, except, of course, subjectively. A close-up of L's face fades to become L standing near the ruins, which fades to reveal L looking at the camera and standing against the railing of a ship, which gives way to L standing near an odalisque, which fades to become L standing near the water, which returns to the first close-up. The window shades cross L's face and close, returning us to N at his window (Jacques Doniol-Valcroze) and an end to the intermittent dogs barking on the sound-track. L stands next to M, a fat man with dark glasses and two dogs on leashes. N asks directions and L offers to give him a ride. She says to him en route: "You are lost. You are in a Turkey of legend." He responds: "As in books." He tells her that he is a professor on leave and invites her to a party the following Sunday. N turns from his window toward the interior of the room, and nobody is there. N turns again, and the room is filled with his party guests. The camera pans the various guests at the party, and these guests turn in the direction the camera is moving, from L's point of view near the window to (illogically) L and N sitting together. Guests walking in front of the camera and filling up the frame allow "cuts" to different spaces, culminating in a cut to a cafe near the water at which N waits for L, with M sitting ominously nearby. The sound-track announces her coming and her dialogue in Turkish before she has arrived in the visuals. The scene is "repeated," and this time she arrives in the visuals and takes N away. On the beach she recites a poem by Sultan Selim for him. When he asks which Sultan Selim, she says: "They're all Selim, they all write the same poem with recurrent fetishes."

She points out that what appears to be a mosque is really the Naval Museum and that everything in the country is false appearances. Briefly in his room, he undoes her blouse, while she stares passively and immobile. There is a cut which returns to the ocean, where she hears the sound of dogs barking and gets up to leave. Yet she goes into the water. They meet inside a mosque, and she explains that women are not allowed in the mosque, that women are considered unclean and only good for making love. She informs him outside that the mosque is not old, that it was reconstructed after the war. In the market-place, after having stopped at an antique store, they pass a pillar with a poster for a belly-dancer. Immediately, the scene shifts to the real belly-dancer and music, with N and L arriving. L is the only woman in a room of fixed and immobile men. N seats L at their table. He remains standing, his hand on L's neck, and her bare back in the foreground is "mirrored" by the bare back of the belly-dancer in the background. A cut to the "outside" reveals L sitting on a bench in a different costume, with N standing behind her in a different costume, both now facing the camera, his hand still on her neck and the sounds of the belly-dance music still on the sound-track. She tells him: "It's not a real scene. It's a backcloth for a love story." He bends to kiss her and she refuses. He asks: "What does it matter if these are not real houses?" He looks up and someone closes a curtain in a window, which becomes N back at his window, turning to the interior of his room where L does a seductive belly-dance, with the Turking belly-dance music still on the sound-track all this time. The camera then pans laterally across a bridge, revealing N and L in different poses at different places along the bridge. Suddenly, they are back in his room, and quick cutting reveals both the eroticism and the sado-masochism in their relationship, as they jump physical spaces in the room with each cut. Back in the woods again, N questions L about her name, her address, her situation, all to no avail. He chases her under a tunnel near the water. A cut reveals them in a boat going through the tunnel. Then the camera pulls back to reveal them against the railing of a bigger boat, with them in the little boat still visible at the corner of the frame. The bigger boat roams the edge of the ruins, already seen in the opening shots. They pass his apartment and the Turkish fisherman down below. L speaks to a Turkish woman who disappears behind her door when N comes near. L is behind some grates, with N standing on the other side, his hand roaming in front of her face, as though he were fondling a mirror image. Then they are seen overlooking some construction below them. She says: "You see, it's false. They're engaged in rebuilding Byzantium." She leaves him there, and he watches her drive off after talking with a young Greek boy, who had asked to give them a tour up above. In the cemetery alone, N sees the various faces of the fisherman, the boy and other secondary characters, punctuated by the headlights of passing cars. N asks his maid about L, then asks the maid her name. Her name is Lâle (meaning "tulip"), the same as L's name. With a distorted Turkish song on the sound-track, N tracks L in the market-place. Through a jump-cut, all figures are frozen, then disappear as L continues walking, then reappears as a crowd carrying a casket with L disappearing. N returns to several of their meeting places: the beach, the cafe by the water. He sees a woman wearing a blouse like L's, one of L's many doubles in the film, at the cafe. N asks Catherine Carayoun about L, and she relates to him a Turkey of legend, of kept women and jealous husbands, of secret harems and tortures, of spies and murders. She denies having talked with L at N's party, when the previous visuals have shown that they did talk. Catherine suggests that her name may be Elyan or Yan. She directs him to a man, who tells him that the woman he seeks is named Lucille, directing him to a man named Socrates, who says that he doesn't know this first man and who warns N of danger. N is sent to a third man who tells him that he's wasting his time. Back at the mosque, the old man (who is also the fisherman) tells him that her name is Madame Yak, but that there is no such person. N goes to the antique dealer, who also denies knowing her. Finally, N walks in the market-place where he sees L with M, then the market-place empties of all its people, then L without M. She hurries him into her car. They drive very fast past his apartment, until one of the dogs appears before them and they crash into a tree. The "dead" L is in a pose identical with the shot of her that opened the film. N asks the police for details about her, but they give none. After several repeated shots of the car and the accident, N buys the "restored" Buick they were driving. In his room, with his hand in a bandage, N rummages through a drawer which reveals money, letters, post-cards of the old man at the mosque and L inside, and a black garter-belt of a woman, presumably L's. N approaches one of L's look-alikes and asks about L and the accident. The woman says it was the man's fault, that he wrenched the wheel away from her and that he died too. N begins seeing L in all the pre-established locales, too present to be a mere apparition and not present enough to be really there. In the cemetery, L's voice is heard but her lips aren't moving: "These are not real graves. They never bury anyone...when they fall they're used to pave the streets...and you walk blissfully across them without giving them a second thought." The corresponding visuals are of N lying on his couch, N looking out the window down on the pavement below, and N walking "blissfully" across the carpet. As N drives off in the "restored" Buick, the Turkish music that began the film reappears, and L's voice comments: "The ramparts of Byzantium must be rebuilt." N veers away from the other dog in the road and crashes, his immobile body in the same pose as that of L in the first "accident." L is seen standing against the railing of the boat. She is laughing in the visuals, but there is no sound of laughter on the sound-track.

Robbe-Grillet suggests that L is imaginary, made up by N, whose stiff gestures and awkward "acting" are an indication outward, away from him and toward what he observes, an indication that the real N is the unseen camera-narrator of the film. The film is a mixture of Pierre Loti, the Thousand and One Nights and the Blue Guide. The layers of real Istanbul, tourist Istanbul and mythical Byzantium are reflected in the various games of narration, jumps in time and space, and punctuated continuity of sound.

Credits:

Producers:	Samy Halfon, Michel Fano (Como Films), Dino de Laurentiis (Cinematografica)
Production:	Franco-Italian co-production: Tamara Films, Como Films, Cocinor (Paris); Cinematografica (Rome)
Director:	Alain Robbe-Grillet
Screenplay:	Alain Robbe-Grillet
Adaptation:	Alain Robbe-Grillet
Photography:	Maurice Barry, Jean-José Richer (black and white)
Camera Operation:	Robert Foucard
Press and still photos:	Catherine Robbe-Grillet
Music:	Georges Delerue, Tashin Kavalcioglu
Sound:	Michel Fano
Editor:	Bob Wade
Director of Production:	Emile Breysse
English Subtitles:	Noelle Gillmor
Cast:	Françoise Brion (L), Jacques Doniol-Valcroze (N), Guido Celano (M), Ulvi Uraz (antique dealer), Catherine Robbe-Grillet (Catherine Carayoun).
Filmed on location in Istanbul, Turkey, in 1961-1962.	
Completed:	1962
Prizes:	Louis Delluc Prize (France, 1963)
Distribution:	Marceau-Cocinor (France), Grove Press (USA, first rights), Films Incorporated (USA, current rights)
Running Time:	90 minutes
Note:	Robbe-Grillet admits that his rigorous scripting prior to the shooting of the film caused innumerable problems. He adds that he had problems with his camera operators and crew, because they couldn't comply with

his directions. He asked them to photograph the frames somewhat independently of the direction of the actors within the frames. Contrary to his instructions, when a character slowed down, the camera operator automatically slowed down too. Thus, Robbe-Grillet suffers when he watches _L'Immortelle_ today. It was this bad experience with the technicians in _L'Immortelle_ that prompted Robbe-Grillet to move away from the detailed script toward a sketch or outline, to be worked on and refined as the shooting progressed. This switch in approach also signaled a temporary hiatus between Robbe-Grillet's film activity and the publication of the corresponding script in _ciné-roman_ form. Not until _Glissements progressifs du plaisir_ (1974) would Robbe-Grillet publish another _ciné-roman_.

3 TRANS-EUROP-EXPRESS (1966)

After stopping to buy two magazines, one of which he pays for and one of which he slips inside the other, Jean (Robbe-Grillet), an author-filmmaker, gets on board the Trans-Europ-Express at the Gare du Nord railroad station in Paris en route to Antwerp with Marc, a movie producer, and Lucette, the assistant to Jean. The reflections of the train's mirrors and windows inspire them to make a film with the train itself as a key setting. Thereafter, intercut with the three summarizing or changing the plot is the story of the film itself. After making the same stop to buy magazines, with the same hiding of one in the other, Jean-Louis Trintignant gets on the same train. He sits briefly in the same compartment with Jean, Marc and Lucette. When he leaves the compartment, Jean imagines him in the role of Elias. Now in the role of Elias, Trintignant reboards the train, this time on a mission of smuggling dope for an international organization. He is going to Antwerp to get a suitcase, supposedly filled with cocaine, to bring back to Paris. In reality the trip is a rehearsal, a test set up by Elias' superiors to gauge his talent and his loyalty. In Antwerp Elias undergoes a series of adventures with false spies, false assassins and false police, the very adventures being dictated by Jean on the train. While the three "authors" are inventing, correcting, replaying and cutting out various scenes in Elias' adventures, Elias establishes himself as a character somewhat apart from his creators with his eccentric sexual obsessions, which drive him to simulate rape and violence with Eva, a prostitute who takes part both in his sexual fantasies and in his drug-smuggling adventures. She finally admits that she has been hired by the organization to watch over him in this test, which causes Elias to distrust everyone, causing him to mistake a policeman for a member of the syndicate. Having confessed the facts of the smuggling to this undercover policeman by mistake, Elias realizes his blunder, but does not notify his boss, Franck, because he is afraid. He returns to Paris with the suitcase that is supposedly filled with cocaine. In Paris he finds out that the suitcase contains powdered sugar. He begins the "real" trip to Antwerp, ironically on the same train with Jean, Marc and Lucette, who are still en route all this time. Elias sees Lorentz, the policeman, who is shadowing his every move. Somewhat driven to derangement, Elias strangles Eva when he learns that she has been working for the police. Lorentz devises a trap for him by placing a notice of the crime in the newspaper with an ad for an erotic cabaret act featuring nudity and chains. Lorentz is there, and so is Franck, who shoots Elias dead. His death coincides with the end of the make-believe film script and the arrival of the real Trans-Europ-Express in Antwerp. As Jean, Marc and Lucette get off the train, they get a newspaper which shows a photo of the strangled Eva with details of a smuggling operation "parallel" to the one they had invented. They also pass the "real" Jean-Louis Trintignant, who has gotten off the same train and who is met by Marie-France Pisier (Eva).

The "plot" of the film is a pretext for Robbe-Grillet to expose the process of fiction, including the viewer in the decisions to remake a scene or to eliminate another scene. The deliberate artificiality of the "film" within the film is counterbalanced by the real Trintignant and Pisier, playing themselves as well as their "fictional" roles. What is cast into doubt in the film is the 19th-century notion of the finished work of art from an omniscient author. That notion, with its corollary concept of "profundity" or "meaning" in the work of art, is replaced by the notion of the "game," in and for itself, with no significance outside the work of art. Involved in this notion of the "game" is a critique of the filmmakers on the train as well as an exposé of the 20th-century's sex- and violence-saturated society.

Credits:

Producer:	Samy Halfon (Como Films)
Production:	Franco-Belgian co-production
Director:	Alain Robbe-Grillet
Screenplay:	Alain Robbe-Grillet
Adaptation:	Alain Robbe-Grillet
Photography:	Willy Kurant (black and white)

Camera Operation:	Jean Orjollet, Armand Marco
Still Photography:	Catherine Robbe-Grillet
Music:	Michel Fano, with a song by Clo Vanesco and musical excerpts from "La Traviata" by Giuseppe Verdi, performed by the Prima Symphony
Sound:	Michel Fano
Sound Engineer:	Raymond Saint-Martin
Editor:	Bob Wade
Assistant Editors:	Annie Mouilleron, Marie-Christine Dijon
Assistant Directors:	Claude Him, Jean-Marie Deconinck
Administrator General:	Jacques Karnas
Asst. Admin. General:	Jean-Claude Durand
Director of Production:	Maurice Urbain
Asst. Dir. of Production:	Jerome Lindon
Hair Styles:	Jean-Louis Saint-Roch
Script:	Nicole Seyler
English Subtitles:	Noelle Gillmor
Cast:	Jean-Louis Trintignant (Elias and himself), Marie-France Pisier (Eva and herself), Charles Millot (Franck, the syndicate man), Christian Barbier (Lorentz, the policeman), Nadine Verdier (hotel maid), Clo Vanesco (singer in cabaret), Alain Robbe-Grillet (Jean, the Director), Samy Halfon (Marc, the Producer), Catherine Robbe-Grillet (Lucette, the Script person), Raoul Guylad (an intermediary), Henri Lambert (a false policeman), Paul Louyet (the producer), Rezy Norbert (the concierge), Gérard Palaprat (Matthieu), Salkin (an intermediary), Ariane Sapriel (a traveler), Prima Symphony (the stripper), Virginie Vignon (the suitcase salesperson), Daniel Emilfork (a false policeman).
Filmed on location in Paris, Belgium and on the Trans-Europ-Express train in 1966.	
Completed:	1966
Distribution:	Lux C.C.F. (France), Kit Parker (USA), Macmillan (USA), United Films (USA), Westcoast Films (USA)
Running Time:	90 minutes
Note:	Contrary to L'Immortelle, which was elaborately scripted before shooting,

Trans-Europ-Express maintains a deliberate rough-cut look, because Robbe-Grillet found that things happened during filming which were totally unexpected but which he wanted to incorporate into the film, especially the interplay between actors. With this film, Robbe-Grillet would begin a new approach to film-making: he would script the film less before shooting, he would collaborate with Michel Fano and Bob Wade in scripting the film and planning the editing on a daily basis, with suggestions from the crew and actors both encouraged and welcomed. This different approach has made it more difficult for Robbe-Grillet to get production financing before shooting. The film created quite a scandal in Italy. Robbe-Grillet was ordered to testify at a pornography trial. His lawyers argued successfully that Robbe-Grillet, were his intentions pornographic or exploitive, would most certainly not have devised such an elaborate plot. He would not have insisted so heavily upon game structures throughout the film nor would he have undercut the erotic scenes with obvious insertions of lies, performance/ritual and shifting points of view. He would not, in sum, have used so many distancing devices between the viewer and the film viewed. He was acquitted. The showing of the film was similarly held up in England, although there were no legal proceedings against him.

4 L'HOMME QUI MENT (The Man Who Lies) (1968)

A young man is pursued in a forest, apparently by Nazi soldiers, but he and the soldiers are never seen in the same frame, so he could be running from himself or his double. This chase is intercut with a game of blind-man's bluff, played by three beautiful women at a chateau in central Europe. The young man is apparently shot. He falls, the light changes on the scene, he gets up, brushes himself off and begins his long narration to the camera, identifying himself alternately as Jean Robin and as Boris Varissa. At the inn in the town, he overhears people talking of Jean Robin and of the three women left behind at the chateau: Maria, the maid; Sylvia, the sister of Jean Robin; and Laura, his wife. Boris goes to the chateau, interrupting the game of blind-man's-bluff, seen previously. He tells them that he was Jean Robin's best friend, but his grasp of details is so tenuous and his accounts so filled with contradictions and inconsistencies that they don't believe him. Nevertheless, Boris is able to seduce Maria, the maid, who both cajoles him for his "lies" and undergoes some sadism and torture, both verbal and physical, in their sex. Aware that Sylvia is eavesdropping on their conversation, Boris announces that Jean Robin was a traitor and a coward, knowing that Sylvia will arrange a meeting with him to confront him. They meet at the cemetery, where Boris leans on the gravestone marked "Boris Varissa" and where many of the names of Robbe-Grillet's fictional characters in his previous novels appear. Boris changes tactics with the sister, admitting that Jean Robin was a hero and that he, Boris Varissa, had betrayed her brother. He seduces her. After an "accident" (perhaps arranged by Boris), in which Jean Robin's father falls from a balcony and dies, Boris moves in as the head of the house and begins to approach Laura, who still believes that Jean Robin will return some day. Just at the moment when Boris has apparently convinced Laura of his sincerity and his affections, Jean Robin walks into the room and shoots Boris three times. He walks out of the room. Laura bends over the body of Boris Varissa, who gets up, brushes himself off and rebegins his story, the story of Jean Robin.

Robbe-Grillet notes that Boris Varissa is a mixture of the Don Juan myth and the various myths of the mad king and usurper king, especially that of Boris Goudounov. He notes that the lesbian relationship that exists between the three women is created by the absence of the man (Jean Robin or Boris Varissa), and that Boris is someone who talks in order to construct his character, his past, his reality. He doesn't lie, he just talks, building his own credibility/reality with his words. There can be no truth or lie if there is no God, and Boris is someone who chooses to invent himself, to take the place of God.

Credits:

Producer:	Samy Halfon (Como Films)
Production:	Franco-Czechoslovakian co-production: Como Films, Lux C.C.F. (Paris); Ceskoslovensky Film (Bratislava)
Director:	Alain Robbe-Grillet
Screenplay:	Alain Robbe-Grillet

Adaptation:	Alain Robbe-Grillet
Photography:	Igor Luther (black and white, 1:1.33)
Still Photography:	Catherine Robbe-Grillet
Set Decoration:	Anton Krajcovic
Music:	Michel Fano
Sound:	Michel Fano, Ondrej Polomsky
Sound Engineer:	Raymond Saint-Martin
Editor:	Bob Wade
Assistant Director:	Jan Tamaskovic
Director of Production:	Maurice Urbain
Czech Representative:	Albert Marencin
English Subtitles:	Richard Howard
Cast:	Jean-Louis Trintignant (Boris Varissa), Ivan Mistrik (Jean Robin), Sylvie Breal (Maria), Sylvia Turbova (Sylvia), Zuzana Kocurikova (Laura), Dominique Prado (Lisa), Catherine Robbe-Grillet (the druggist), Josef Kroner (Frantz), Josev Cierny (the father), Dusan Blaskovic (the inn-keeper), Bada (a member of the resistance), Julius Vasek (a man).
Filmed on location in Czechoslovakia in the summer of 1967, at the chateau of the Baroness von Czobel.	
Completed:	1967
First French Showing:	April (1968) in Paris at the Studio St.-Germain
First American Showing:	1969 at the Grove Press Film Festival
Prizes:	Best Actor (Jean-Louis Trintignant) at the Berlin Film Festival (1969)
Distribution:	Lux C.C.F. (France), Grove Press (USA, first rights), Films Incorporated (USA, current rights)
Running Time:	95 minutes
Note:	Robbe-Grillet notes that in the film there is a German officer reading <u>Pravda</u>. This German officer can only be a lie, since he is reading a newspaper which was not in existence during the war, and yet at the same time the word "Pravda" means "truth" in Slovak and in other Slavic languages; thus, it is the word "truth" which is the proof of the lie. The film opened in Czechoslovakia on the very day

that Soviet troops invaded in 1968 and put an end to the liberal Dubcek regime. On the film posters all over the city, people wrote: "Breshnev, The Man Who Lies." Now there were East German officers in Prague wearing uniforms similar to those worn by the German officers in the film. And they were reading Pravda. Thus, the "lie" of the film had become the truth.

Robbe-Grillet has remarked that the film was conceived as a vehicle for Trintignant, a film in which Trintignant could display the complete range of his acting talents.

5 L'EDEN ET APRÈS (Eden and After) (1971)

The film opens on highlighted words intercut with the credits and punctuated by neon lights and darkness: "object," "game," "blood," "rape," "labyrinth," "sex," "Eden," "fantasy," "objective," "subjective," "injective," "surjective." The red lights come from the Eden cafe, supposedly in Paris, and a group of students are in the process of playing a game in the labyrinth of red Mondrian-like sets. The familiar signs of "Coca Cola" and "Camel" are mixed with signs like "Buvez du sang" ("Drink blood"). Unrelated spatial scenes are cut together with the link being Violette (Catherine Jourdan). The students play a game of simulated Russian roulette. They announce that they're going to sell the painting (composition #234) that Violette's uncle left her to the Americans. They play a game in which Boris, one of the students, is "poisoned," and they announce that the Cafe Eden is where they play their games, but in reality nothing ever happens. Frantz, the waiter, serves cocaine fizzes to these bored students. One of the students comments that he's not called Frantz always and that he's probably Dupont or Jean Robin (a fictional character in The Man Who Lies). The Stranger arrives at the Cafe Eden, teaches them a game in which one of the students is asked to pick up the pieces of a broken glass, gets bloodied and then "healed" by the Stranger, who announces that it's a trick he learned in Africa, the "land of your nightmares and sacred dances through fire." Each of the students imagines himself or herself in Africa. Duchemin, the Stranger, gives Violette "fear" powder, and her fantasies and fears of rape, chains, cages and murder are all visualized. He arranges a meeting with her for that night by the canal near the factory. Near the factory she encounters all the students in various fantastic, imaginary or menacing guises. The encounters involve cuts to shots of a gun hanging from a wire, of sperm dripping, of powder falling. A woman says to Violette: "You're in the center of a figure-eight. You'll get lost forever." After allusions to Hamlet (Ophelia and the river bed) and Macbeth (red paint stains on her hand), Violette finds Duchemin's "dead" body at the canal. She takes a blue-and-white post-card of Tunisia from his pocket, which seems to suggest a later rendez-vous. When she recounts this to the students, they deny being there. The body has disappeared as well as Duchemin's key. Violette goes to a film on Tunisia, and suddenly she is in the film: she is in Djerba and Robbe-Grillet is seen watching the "film" from the audience. The same actor who played Frantz is now in Djerba, giving her directions. All the students are there too in search of the lost and valuable painting, plotting Violette's torture and death. Violette goes to Duchemin, now called Dutchman, a sculptor who uses junk objects, cages, torture and nude models in cages. The Stranger makes love with her before three nude women in cages. Violette and Dutchman constantly switch costumes between scenes. Violette is asked what she is looking for. She answers: "Nothing. And I found it." Violette dances erotically around an evening campfire and is then abducted by horsemen wearing turbans. Dutchman won't surrender the painting in exchange for Violette. Boris is poisoned a second time. Violette finds the body of Sonia near a bathtub. Violette drags her body through the desert sand, intercut with shots of the dance around the fire, the horsemen and the abduction. Violette's double appears and gives her the dress she wore at the Cafe Eden. They kiss and touch each other's lips. Marc-Antoine fights with another student and is drowned in the water. Dutchman reappears near the water. Violette goes toward him and he dies a second time. The painting is there on the ground. Violette moans that Marc-Antoine, Sonia, Marie-Eve and Duchemin have all died for that painting. Violette walks out into the water, and the frame goes to white. Violette is back in her room, saying: "I'm alone in my room. Nothing has happened. Soon I'll go to the Eden. We shall drink cocaine fizzes. At the end of the evening, we shall fall silent. We will notice the Stranger with pale eyes opening the door."

Robbe-Grillet constructed the film around a serial arrangement of twelve themes in series of ten, all themes coming to play in each series. The series are: (1) credits; (2) the Cafe Eden before the Stranger comes; (3) the fear potion and the hallucinations; (4) the Cafe Eden after the Stranger's arrival; (5) the factory; (6) the projected film on Tunisia; (7) the Tunisian village of Djerba; (8) the house of Dutchman; (9) the prison; (10) the various mirages of Violette lost in the desert. The twelve themes are: (1) the painting, which is also a post-card and a Tunisian village; (2) blood: the game at the Cafe Eden, the suicide of Sonia, the wounds; (3) the double: double poisoning of Boris, double drowning of

Duchemin, a double dance by Violette and her meeting with the double; (4) the dance; (5) light; (6) the labyrinth; (7) the prison; (8) images and symbols of sperm; (9) eroticism; (10) death, simulated or imagined; (11) water; and (12) doors.

Robbe-Grillet suggests that the film is a cross between Justine of Sade and Alice in Wonderland of Lewis Carroll, with many borrowed elements from chivalric romance, such as the changing of costumes, the notion of "tests," and the serial arrangement, as in le jeu des lois, in which each incident is related to a certain myth. Robbe-Grillet notes that the film is Violette's series of tests to free herself of society's sexual repression and to free herself of her own personality. To do so, she must become a "prisoner" (her dress is taken off) and then free herself (her double restores her dress).

Credits:

Producer:	Samy Halfon (Como Films)
Production:	Franco-Czechoslovakian-Tunisian co-production: Como Films (Paris); Ceskoslovensky Film (Bratislava)
Director:	Alain Robbe-Grillet
Screenplay:	Alain Robbe-Grillet
Adaptation:	Alain Robbe-Grillet
Photography:	Igor Luther (Eastmancolor)
Still Photography:	Catherine Robbe-Grillet
Set Decoration:	Anton Krajcovic
Music:	Michel Fano
Sound:	Michel Fano
Editor:	Bob Wade
Cast:	Catherine Jourdan (Violette), Pierre Zimmer (The Stranger, Duchemin, Dutchman), Richard Leduc (Marc-Antoine), Lorraine Rainer (Marie-Eve), Sylvain Corthay (Jean-Pierre), Juraj Kukura (Boris), Yarmila Kolenicova (the suicide).
Filmed on location in Czechoslovakia and Tunisia and in specially constructed studio sets in Bratislava in 1970.	
Completed:	1971
Distribution:	Plan Film (France), Mundial Films (USA)
Running Time:	100 minutes
Note:	Catherine Jourdan was not Robbe-Grillet's first choice to play the part of Violette. She was a last-minute replacement. The play of "chance" obviously pleased Robbe-Grillet, for he says that Jourdan

makes the film her own. Nor was the idea of Violette's "double" foreseen in the script; it grew out of an accident to Catherine Jourdan's wardrobe in Djerba. Robbe-Grillet was forced to adjust his rigidly scripted series of generative themes and segments to accommodate this and other "happenings" that occurred during the shooting and which were incorporated into the film. Thus, instead of the original seven themes in a series of five, there were twelve themes in a series of ten. Robbe-Grillet notes that this expansion was the creation of four people: (1) himself; (2) Catherine Jourdan, whose role increased considerably during the shooting; (3) the Czech camera operator; and (4) Robbe-Grillet's Tunisian assistant, who began the film as the third assistant.

*6 N A PRIS LES DES (N Took The Dice) (1971)

The film was made for French television. The title of the film is an anagram, generated from L'Eden et après. The footage for the film came from L'Eden et après, with the exception of the ending, which Robbe-Grillet conceived especially for French television. The protagonist of the film, as in L'Eden et après, is a young girl who has a series of adventures. At the end, she realized that her adventures have all been part of a televised game. The film was never shown, either on television or commercially.

Credits:

Producer:	Samy Halfon (Como Films)
Production:	Como Films, L'O.R.T.F. (French Television)
Director:	Alain Robbe-Grillet
Screenplay:	Alain Robbe-Grillet
Adaptation:	Alain Robbe-Grillet
Photography:	Igor Luther (Eastmancolor)
Still Photography:	Catherine Robbe-Grillet
Set Decoration:	Anton Krajcovic
Music:	Michel Fano
Sound:	Michel Fano
Editor:	Bob Wade
Cast:	Catherine Jourdan (Violette),

	Pierre Zimmer (The Stranger, Duchemin, Dutchman), Richard Leduc (Marc-Antoine), Lorraine Rainer (Marie-Eve), Sylvain Corthay (Jean-Pierre), Juraj Kukura (Boris), Yarmila Kolenicova (the suicide).
Constructed from out-takes from the film <u>L'Eden et après</u>, with the same cast as for that film. Only the fictional names of the characters change.	
Completed:	1971 (never shown)

7 GLISSEMENTS PROGRESSIFS DU PLAISIR (<u>The Slow Slide Into Pleasure</u>) (1974)

A young woman named Alice (Anicée Alvina) is charged with murder and imprisoned in an institution for delinquent girls run by a religious order. She denies having murdered Nora (Olga Georges-Picot), the woman with whom she has been living. Both women were apparently prostitutes and involved as well in a lesbian relationship. The Inspector of Police (Jean-Louis Trintignant) arrives at the apartment to find the body of Nora tied to the bed and stabbed in the heart with a pair of dressmaker's scissors. The Inspector grills Alice with a series of apparently illogical questions, all of which will take on meaning and relevance later in the film: "Where did you spend your vacations?" "Do you know a certain Boris?" "Do you know about a glass shoe?" "At what age did you make your first communion?" "What are you, an actress? A dancer? A call-girl? A script-girl?" Alice answers vaguely that the ocean is breaking at her feet. Alice then appears in her prison cell, which is white and bare like the apartment, but it is claustrophobic where the apartment was airy. Alice seems more relaxed, smiles more, talks more freely, but she is as unconcerned as before about logic in her answers, or morality in her behavior, or even simple modesty. She tells her next interrogator, the magistrate (Michel Lonsdale), that the real assassin was a stranger, a man, probably insane, who suddenly burst into their apartment. But Alice cannot substantiate her story, she is hesitant about key points, she is sometimes silent, she offers contradictory explanations, she bares her breast and teases the magistrate, all of which seems to implicate Alice in the crime. In addition, she takes delight in inventing far-fetched theories on the pretext of helping the magistrate to uncover the truth; yet it is clear that she is totally unconcerned with the truth. What becomes apparent in successive scenes is that, whether she is guilty or innocent, Alice is obsessed with the idea of blood: the blood of the victim, the blood of the feminine cycle, the blood of lost virginity, even with drinking the blood of others or with making others drink her blood. Ironically, it is the "crime" which engenders a series of "crimes," leaving a trail of victims who were first Alice's interrogators. The first to succumb is the magistrate. He gradually loses his reason and becomes angry, both at her contradictory answers and at her offer of seduction. As though in a dream, he agrees to lick a small cut on Alice's foot. Alice says: "You want to rape me to make me confess?" When the head nun comes in, Alice says to her: "All men are maniacs." The too-trusting nun asks her: "Maybe you're going to assassinate me too?" Alice answers: "You're not pretty enough." She tells the nun about her school-girl days and her yearning to be alone with a girl named Laura on a hill overlooking the ocean. Alice apparently pushed Laura off the cliff, then sucked the blood of Laura. When the magistrate sucks Alice's blood, Alice tells him: "It's you now who are going to die. You have blood on your lips." Continually, there are cuts to the ocean, revealing different objects in that setting: a glass slipper, a kneeler, eggs, a brass bed. The camera tilts up from the ocean to the blue sky: the camera tilts up, from the naked genitals of Nora to her sailor-shirt. Back in the cell, the horrified nun, seeing the hysterical magistrate, makes the sign of the cross. Cut back to Nora with a "customer," who whips off his belt and breaks a wine bottle against the bed, in preparation for sex-violence with Alice. He says to Nora: "You're also a prostitute?" She answers: "Yes, like everyone else these days." She flicks cigarette ash into her own navel. As Alice's changing stories of her life with Nora unfold (in the white apartment, on an empty beach, in an old country churchyard) there is developed, beside this taste for blood and for games, a shifting narrative formed by the sliding together (glissements) of the various objects that have been part of the investigation. They are like incriminating pieces of evidence, which seemed at first without any apparent meaning or function: a sandal, a kneeler, a broken bottle, a grave-digger's spade, an unnaturally red glass of grenadine, three eggs in a bowl. Next the head nun succumbs to her pleas for sex and to an exorcism to take away her sexual feelings. Finally, a young woman enters the cell. She is Alice's lawyer, and her features, appearance and clothes are all reminiscent of Nora (Olga Georges-Picot plays both roles). Enmeshed in Alice's experiences of the past and her accounts of what is going on in the institution outside of the cell (images inspired by the popular romances of the Middle Ages, in which, under the cold eyes of a religious superior, lesbian affairs, ritual humiliations and the tortures of the Inquisition are prevalent), the lawyer is drawn into this world of chains, fire, embraces and cruelty, identifying more and more with Alice and with Nora as victim. Eventually, the lawyer is accidentally stabbed and dies, bringing the murder of Nora full-circle. At that moment, the Inspector of Police (Trintignant) comes in and announces: "The investigation is over. We found the murderer." Seeing the lawyer, he says: "Ah yes, then everything must start again." The last shot of the film is of an empty beach, the first time it has been empty during the whole film.

Robbe-Grillet notes that the character of Alice is based on the "sorceress" figure of Jules Michelet, a figure who, accused of a crime, is really accusing the society that engenders such crimes and whose laws petrify creative imagination. Robbe-Grillet adds that the Alice character also stems from Nabokov's Lolita, from Lewis Carroll's Alice, from Queneau's Zazie. He emphasizes the shift from the "given" and closed truth of the traditional detective narrative to the shifting, sliding truths of Alice inventing her narratives and unrelated objects accumulating "histories" unto themselves. Beyond Alice's recounting the various versions of the story and possible explanations for the crimes, the structure of the film is based on jump-cutting that involves the use of "object-cuts" as punctuation, the breaking up of narrative scenes with short shots of objects out of their usual context (the brass bed on the ocean shore, for example). The doubling of characters (Nora-lawyer), the succession of investigators as victims, the enigmatic entries of Trintignant at the beginning and end of the film, and the circular return to the first crime with the last crime, are all a pretext for Robbe-Grillet to "reconstruct" the traditional detective narrative into serial hypotheses with punctuated object-cuts.

Credits:

Producers:	André Cohen, Marcel Sebaoun (Cosēfa Films)
Production Delegate:	Roger Boublil (Cosēfa/S.N.E.T.C.)
Director:	Alain Robbe-Grillet
Screenplay:	Alain Robbe-Grillet
Adaptation:	Alain Robbe-Grillet
Photography:	Yves Lafaye (Eastmancolor, 1:1.66)
Assistant Photography:	Michèle Ferrand
Camera Operation:	A. Canda
Still Photography:	Catherine Robbe-Grillet
Music:	Michel Fano
Sound:	Michel Fano
Assistant Sound:	Jean-Philippe Le Roux
Mix:	Jacques Ort
Editor:	Bob Wade
Assistant Editor:	Martine Rousseau
Script:	Bob Wade, Martine Rousseau
Assistant Directors:	Luc Béraud, Franck Verpillat
Chief Electrician:	J.-P. Dabosville
Director of Production:	Hubert Niogret
Make-up:	Jacky Bouban

Lab:	L.T.C.
Sound Lab:	Avia-Film
Cast:	Anicée Alvina (Alice, the prisoner), Olga Georges-Picot (Nora and the lawyer), Michel Lonsdale (the magistrate), Jean-Louis Trintignant (the police inspector), Jean Martin (the pastor), Mariane Egerickx (Claudia), Claude Marcault (Sister Julia), Nathalie Zeiger (Sister Maria), Maxence Mailfort (the client), Bob Wade (the grave-digger), Hubert Niogret (the photographer), Franck Verpillat (the porter-voyeur), Alain Robbe-Grillet (a passer-by), Catherine Robbe-Grillet (a nun).
Filmed on location in Paris and Carteret and in the Dovidis Studios in Paris in 1974.	
Completed:	1974
First French Showing:	March 7, 1974 in the following Paris film theaters: Elysses-Lincoln, Quartier Latin, Dragon, St.-Lazare-Pasquier, Hollywood Boulevard, Gaumont-Sud, Cambronne, Gaumont Gambetta
First American Showing:	1975 (New York)
Distribution:	Fox-Lira (France), Mundial Films (USA)
Running Time:	104 minutes
Original Title:	DEPLACEMENTS PROGRESSIFS DU PLAISIR
Note:	Another pornography trial was instigated in Italy for *Glissements*. Robbe-Grillet told me that he never appeared on his own behalf. With a smile and a somewhat vague explanation, he explained that the right people were taken care of, so nothing came of the proceedings. As with his other color films, Robbe-Grillet has had trouble placing *Glissements* with major distributors outside of France.

*8 LE JEU AVEC LE FEU (*Playing With Fire*) (1975)

A wealthy banker Georges de Saxe (Philippe Noiret) hires Frantz (Jean-Louis Trintignant) to find his daughter Caroline (Anicée Alvina) who has been abducted. The trail leads to a house of prostitution, at which a wide variety of sexual aberrations, tortures, simulated murders and even apparent cannibalism take place. What becomes clear is that, far from acting like a prisoner, Caroline actually enjoys her stay and is not really the victim of an abduction, as had been assumed. The "games" enjoyed by the people at the pleasure-house are complicated by a complex interweaving of character doubles. Caroline seems to have three or four doubles, her identity merging with that of Christine and Lisa. The doubling creates the possibility that Georges de Saxe (it could be a double) has incest with his daughter (it could be a double). Finally, Frantz becomes Francis (still played by Trintignant) in the second half of the film. Francis and Caroline have apparently constructed this elaborate abduction in order to get ransom money from de Saxe, with which they escape at the end of the film.

Robbe-Grillet suggests that the major theme of the film is that of incest, which merges with the mixed musical themes on the sound-track: an air of Verdi, from an opera that involves many similarities with the story-line of the film, and a Brazilian air, with a song by Chico Buarque. The film is an attempt at film-opera, and it is Robbe-Grillet's most edited film, containing more shots than any other.

Credits:

Producers:	Alain Coiffer, Philippe Ogouz (Arcadie)
Production:	UGC-CFDC Release of Arcadie Productions; Madeleine Films, Ciné Compagnie Productions
Director:	Alain Robbe-Grillet
Screenplay:	Alain Robbe-Grillet
Adaptation:	Alain Robbe-Grillet
Photography:	Yves Lafaye (Eastmancolor)
Art Director:	Hilton MacConnico
Music:	Michel Fano
Additional Music:	Excerpts from Giuseppe Verdi, from a Brazilian air, song by Chico Buarque
Sound:	Michel Fano
Editor:	Bob Wade
Cast:	Jean-Louis Trintignant (Frantz and Francis), Philippe Noiret (Georges de Saxe and his doubles), Anicée Alvina (Caroline de Saxe), Philippe Ogouz (Pierre Garin), Agostina Belli (Maria, the de Saxes' maid), Sylvia Kristel (Diana va den Berg), Serge Marquand (Matthias), Christine Boisson (Christina, the woman in the trunk), Nathalie Zeiger (the woman

	with the dogs), Jacques Doniol-Valcroze (Inspector Laurent).
Filmed in and around Paris in 1974.	
Completed:	1974
First French Showing:	January 1975 at the Antegor Theatre in Paris
First American Showing:	November 1975 at New York University where Robbe-Grillet was teaching
Distribution:	Arcadie (France), International Film Exchange (USA; Jerry Rappaport)
Running Time:	109 minutes
Note:	This film is perhaps the most "personal" of all his films in a very pragmatic sense, in that, for the first time, Robbe-Grillet largely financed a film himself. And, for the first time, he experienced difficulties in getting one of his films subtitled. Understandably, he is dismayed that the film has not been shown in this country, outside of a few limited showings, instigated by him, in New York while teaching at New York University.

*9 PIEGE A FOURRURE (Fur Trap) (1977)

The film is not finished yet. The synopsis here presented has been supplied by Robbe-Grillet. The film begins on a close-up of Néro (his full name is Néroby) watching a film or a slide presentation of the "generative signs," upon which the film is structurally built, and which in the film serve as "clues" for Néro. Those generative signs include men's shoes and the tip of a cane advancing in a corridor, a fur coat that moves on a bed, a bedroom door that opens slowly, a hand holding a hunting knife, a head of a young woman who turns toward the camera and begins a scream of terror. Néro, an investigator, goes to meet Ava L., who arrives on a motor-bike. She gives him a fur coat that Néro must transport to a certain man named Van de Reeves. Never stated, it is nonetheless clear that the fur coat somehow contains a message for Van de Reeves. En route Néro comes across the body of a young woman named Christa on the road. She seems to have been deflowered (she has blood all around her genital area), and she is apparently mute or else traumatized by the experience into silence, since she can answer none of Néro's questions. He tells her that he is on an important mission and that he will drop her off at the first convenient house, which turns out to be the mysterious "Villa Seconde," where nobody understands either French or

English, but where no questions are asked about Christa's condition or about the reasons for her staying there. Only too late will Néro discover that this apparent "accident" was really the mission itself and that Néro's attempts to avoid involvement in this "distraction" will have fatal consequences.

The detective-fiction format is a "pretext" for Robbe-Grillet to apply the principles of serialism to the cinema. The film will be based on nine generative signs, each one related to the others in a serial arrangement: footsteps, fur, opening, knife, scream, penetration, fall, dripping, viscuous spot or stain. If the series is shown in this given order, there is in that order a metaphor for sexual aggression, which culminates in a deflowering or an assassination. Thus, the nine generative signs are what constitute the investigator's mission. He will consider them as pieces in a puzzle. But they function quite differently from the causal relationships of the traditional detective novel. They are related associatively, not logically, and in a serial, not causal, arrangement. The film will be divided into nine episodes, which are each begun by the succession of the nine generative signs, each time in a different order, so that each of the generative signs will begin one episode and end one episode. There will be a masculine narrating voice (probably Robbe-Grillet's), which will both comment directly on the action of the film and give camera and acting indications.

Writings about Robbe-Grillet

Entries preceded by an asterisk (*) refer to unconsulted works. The sources for such entries are listed in parentheses. Where those sources are themselves entries elsewhere, the entry number is given. Otherwise, the reader should refer to the list of sources at the end of the Preface. The notation (n.p.) indicates that page numbers were unavailable or were not precise enough to list. Entries with multiple authors are not cross-listed within a given year, but they are cross-listed in the Index.

1958

10 ASTRE, GEORGES-ALBERT. "Les deux langages." La Revue des Lettres Modernes (Cinéma et Roman), 5, Nos. 36-38 (Summer), 135-49.

Article about the specificity of literary language as opposed to film language. Astre is primarily a literary critic; thus, his separation of the media is from that bias and, consequently, not very helpful toward understanding Robbe-Grillet's efforts in both languages.

11 AUDRY, COLETTE. "La Caméra d'Alain Robbe-Grillet." La Revue des Lettres Modernes (Cinéma et Roman), 5, Nos. 36-38 (Summer), 259-69.

Other than Robbe-Grillet's article in this issue of La Revue des Lettres Modernes, Audry's article has had the most long-reaching impact on other critics, despite the fact that her position is not compatible with that of Robbe-Grillet. Audry traces the cinematographic devices already apparent in Robbe-Grillet's novels, concluding that these novels are already films in disguise.

12 BORY, JEAN-LOUIS. "Le Cinéma: périlleux salut du roman." La Revue des Lettres Modernes (Cinéma et Roman), 5, Nos. 36-38 (Summer), 249-55.

Bory is one of the few legitimate film critics in this issue; yet, his criticism is impressionistic and opinionated. He cautions against adaptations, against the cinema becoming too literary or the novel becoming too cinematic.

13 BOUCHAREINE, R. "Film, roman et entourage concret: lumières sur l'univers quotidien." La Revue des Lettres Modernes (Cinéma et Roman), 5, Nos. 36-38 (Summer), 166-85.

Film and novel both tied here to the carcass of being "recorders" of reality, without much allowance for the subjective possibilities of each.

14 DURAND, PHILIPPE. "Cinéma et roman." La Revue des Lettres Modernes (Cinéma et Roman), 5, Nos. 36-38 (Summer), 186-94.

Interesting article by a critic capable of dealing equally well with literature and film, although his views are not in accord with Robbe-Grillet's.

15 DUVIGNAUD, JEAN. "Dialogue ininterrompu." La Revue des Lettres Modernes (Cinéma et Roman), 5, Nos. 36-38 (Summer), 150-54.

Uninteresting comparisons between film and literature by a very influential critic.

16 GAUTEUR, CLAUDE. "Eloge de la spécificité." La Revue des Lettres Modernes (Cinéma et Roman), 5, Nos. 36-38 (Summer), 208-15.

The question of specificity is an interesting one, especially in light of Robbe-Grillet's later reliance on intertextuality, on cross-feeding between film and literature, to generate new works. Within the context of this issue, Gauteur's article is not very helpful, but if the specificity problem is related to intertextuality, then Gauteur's article is useful.

17 LABARTHE, ANDRÉ-S. "Histoire d'un échec." La Revue des Lettres Modernes (Cinéma et Roman), 5, Nos. 36-38 (Summer), 304-306.

Labarthe discusses Robbe-Grillet's objects, noting that they are no longer "named"; rather, they are described in minute and geometric detail. Labarthe sees in Robbe-Grillet's novels the obvious failure of the traditional novel, the dependence of the novel upon the cinema and, hence, the failure of the novel of the future.

18 LAGROLET, JEAN. "Nouveau réalisme?" La Nef, 15, No. 13 (January), 62-70.

Primarily dealing with literature and highly critical of Robbe-Grillet, the article does point out Robbe-Grillet's cinematographic vision in his novels.

19 MOURLET, MICHEL. "Cinéma contre roman." La Revue des Lettres Modernes (Cinéma et Roman), 5, Nos. 36-38 (Summer), 155-65.
More insistence upon the role of objects, the primacy of the visual image and exteriorized psychology, as those three areas categorize the entire issue and its generally literary approach to the relationships between film and the novel.

20 PIZZORUSSO, ARNALDO. "La Jalousie." Letteratura (January-April), p. 183.
Discussion of cinematic devices in La Jalousie.

21 ROBBE-GRILLET, ALAIN. "Notes sur la localisation et les déplacements du point de vue dans la description romanesque." La Revue des Lettres Modernes (Cinéma et Roman), 5, Nos. 36-38 (Summer), 256-58.
Robbe-Grillet here emphasizes point of view in fiction and in film as a link between the objective and the subjective.

22 TRUFFAUT, FRANÇOIS. "L'Adaptation littéraire au cinéma." La Revue des Lettres Modernes (Cinéma et Roman), 5, Nos. 36-38 (Summer), 243-48.
Article has very little to do with Robbe-Grillet, except by opposition. Truffaut was one of the leading voices for the then young New Wave, and his attacks on the "well-made" films of the 1930-1940 period, with their emphasis upon screenplay over direction, are an interesting parallel to Robbe-Grillet's development of a "literary" cinema, based on the transposition of literary techniques and not literary plots.

1959

23 AUDRY, COLETTE. "The Camera and Robbe-Grillet." Forum, 3, No. 2 (Spring), 13-17.
Translation and reprint of Audrey's article from La Revue des Lettres Modernes (See: 11).

1960

24 ANON. "In the Picture: News From Paris." Sight and Sound, 29, No. 4 (Autumn), 176-79.
Review of upcoming films, including an announcement of L'Année dernière à Marienbad before its release. "The subject sounds conventional enough, a variation on the husband-wife-lover eternal triangle, but the idea is to treat it with total objectivity." Quotes director Alain Resnais as saying: "I would like people to see the film rather as

they would a piece of sculpture. It can be looked at from all angles, and the final choice is up to the spectator."

25 ANON. "L'Année dernière à Marienbad." Sight and Sound, 30, No. 1 (Winter), 25.

Pictorial supplement on the film, still before its release. Quotes Resnais and Robbe-Grillet: "The composition of images, their linking, the sound that accompanies them need no longer be subject to the tyranny of common sense. When one hears a word, one doesn't always know who's speaking, or where the sound comes from, or even what it means; when one looks at a scene, one doesn't always know where it's taking place, or when, or exactly what it represents.... Nevertheless, through these strangenesses and uncertainties, the images and sounds...should impose themselves with enough force, enough evident necessity, to define a contemporary realism, breaking down the old opposition between realistic and poetic cinema...."

26 AUTRUSSEAU, J. "Le Nouveau Cinéma et le nouveau roman." Les Lettres Françaises, No. 837 (August 18-24), pp. 1, 8.

Interview with Robbe-Grillet, centering on the preoccupations of film directors like Resnais and parallels between those concerns and the concerns of the new novelists.

27 GESSNER, ROBERT. "The Film: A Source of New Vitality for the Novel." New York Times Book Review (August 7), pp. 4, 20-21.

Brief mention of Resnais and his literary collaborators (Marguerite Duras, Robbe-Grillet).

28 ROBBE-GRILLET, ALAIN. "L'Acteur peut devenir une sorte de personnage mythique." Le Monde (August 13), (n.p.)

Interesting account by Robbe-Grillet, since it continues his move away from purely objective concerns and toward subjectivity in both fiction and film.

29 WEIGHTMAN, J. G. "New Wave in French Culture." Commentary, 30 (September), 230-40.

Article notes the rampant romanticism in the films of the New Wave and likens them to the nouveau roman in that they both represent a retreat from political and social commitment. Weightman notes that Robbe-Grillet has obviously borrowed from the cinema and the detective novel for his fiction, but not their concern with immediate social reality. "His attention dwells on the external world with the insistence and impartiality of a cinema camera making a documentary exploration." Weightman concludes that the best forms of art are those that come to grips with social reality, whereas films and novels in France of 1960 are trying to avoid that reality.

1961

30 ANON. "Sounding the Sixties--Three Outside English." The Times Literary Supplement, No. 3318 (September 30), pp. 830-41.
Brief discussion of Marienbad, primarily as plot summary.

31 ARISTARCO, GUIDO. "Senza passato nē prospettiva l'oro' di Marienbad." Cinema Nuovo, 10, No. 153 (September-October), 399-400.
Analysis of Last Year at Marienbad, specifically of time and point of view in the film. Aristarco notes that the image is entirely in the present tense. "There is no real looking back, no moving towards the past or remembering by means of blurring or other technical devices." Suggests that the past and future seen by A are purely imaginary, that A is not reliving the past, but rather sees a present that X narrates to her as if past.

*32 _____. "Venezia 61." Cinema Nuovo, No. 153 (September-October), (n.p.)
Unseen. Cited in Pingaud, p. 93 (See: 65). Review of the films in the Venice Film Festival of 1961, including Marienbad, which won the Golden Lion of St. Mark Prize in that festival.

*33 BABY, YVONNE. "L'Année dernière à Marienbad." Le Monde (August 29).
Unseen. Cited in Pingaud, pp. 80-82 (See: 65). Interview with Resnais and Robbe-Grillet about Marienbad.

*34 BERETTA, VINICIO. "Le due anime di Alain Resnais." Settimo Giorno, 14, No. 37 (September 12).
Unseen. Cited in Pingaud, p. 93 (See: 65). Interview with Resnais about the film and about working with Robbe-Grillet.

*35 BIANCHI, PIETRO. "Resnais distrugge il tempo in un film rompicapo." Il Giorno (August 30).
Unseen. Cited in Pingaud, p. 93 (See: 65). Discussion of Resnais' time distortions in Marienbad.

36 BILLARD, PIERRE. "Entrevue avec Alain Resnais et Alain Robbe-Grillet." Cinéma 61, No. 61 (November-December), (n.p.)
Interview with Resnais and Robbe-Grillet on Marienbad.

*37 BOLLÈME, GENEVIÈVE. "L'Année dernière à Marienbad: essai d'interprétation." Les Temps Modernes, No. 183 (July), pp. 177-79.
Unseen. Cited in French VII, 1962, #27667 (See: Source List).

38 BONNOT, GERARD. "Marienbad ou le parti de Dieu." Les Temps Modernes, No. 187 (December), pp. 752-68.

Notes that the film is in fashion, an anti-film in the way that the nouveau roman was the anti-novel. Thus, there is no pretense to action or character development...the two men and the woman are reduced to their physical appearances and are given only initials, not whole names. "And if it's true that a human being is only the sum of what happens to him or her, then these people don't even exist." Bonnot believes the hotel is an artificial environment, that the time-period is unstable and indeterminate. He suggests that Resnais is paying homage to the experimental directors of the 1920's: Marcel L'Herbier, Germaine Dulac, Jean Epstein. According to Bonnot, if even one of the actors acted in a realistic way, the whole network of artificial symbols would fall apart. With realism gone, all that is left is the game, all the games in the film and the film itself as a stylized game. Bonnot complains insightfully about the editing, suggesting that Marienbad is not a single film, but a compilation film. The frenetic editing represents a composite, a kind of newsreel tribute to all the films of the silent era. There are various interpretations of the "story" and various interpretations of the statue in the garden. Bonnot does not criticize the film for its technical virtuosity and its innovative camera movements and editing displacements, but he does criticize the film, because such technique carries with it a total lack of concern with everyday reality, with daily problems, offering instead only a void of ambiguous possiblities: in short, a game.

In the second half of the article, Bonnot suggests that even the technical aspects of the film were borrowed from earlier films. He then contrasts Marienbad with Hiroshima mon amour, the former unfavorably with the latter. The "look of God" of the article's title refers to the lucid but disinterested overview of Resnais and Robbe-Grillet toward their material, as opposed to the passionate commitment to portraying human tragedy in Hiroshima. From this existentialist perspective, Bonnot indicts Resnais and Robbe-Grillet on the basis of their extreme formalism being an avoidance of human nature.

*39 BURGUET, FR.-A. "L'Année dernière à Marienbad." L'Arc, No. 16 (Fall), pp. 23-26.

Unseen. Cited in Klapp, 1961-62, p. 44 (See: Source List).

40 BUTOR, MICHEL and CLAUDE OLLIER, JEAN RICARDOU et al. "Enquête," in Premier Plan (Alain Resnais). Edited by Bernard Pingaud, No. 18 (October), pp. 25-35.

A college-questionnaire, responded to by various novelists, concerning the influence of Resnais in particular and the cinema in general on their writing. Other novelists who responded were Claude Simon, Philippe Sollers and Jean Thibaudeau.

*41 CASIRAGHI, UGO: "Gli enigmi di Resnais." L'Unità (August 30).
Unseen. Cited in Pingaud, p. 93 (See: 65). Review of Marienbad, stressing the film's enigmatic qualities.

42 COLLET, JEAN. "Peut-on se perdre dans les jardins de Marienbad?" Signes du Temps, No. 11 (November), pp. 30-32.
Review of Marienbad, noting the spectator's inevitable confusion and inability to find one workable interpretation of the film.

43 DECAUDIN, MICHEL. "Roman et cinéma." Revue des Sciences Humaines, No. 104 (October-December), pp. 623-28.
Discusses Robbe-Grillet both as an author who has turned filmmaker and as an author whose novels contain film techniques: "The look of the novelist is assimilated in the camera lens, and perception is left open to a new kind of film-eye." What concerns Decaudin most are equivalency problems in the transposition from one medium to the other: what is the equivalent of the novelistic "I" in film; how can film convey sentiments of characters in a novel; how can the time of the novel be adapted to film; how can stylistic devices, such as Flaubert's verbs, be transferred to film.

44 EGLY, MAX. "L'Année dernière à Marienbad." Image et Son, No. 144 (October), pp. 241-42.
Brief review of the film.

*45 ELSEN, CL. "Le 'Nouveau Cinéma' n'est pas celui qu'on pense." Ecrits de Paris, No. 198 (November), pp. 103-107.
Unseen. Cited in Klapp, 1961-62, p. 44 (See: Source List).

46 FUSCO, MARIO. "Alain Robbe-Grillet." Les Lettres Modernes, 2:784-88.
Survey discussion of Robbe-Grillet as novelist-turned-filmmaker and a review of Last Year at Marienbad.

*47 GRAMONT, SANCHE DE. "The Paris Scene." Olympia, No. 1, pp. 1-3.
Unseen. Cited in French VII, 1967, #65733 (See: Source List). Discussion of the Resnais-Robbe-Grillet collaboration, with brief comments on Last Year at Marienbad.

48 GRENIER, CYNTHIA. "Alain Resnais of France--Explorations in the Unconscious." Saturday Review (December 23), pp. 37-38.

Brief discussion of novel and film in France, with comments on Hiroshima mon amour and then on Last Year at Marienbad as representative examples of Resnais' effort to portray mental states (dreams, imagination, memory) in film.

49 HALLIER, JEAN-EDERN. "Toute une vie à Marienbad." Tel Quel, No. 7 (Fall), pp. 49-52.

Article on Last Year at Marienbad. Hallier says that the film comes somewhere out of Mallarmé and Valery idolatry. He objects to the cinema, its sudden images, its "diminution" of reality's ambiguity. How can an image of a clock without hands (Bergman's Wild Strawberries) depict a mental state without either stereotyping that state or impoverishing it? From the Surrealists to Bergman and Resnais/Robbe-Grillet, Hallier sees an uneasy polarity between the random element and the simplistic treatment of complex psychological states. He cites a shot of the garden in Marienbad, in which the immobile characters have shadows, while the trees and statues don't. He notes the "reality" of the hotel in opposition to the half-dead characters. The corridors of the hotel become "time" rendered spatially. The mirrors become symbols for infinity. "Reality" is theatrical within the film, between the film and the spectator. Inexplicably, Hallier sees hope for the cinema in this closed work of a "whole life" at Marienbad, in which everything is reduced to form, the form of a mathematical series or of serial music.

50 HOUSTON, PENELOPE and GEOFFREY NOWELL-SMITH. "Resnais' L'Année dernière à Marienbad; Antonioni's La Notte." Sight and Sound, 31, No. 1 (Winter), 26-31.

The article is in two parts: Houston reviews Marienbad, while Nowell-Smith reviews La Notte and relates it to Marienbad. Houston suggests that Last Year at Marienbad involves the audience as much as it does the people on screen. It invites total acceptance or rejection. Among the several reasons for rejecting the film: a film whose every shot of the heroine is a fashion photograph is suspect; a film which shows no characters working, eating, thinking or talking about any aspect of the "outside" world doesn't have much directly to say about that world. "Resnais was accused of being trivial about a big theme in Hiroshima mon amour, and this time he's criticized for being pretentious about a little one." Houston traces the hypnotic effects of the film's opening sequences, from the organ music and panning camera to the voice of the narrator fusing with the voices of the play within the film. The organ music drowns the voice, then it returns, then the music rises over it again. She then discusses spatial symbolism: the Stranger's territory is that formal, continental garden with its neatly clipped trees, "gravel paths, ornamental lakes and neoclassical statuary"; the ground floor of the hotel is "neutral" ground; A's bedroom is her territory, which she cedes to the Stranger with the "persuasion" of his story. Houston notes the ambiguity of the film's ending, in which A seems to have traded one lost self for another, and, thus, the chateau appears more like a refuge than a prison. She calls the Albertazzi figure (X) a personification of moral force; A's attitudes are "hieratic"; Sacha Pitoeff (M) is a "deep, resonant voice speaking from an elongated black and white form." All are "automatons"; A doesn't go away with X; she accepts her necessary place in his dream. Houston is reminded of Iris Murdoch's novels. She suggests that, if written as a novel, Last Year at Marienbad would seem less audacious and challenging.

*51 JUIN, HERBERT. "Introduction à la méthode d'Alain Resnais et d'Alain Robbe-Grillet." Les Lettres Françaises, No. 888 (August 10-24), pp. 1, 5.
Unseen. Cited in Besses, p. 88 (See: 377); French VII, 1962, #27673 (See: Source List).

52 KANTERS, R. "Quand l'allittérature se fait a-cinéma." Le Figaro Littéraire (September 23), p. 2.
Brief discussion of the link between the so-called anti-novel and the new "anti-cinema," as typified by Last Year at Marienbad.

*53 KAST, PIERRE. "A Venise, Alain Resnais a gagné la bataille de Marienbad." Arts, No. 833 (September 6-13).
Unseen. Cited in Pingaud, p. 93 (See: 65).

*54 KYROU, ADO. "L'Année dernière à Marienbad." Positif, No. 40 (June).
Unseen. Cited in Pingaud, p. 93 (See: 65). Kyrou discusses myth- and symbol-making in Last Year at Marienbad, seeing in both an extension of the work of the Surrealists.

55 LABARTHE, A.-S. and JACQUES RIVETTE. "Entretien avec Resnais et Robbe-Grillet." Cahiers du Cinéma, No. 123 (September), pp. 1-18.
The most extensive and most useful interview given by Resnais and Robbe-Grillet on Last Year at Marienbad. Initially, Resnais was interviewed alone. Then both Resnais and Robbe-Grillet were interviewed. The two interviews were then synthesized and published as one. Resnais was asked about the Nim game and the concept of the game as a trap. Resnais suggests that Albertazzi (X) loses voluntarily and in a calculated manner, due in part to what Resnais sees as the schizophrenic or double nature of X's character. What interested Resnais in terms of possible

interpretations of the film was the idea of parallel universes, the idea that all characters could be right. He alludes to automatic writing and the Surrealists. Robbe-Grillet's writing reminded Resnais of the Douanier Rousseau's way of painting. Resnais further notes that moments of invented or interior reality in the film occur when the image corresponds to, or coincides with, the dialogue; the interior monologue is never on the sound-track; it is almost always on the image-track, which, even when it represents the past, corresponds always to the present in the mind of the character. There is a discussion of various mythical and symbolic interpretations of the film. Resnais suggests that the first part of the film is "real" and maybe the end is real. He suggests that when A ties her shoe, she remembers. From that moment on, the past (what's related as "past") is true for her. Robbe-Grillet notes that the harshest critics of the film as being "artificial" were those who sensed a spontaneity in works which are the most fabricated, formulaic, codified and respectful of traditional rules of composition. Resnais explains the image of the broken balcony as a false image projected from A's point of view. He says the Fantomas or Feuillade look of the scene came naturally from her recourse to popular fiction as a means of protecting herself from her fears. Robbe-Grillet explains that in the scenario there are indications for dissolves between two present moments, whereas there are abrupt shifts between scenes in which one is "past" and one "present" in the final film. Robbe-Grillet's dissolves never got into the film. He explains the "hole," the idea that Bruce Morrissette would later explain so well in terms of Robbe-Grillet's generative images. The "hole" in Marienbad is "last year" and the uncertainty about the time frame, even as it unfolds in the present. Robbe-Grillet offers the phrase "Larvatus prodeo": "I advance masked, all the while exposing my mask." In like fashion, the cinema is a technique or process which designs itself.

56 LABARTHE, A.-S. "Marienbad année zéro." Cahiers du Cinéma, No. 123 (September), pp. 28-31.

Rather than point out that Marienbad is an exceptional film (defined as radical or innovative), Labarthe suggests that it is in a sense a dated work, belonging to certain traditions; specifically, it is the last of the great neo-realist films. Neo-realist film is here defined in opposition to more traditional films as a film having an open scenario, fragmented scenes or an episodic narrative, all of which demand an active spectator for completion in terms of coherence. Labarthe compares Last Year at Marienbad with Rossellini's Paisa. Traditional narrative films erased all ambiguities. There was no need of a spectator, since the viewing process was all foreseen and included in the making of the film. Filmmakers like Orson Welles and the Neo-realists forced the spectator to participate in creating meaning for the films they made. In keeping with the Neo-realist analogy, Labarthe suggests that Marienbad is a documentary, but we as spectators never know that. Like the Neo-realist films, Marienbad does not resort to flashbacks. The greatness of a Welles, an Ophuls or a Resnais lies partly in the fact that when such as these do use flashbacks, they are not to secure film continuity (as flashbacks are traditionally used), but rather to emphasize discontinuity. Labarthe likens Last Year at Marienbad to a Rorschach test. The film is a two-dimensional object. The spectator must create perspective, giving the film its third and other dimensions.

*57 LANOCITA, ARTURO. "Il film difficile è nato dalla memoria troppo labile." Corriere della Sera (August 30).
Unseen. Cited in Pingaud, p. 93 (See: 65).

58 MAZARS, PIERRE. "...comme au sortir d'un rêve." Le Figaro Littéraire (October 7), p. 16.
Discussion of Last Year at Marienbad as a puzzle-film, which can be explained as a dream; thus, the interconnections between shadowy characters, the baroque hotel, time and memory of an hypothetical "last year" make sense, if the film is taken as an elaborate dream structure.

*59 MICCICHÉ, LINO. "Un film dove non succede niente ma che potrebbe continuare all' infinito." Avanti! (August 30).
Unseen. Cited in Pingaud, p. 93 (See: 65).

*60 MORANDINI, MORANDO. "Difficile da capire come un quadro cubista." La Notte (August 30-31).
Unseen. Cited in Pingaud, p. 93 (See: 65). Last Year at Marienbad can be looked at like a cubist painting: that is, from multiple perspectives, so that meaning depends upon the angle of vision from which one looks at the film.

61 MORRISSETTE, BRUCE. "Roman et cinéma: le cas de Robbe-Grillet." Symposium, 15, No. 2 (Summer), 85-103.
Morrissette begins by tracing historically what cinematic techniques have most interested writers from the Expressionists to the present. The rest of his article is a critique of the special "Cinéma et Roman" issue of La Revue des Lettres Modernes (Summer 1958). He takes this issue to point out, one by one, the fallacies involved in not respecting the specificity of each medium in false comparisons. He notes that all of the articles in that issue focus on three areas of comparison: point of view, the priority of the visual image and the development of an

exteriorized psychology. He takes issue with G.-A. Astre, who is against Robbe-Grillet as a voyeur who doesn't let the reader participate; he takes issue with Michel Mourlet, who objects to Robbe-Grillet's attempts to reproduce film images in words; he takes issue with Jean-Louis Bory, who sees Robbe-Grillet's images as photographs; and, most of all, he takes issue with Colette Audry, who sees Robbe-Grillet's style as cinematic for a narrative content that is non-cinematic. Morrissette compares La Jalousie with the film Lady in the Lake in terms of the failed gamble in that film of the subjective camera. He defends Robbe-Grillet's style as literary and suggests in his notes a trend of novelistic adaptations of films.

62 OLLIER, CLAUDE. "Ce soir à Marienbad." La Nouvelle Revue Française (October), pp. 711-19.

Often critics have affirmed that the "modern" cinema is the art of capturing reality without ever defining what that "reality" is. Usually, the "reality" turns out to be similar to the plot of a traditional novel. On the other hand, by exalting "artifice," Resnais and Robbe-Grillet have made a "true" and "real" film with Last Year at Marienbad. Ollier notes six kinds of fictional structures in the film: (1) frames presented as image-memories (as though they came from "last year" at Marienbad) and which correspond to X's accounts; (2) frames presented as image-memories, but which don't correspond exactly to X's accounts. Small details are changed within the frames, which, nevertheless, still confirm X on the whole. Then there are (3) frames of supposed image-memories, which are absolutely incompatible with X's accounts. In such frames a character may refuse to do what the text affirms he or she did (curiously, the image carries more weight than the words which contradict it). There are (4) frames of images which correspond to the wishes or desires of X, to X's emotional states, but which are outside of any "reality" of his accounts of the past. There are (5) frames of image-desires combining with frames of image-memories. And there are (6) frames of image-desires combining with image-memories whose accumulation and linkage are such that they compose oneiric "suites" without any realistic rapport between them and the events that supposedly brought them on. The music and the sounds add other elements to these six. The music adds two aspects which sometimes merge and sometimes oppose each other: the organ in the form of a prelude or waltz is linked to the idea of wandering; the symphonic orchestra, with its romantic style, is related to the idea of triumph or confirmation. As for the sounds, they sometimes correspond to their real-life referents; at other times, they are used simply for their expressive value. Sometimes an event is shown in the images without commentary by the text, when one would normally expect some commentary. Sometimes such commentary is so full of errors in the details of a scene or so charged with distorted emotion that the spectator doubts both the image and the commentary. Even within the frames, the principal character is often shown to one corner of the frame or in the background or is suddenly masked. Ollier shows how doubt is instilled in us as to "last year" or when and as to Marienbad or where, which leads him to insist upon the present tense of this film of persuasion. X's voice seems to convince by repetition and incantation. The voices are progressive: (1) X himself in the first third of the film, (2) A in the second third and finally (3) M, who watches X and A go off together without trying to intervene. According to Ollier, M is rational, X is irrational; X always loses to M in games but always wins A; X is impotent, while M is virile.

63 _____. "Ce soir à Marienbad." La Nouvelle Revue Française (November), pp. 906-912.

The sequel to the longer October article of the same title. In this second part, Ollier suggests that the voice of X creates fear, then point of view in A. Sounds of water when the balcony crumbles reinforce the oneiric rather than the realistic passion. Other sounds, such as wind, deep thumps in the corridors, are also independent of any visual source. Ollier notes the absence of windows and the overabundance of mirrors which fix people, double them, multiply and distort them. Thus, multiple interpretations are possible. The last scene, for example, is narrated in the past by X, as though it belonged to "last year." Time then becomes cyclical: each time there is a play put on at night and X crosses the threshold alone, this series of evocations, memories and imaginings takes place. Ollier compares Last Year at Marienbad with Bioy Casares' L'Invention de Morel. With so many possible interpretations, the film appears as a musical composition for three voices, organ and orchestra. The two "male" voices are accented, while the voice of Delphine Seyrig is somber and romanticized. In this film-exploration, the authors, the actors and the spectators all "know" what there is to know at the same moment, with no one of them having an advantage of prior knowing over the other.

*64 PESTELLI, LEO. "Un film raffinato e difficile." La Stampa (August 30).

Unseen. Cited in Pingaud, p. 93 (See: 65).

65 PINGAUD, BERNARD. "Alain Resnais." Premier Plan (Alain Resnais), No. 18 (Autumn), pp. 3-24.

Pingaud opposes Hiroshima mon amour with Last Year at Marienbad, since memory is a phenomenon which, from a certain standpoint, is the opposite of remembering; thus, one can imagine false memories as being as peopled and as rich as real ones. Pingaud suggests there are four possible interpretations of Last Year at Marienbad: (1) they (X and A) met and loved last year, but A forgot and X makes her remember; (2) X had an affair the preceding year but with another woman or A had an affair the preceding year but with another man, perhaps Franck or Frank, whose name is repeated several times; (3) X insists and the force of his convictions convinces A, but nothing is verifiable; and (4) the flight of the two lovers is told in the past, the whole film having been meant to be repeated infinitely, since the end leads into the beginning. Pingaud studies counterpoint as it is used between the verbal narration and the visuals. He notes the various interpretations given to the film by Claude Ollier, François Weyergans and Roger Tailleur. He then suggests that the images of Marienbad struggle throughout the film against the verbal narration, only to coincide finally with a now confused, less definite narration. X's truth has no references in reality, only in theatre. His life is an acted-out role from a play. Pingaud concludes that Hiroshima mon amour extends a tradition of a "literary" cinema, while Last Year at Marienbad begins a kind of "pure" cinema. He adds that a film like Last Year at Marienbad cannot be "read"; it can only be looked at. By that Pingaud means that the passivity of the spectator is for the first time encouraged in film.

66 _____. "Le Cinéma. Dans le labyrinthe." Preuves, No. 128 (October), pp. 65-69.

The title is deceptive, since the article has very little to do with Robbe-Grillet's novel In the Labyrinth. Instead, the article is about Last Year in Marienbad. Pingaud suggests that the film combines the situations found in Robbe-Grillet's two earlier novels: In the Labyrinth and Jealousy. He also suggests that the structure of the "modern" work of art is the labyrinth. He announces that Marienbad is the film which "inaugurates" the cinema, the first film whose beauty is self-contained and which dares to proclaim itself as an autonomous work, exclusive of all the literary forms with which the cinema, until then, had compromised itself in order to justify itself as an art form and gain respectability. Pingaud explains the various examples of displacement between the image-track and the sound-track in the film, concluding with the "false" endings proposed by these displacements: the husband-figure kills the woman; a balcony crumbles behind the protagonist; etc. All the fantasy images of suicide, rape and murder are shown as "real"; the "white" scenes of the bedroom and corridor do not demarcate the past from the present nor the imaginary from the real. They mark the moments of heightened emotion, which are less concerned with proving themselves than with convincing. Because the film is so meticulously photographed, one gets the impression, even though there is a great deal of dialogue, that Last Year at Marienbad is a silent film, especially in the sense that only the faces "talked" in silent films. The script is so rigorous and meticulous that it's as though Robbe-Grillet had scripted a film that had already been made. And although the structure of the film is very complex, the original theme is simple.

67 QUÉVAL, JEAN. "L'Année dernière à Marienbad." Mercure de France, No. 1180 (December), pp. 692-98.
Quéval is against the content of the film: too much work without rewards. He can't get interested. He suggests that there are two films here: the one he doesn't like, which is boring and full of "stories of deaf-mutes"; the other he does like, which is a film-opera. In the first, there isn't any dialogue; there are two monologues enjoined. He discounts the so-called poetry of the narration as mere enumeration of objects. What spectator will be able to participate, even when invited to, he asks. He discusses opera and infra-film and criticizes Robbe-Grillet as empty-headed, vacuous and tiresome, but he finds it encouraging that Robbe-Grillet has gotten involved in film where, according to Quéval, his fiction belonged all the time. He praises Resnais and Henri Colpi, the editor. He describes the film's music: "as though the orchestra had devoured the opera." He is reminded of Henri Storck's Le Monde de Paul Delvaux (music by André Souris and text by Paul Eluard), which he finds sensuous, sexual, full of passion, all contrary to Marienbad. He concludes by saying that he awaits a film that is by Resnais and not by his literary collaborators.

68 REID, GORDON. "The Experimental Novel and Film." Continental Film Review (January), pp. 10-11.
Ostensibly a review of Last Year at Marienbad, Reid quotes extensively from Resnais and Robbe-Grillet in telegraph fashion, only to emphasize the demand on the viewer to be a reader in order to participate in the film. Reid compares Robbe-Grillet's novel The Voyeur to Faulkner's The Sound and the Fury, among other whims. No analysis of the film, since the article was written prior to the author's having seen the film.

69 RESNAIS, ALAIN. "Alain Resnais à la question." Premier Plan (Alain Resnais), No. 18 (October), pp. 36-89.
Excerpts from interviews with Resnais about Hiroshima mon amour and Last Year at Marienbad, first printed elsewhere and here collected and put together in collage fashion by Bernard Pingaud.

70 _____. "L'Année dernière à Marienbad." Cinéma 61, No. 61 (December), (n.p.).

Resnais explains what has often been quoted elsewhere: his intentions and those of Robbe-Grillet in making Last Year at Marienbad and how he would like the spectator to "receive" the film.

71 ROBBE-GRILLET, ALAIN. "Alain Robbe-Grillet vous parle de L'Année dernière à Marienbad." Réalités, No. 184 (May), pp. 95-98, 111-15.

Reprise of Robbe-Grillet's writings elsewhere on how he and Resnais worked on Last Year in Marienbad and the implications of that collaboration. Robbe-Grillet notes that usually there is a division of labor between scenarist and director, which means that there is a separation between the scenario and the images, between the story and the style, between content and form. Robbe-Grillet says that he and Resnais worked so closely on the film that they co-directed it, even though Robbe-Grillet was never present on the set during the shooting of the film. He defines the cinema as an art form in proportion to the reality it creates with its forms. Content must be sought and found in the forms. For Robbe-Grillet, to conceive a story in terms of making an eventual film of it is already to conceive it in terms of images, not words. He itemizes what he admired in Resnais' style before working with him: a style of composition that was both conceptual and personal, that was rigorous and not overly worried about public taste; a certain ritual solidity; a certain weight; a sense of the "theatrical" in terms of fixed poses, rigid gestures and decors, which made one think of an opera; finally, the attempt to build a space and time that would be purely mental or "interior" as in a dream or a memory. Robbe-Grillet says he never wrote a "story" for Last Year at Marienbad; from the outset, he wrote a scenario, image by image, with camera indications defined and clearly marked. He then provides an excellent synopsis of the film. Finally, he gives his somewhat facile justifications for Marienbad being the easiest, truest, most realistic film the spectator will ever see, provided the spectator can let go of preconceived ideas and avoid doing a psychological profile on the film. At the end of Robbe-Grillet's statements, there is an attached fragment from the scenario for the film.

72 _____. "Comment j'ai écrit L'Année dernière à Marienbad." Les Nouvelles Littéraires, No. 1775 (September 7), p. 1.

Description of Robbe-Grillet's working methods in writing the scenario for Last Year at Marienbad: how he wrote it as a film, image by image, instead of conceptually, in terms of words; how he worked with Resnais in the preparation of the scenario.

73 ______. L'Année dernière à Marienbad. Paris: Minuit, 172 pp., 48 photographs.

The published ciné-roman (film-novel) for Last Year at Marienbad, including a brief introduction and synopsis by Robbe-Grillet, as well as the scenario (minus the camera indications) for the film. This published ciné-roman combined Robbe-Grillet's twin positions as screenwriter for the film and as literary editor at the Editions de Minuit publishing house.

74 ______. "L'Année dernière à Marienbad." Cinéma 61, No. 56 (May), (n.p.).

Statements repeated elsewhere concerning Robbe-Grillet's involvement with Resnais, the extent to which Robbe-Grillet was the "author" of the film, how he viewed the film.

75 ______. "L'Année dernière à Marienbad." Sight and Sound, 30, No. 4 (Autumn), 176-79.

Robbe-Grillet discusses the different relations possible between the scriptwriter and the director of a film: there are many possibilities as there are films. He lauds Resnais, speaks of their close relationship, mentions some of the changes Resnais made in the shooting of the film, while Robbe-Grillet was in Istanbul working on L'Immortelle. He contrasts his work as a screenwriter with his work as a novelist. "The writer's idea when he begins work on a novel allows both for the story and for the way he's going to tell it. Often it's the latter which first takes shape in his mind, in the same way that a painter might think of a canvas composed entirely in vertical lines before deciding that what he's actually going to paint is a group of skyscrapers." He gives his reasons for admiring Resnais as a director, provides a synopsis for the film and concludes with a discussion of the differences between film tenses (rooted in the present) and literary tenses.

76 ______. L'Anno scorso a Marienbad. Translated by C. Cignetti and A. Savini. Torino: Einaudi, 183 pp.

The Italian translation of Robbe-Grillet's ciné-roman.

77 ______. "Le 'nouveau roman.'" La Revue de Paris (September), pp. 119-21.

Discussion of point of view in the nouveau roman, with examples from Last Year at Marienbad to show the camera as omniscient, like a God. "Who is this omniscient and ever-present spectator who is situated everywhere at the same time and who sees simultaneously the inside and outside of things, who simultaneously unifies the movements of the face and those of the conscience, who knows simultaneously the present, the past and the future of every event? It can only be God."

*78 ROSSETTI, ENRICO. "Hanno premiato un gelido sogno." L'Espresso, 7, No. 37 (September).
Unseen. Cited in Pingaud, p. 93 (See: 65).

79 SADOUL, GEORGES. "Eurydice à Marienbad." Les Lettres Françaises (October 5), pp. 1, 7.
Discussion of Last Year at Marienbad as an allegorical presentation of the Orpheus-Eurydice myth, the descent into the underworld, the reprieve from death, M as Pluto and the baroque hotel as Hades.

*80 SALA, ALBERICO. "Il film più discusso." Corriere d'Informazione (August 30-31).
Unseen. Cited in Pingaud, p. 93 (See: 65).

81 SAMPAYO, NUNO DE. "O romance da 'Nouvelle Vague.'" Rumo, 5:254-59.
Only indirectly applicable to Robbe-Grillet.

82 SICLIER, JACQUES. "New Wave and French Cinema." Sight and Sound, 30, No. 3 (Summer), 116-20.
From 1959 to 1961, in two years, the original enthusiasm for the New Wave disappeared. Siclier discusses the sheer numbers of new filmmakers who emerged during that time. Just as everyone wanted to write novels and poems after the war in 1945, so too everyone wants to make films after 1959 in France. The deterioration and growing public disapproval of the New Wave in France was due in part to its intellectual calibre. Hiroshima mon amour and Le Bel Age are cited as examples. There was a reaction against the scandalous or exhibitionist aspects of the films. Producers turned the New Wave style into a cliché. Robbe-Grillet is cited as a cinéma d'art et essai director, making films for limited audiences. He also notes that André Labarthe saw a link between the new French novel and the new cinema (Robbe-Grillet, Butor, Sarraute are cited): "a literary cinema of individual expression." Siclier passes severe judgment on the New Wave (excluding Truffaut), for "turning their backs on social reality.... There exists no other ideal than the acte gratuit; and force always wins out over intelligence.... The only moral is an aesthetic one." About Last Year at Marienbad, Siclier concludes: "Images finally become little more than a succession of anagrams. Actors, often enough, are accorded no more and no less aesthetic meaning than the painted ceilings and columns, the gilded doors, the fountains and statues which surround them. If the film, in so far as screen language is concerned, is an advance on Hiroshima, it also marks a step back for the actual world."

83 TAILLEUR, ROGER. "L'Année dernière à Marienbad d'Alain Resnais." Les Lettres Nouvelles, No. 16 (July-September), pp. 164-69.

Tailleur suggests that Resnais and Robbe-Grillet were meant to collaborate, to judge from the similarities in their styles. Trying to reconstruct the film of Last Year at Marienbad chronologically is not the point, nor is it sufficient just to say the film is a puzzle like Citizen Kane. Marienbad is "the Citizen Kane of the fourth dimension." What's asked of the spectator is the ability to incorporate a mind-set of dissolves. Tailleur insists upon the "either-or" of Robbe-Grillet's critical pronouncements: both are possible. The spectator must react while submitting, must participate while being manipulated, etc. Tailleur sees both X and A as sincere: X in his beliefs about a meeting the previous year, and A in not remembering any such meeting. Tailleur suggests that all the characters in the film come from Robbe-Grillet's novel La Jalousie. If one uses that novel as a possibility for interpretation, then A may very well have been with another man "last year," but it was not X. The film was scripted cinematically by Robbe-Grillet, but it could only have been filmed in such a radical way by Resnais, especially with the unmistakable stamp of the end of the silent era: the plastic qualities, the refined photography, the daring symbols, the decor and rhythm, all of which, according to Tailleur, are gone in today's films. Everything is "dated" in this ultra-modernist film, from the costumes and make-up to the furniture and architecture, from the use of shadows à la Chirico to the baroque ornamentation. Tailleur concludes that, by making the most uncommercial film possible, Resnais and Robbe-Grillet have crossed the Rubicon of film rules and have destroyed any distance left between creator and spectator.

84 TILLIETTE, XAVIER. "Marienbad ou le nouveau cinéma." Etudes, 312 (December), (n.p.).

Discussion of Last Year at Marienbad as representative of a radically new kind of cinema.

85 VILLELAUR, A. "Marienbad, ciné-roman et univers mental." Les Lettres Françaises (November 9), pp. 1, 5.

Discussion of the phenomenon of the ciné-roman, revived by Robbe-Grillet with Last Year at Marienbad, and of the film as projecting a mental universe that has little to do with physical reality.

86 WEYERGANS, FRANÇOIS. "Dans le dédale." Cahiers du Cinéma, No. 123 (September), pp. 22-27.

Last Year at Marienbad reminded Weyergans of Baldung Grien's painting entitled "Death Giving a Kiss to a Naked Woman in Front of an Open Grave." Weyergans notes that the function of criticism is already inside the work and not the reverse. The film presents a closed world in which time functions, not like clock time, but like musical time. The film is a kind of movable feast or mobile, dependent upon the spectator to animate it, to give it life. He uses Freudian terms to explain the film as a dream, the dream of A split into three characters (X as her id, M as her superego and A herself as the ego). The film also incites the primitive instincts of Eros and Death in the spectator in a kind of duality. He suggests that the moments of the film most likely to be "real" moments are those in which Sacha Pitoeff (M) is present. Thus, the film is not a game of interplay between past and present so much as it is between dream and reality. He notes that without recourse to myths and without the various symbolic interpretations of the film as some kind of dream, the critic is forced to make allusions to other works and authors. So, acknowledging his frustration, Weyergans alludes to Gaston Bachelard, Pierre Klossowski and Bioy Casares. He concludes by admitting that all meaning is there, integral, within the film and that it can't be deciphered by fragmented analyses.

87 ZAND, NICOLE. "Un Entretien avec Alain Resnais et Alain Robbe-Grillet." France-Observateur, No. 576 (May 18), (n.p.).
Brief interview with Resnais and Robbe-Grillet, in which Resnais suggests that the film fascinates him so much that there must be "hidden forces" in it.

1962

88 ALLOMBERT, GUY. "Entretien avec Alain Robbe-Grillet." La Cinématographie Française (December 22), (n.p.).
Interview with Robbe-Grillet about Last Year at Marienbad and L'Immortelle.

89 ALPERT, HOLLIS. "Maybe Last Year." Saturday Review (March 10), (n.p.).
Review of Last Year at Marienbad. Alpert suggests the subtle film techniques become almost an end unto themselves. "Neither a factual or chronological understanding of the story is sought by Resnais, who instead creates a romantically formalized world, perceived as though broken into fragments which now rest on varying levels of time and which can presumably be reassembled as desired by the individual viewer."

90 ANON: "Cinema: All Things to All Men." Time (March 16), p. 56.
Review of Last Year at Marienbad. The author compares the film with Pirandello. Quotes Resnais as suggesting that reality is a Platonic allegory. The hero and heroine

represent the Eternal Masculine and Eternal Feminine, which stand impersonal in stone in the garden. Notes the various symbolic interpretations of the film: death and the maiden; Sleeping Beauty and an awakening Prince, etc. Suggests that Resnais and Robbe-Grillet applied the principles of relativity to film as Picasso had done to painting and Schönberg to music. "The result is true cubistic cinema, in which reality is dismantled." Concludes by saying watching the film is like listening to ninety-three minutes of twelve-tone music: it's exhausting.

91 ANON: "At the Pictures." Punch (March 7), p. 402.
Review of Last Year at Marienbad. Quoting Ingmar Bergman, the author suggests that Marienbad be seen in its affinities with music. Thus, the film needs no more justification or explanation than the pleasure or displeasure given by a piece of music.

92 ANON. "Film of Subtlety and Fascination." The Times, No. 55320 (February 20), p. 13.
Review of Last Year at Marienbad, suggesting that it is both challenging and rewarding.

93 ANON. "Keeping Faith." The Observer Weekend Review (Sunday, February 25), (n.p.).
Review of Last Year at Marienbad. The author depends more upon a cute turn of phrase than upon any close analysis of the film. "Unfortunately, it (the film) renders the enthralling mess of our emotional lives in such a cold, glazed style that it is as hard to respond to the raw state of the material as it would be to accept a dropped hem in a fashion picture."

94 ANON. "Last Year at Marienbad." Filmfacts, 5, No. 9 (March 30), 47-49.
Synopsis of the film with excerpts from some of the New York newspaper and magazine reviews of the film.

95 ANON. "Last Year at Marienbad." New York Post (March 8), (n.p.).
The author feels that Last Year at Marienbad is too much trouble, more trying than Antonioni, less rewarding than Resnais' Hiroshima mon amour. Impressed with the form, he is unable to allow the work needed to appreciate the film. He concludes: "If this seems slightly clouded, so is the picture."

96 ANON. "Last Year at Marienbad." Show (March), p. 32.
The author labels the film "revolutionary" and sees the aim of the film as the "destruction of conventional chronology." He notes that Resnais believed that X and A had actually met "last year," while Robbe-Grillet did not.

97 ANON. "Persuasion." The Times Literary Supplement (February 9), p. 90.
Review of Last Year at Marienbad, using Robbe-Grillet's definition that the film could be summed up as the theme of persuasion.

98 ANON. "The World of the Cinema." The Illustrated London News, 240, No. 6398 (March 17), 428.
Brief mention of Last Year at Marienbad.

99 BARILLI, RENATO. "A proposito di Marienbad: una diffida." Il Verri, No. 1 (February), pp. 135-38.
Discussion of Last Year at Marienbad.

100 BECKLEY, PAUL V. "A Place, a Time and No Signposts." New York Herald Tribune (March 11), (n.p.).
No analysis here, not even a good plot summary. Beckley can do no better than to say: "Simply relax and enjoy it." Concludes by suggesting that the viewer see the film as a modern morality play.

101 _____. "Last Year at Marienbad." New York Herald Tribune (March 8), (n.p.).
Beckley suggests that Last Year at Marienbad is the story of a specific passion at the same time as it is an abstraction of all such passions. Notes that "unlucky at cards, lucky at love" could be the major theme of the film.

102 BENAYOUN, ROBERT. "Marienbad ou les exorcismes du réel." Positif, No. 44 (March), pp. 36-44.
A remarkable article, despite Benayoun's insistence upon placing Last Year at Marienbad in the tradition of André Breton, the Surrealists and l'amour fou. That insistence upon Surrealism is characteristic of Ado Kyrou, Gerard Legrand, Benayoun and other critics at Positif in the early 1960's. Benayoun suggests that Resnais and Robbe-Grillet created a Pandora's box with the film, without determining what was inside, and the pleasure for the viewer comes from opening the box. There are simultaneous solutions suggested and authorized. From the outset, the film presents a reality that is suspicious, the exact opposite of The Cabinet of Dr. Caligari, in which the suspicious reality is withheld until the doubtful ending. Benayoun quotes from André Breton: "What does it matter to me what one says of me, since I don't know who is speaking, to whom I'm speaking or in the interest of whom we are speaking? I forget, I speak of what I've already forgotten. I have systematically forgotten everything that has happened to me that was either happy or unhappy. I have saved only the indifferent things. It's toward indifference that I have aimed my memory, toward the tales without morality, to neutral feelings, to

incomplete statistics." Benayoun then notes the different forms of theatricality in the film: the play, the fragmented snatches of conversations and the statues. According to Benayoun, the camera is the real narrator of the film. X's accent sets up a distance between him and the spectator, and the visuals of him often run ahead of, or trail behind, the commentary, when they are not actually contradicting that commentary. The Nim game is seen as being related to the illusory aspects of the film, and Benayoun believes X loses on purpose. In fact, the characters in the film are like cards that are being played by someone unseen. Benayoun notes that several ruptures between the image and the sound are later "corrected" in inverse order: X describes the episode of the broken shoe during a party reception scene, which itself will be described by a voice-over commentary during a scene in which we see A trip on the pavement. After noting the various influences (Roussel, Pirandello, the Malombra of Soldati) and some of the possible mythical interpretations (Sleeping Beauty, Cinderella), Benayoun concludes that Marienbad is a dream, in which time and space are illusory. Albertazzi (X) has the power to reproduce the objects necessary to his desire (the reproduced photos, for example). Benayoun relates Albertazzi's ability to actualize his accounts in the images with his disconcerting memory lapses. Benayoun suggests that the meeting did take place last year, but that meeting was in a dream, X's dream; thus, A would not recognize him. The longer X insists in the present, the more that present reality affects and modulates his past dream. Finally, he realizes that the present itself is an illusion. Applying Freud's principle of false recognition, Benayoun suggests that the dream takes place for the first and only time in the present and that X merely thinks he remembers it as past.

103 BONDY, FRANÇOIS. "The Audience Makes Up the Story." Thought, 14, No. 3 (January 20), 13-14.

Brief review of Last Year at Marienbad as a puzzle-film which the spectator must co-create in order to derive meaning.

104 BONNEFOY, CLAUDE. "Des Ecrivains chasseurs d'images. Que photographiez-vous? La photographie vous sert-elle pour ce que vous écrivez?" Arts, No. 890 (November 14-20), p. 3.

Brief questionnaire for several writers, Robbe-Grillet included, about the subjects of their photography and about the role of photography in their writing. Robbe-Grillet noted his many trips and put his photographs into three categories: monuments and the typical tourist attractions; crowd scenes; pictures of vegetation and plant life. He stated that there was no connection between what he photographed and what he wrote, only an interconnection between the acts of photography and writing.

105 BORDE, RAYMOND. "Attention, Littérature!" Positif, No. 44 (March), pp. 47-51.

Borde criticizes the baroque cinema, a cinema of objects and decors, in the tradition of Marcel L'Herbier's L'Inhumaine and Max Ophuls' Lola Montès. Both L'Herbier and Ophuls are accused of seeking an abstract and dehumanized cinema. Borde then criticizes the New Wave films and praises the "literary" New Wave, specifically Resnais' and Robbe-Grillet's Last Year at Marienbad, Antonioni's La Notte and Henri Colpi's Une aussi longue absence. Then he criticizes these three films for being too "literary," for placing too much emphasis on the spoken text and not enough trust in the images. In speaking of Marienbad, Borde affirms: "We enter the world of the American avant-garde, with its mannequins, its fixed stares, its immobile widows on deserted beaches. As with Cocteau, the height of the human becomes the void of statues." Borde believes that films like Marienbad vaunt their ambiguities, "cultivating the question mark." He concludes by affirming that the complex formal structures of Hiroshima mon amour were necessary and justified by the emotions of love and fear, but the complex, extremely formal structure of Last Year at Marienbad has no justifications and is a game, a secret code. He notes that it is ironic that the most intellectual films of this century stem from some of the worst literature, an obvious attack on Robbe-Grillet.

106 BOUNOURE, GASTON. Alain Resnais (Cinéma d'aujourd'hui, No. 5). Paris: Seghers, 222 pp.

Section on Last Year at Marienbad. One of the three or four book-length studies of Resnais with a chapter devoted to Marienbad.

107 BRAY, BARBARA. "Robbe-Grillet Talks to Barbara Bray." The Observer, 942, No. 8 (November 18), 23.

Interview with Robbe-Grillet on L'Immortelle. Supposedly, these were Robbe-Grillet's first public statements on L'Immortelle. Robbe-Grillet says the script for that film was done before he wrote the script for Last Year at Marienbad for Resnais, and that while Resnais was filming Marienbad, he was already in Turkey working on L'Immortelle, thus denying somewhat many critics' contention that Robbe-Grillet's first film was overly influenced by Resnais' film. Robbe-Grillet explains: "What I've been trying to do is break away from the idea that a film must be based on an anecdote. I think a film needs to be organized according to cinematic logic and not any other kind, and it may be quite false, in terms of this cinematic logic, to stick to ordinary chronological time and sequence.... I don't believe a work of art has reference to anything outside itself." He contrasts L'Immortelle (less "enclosed," only one room that's shut in) with Marienbad ("even the garden was hardly a real exterior"). He contrasts description in a novel with that in a film: "At any rate when I write a description in a novel it's not to replace an image, it may even be to destroy one. Whereas what you get in a film script are merely designs for images." He notes that there is much less dialogue in L'Immortelle than in Marienbad and suggests that he is concentrating more on images than on words.

108 BRUNIUS, JACQUES. "Every Year in Marienbad or the Discipline of Certainty." Sight and Sound, 31, No. 3 (Summer), 122-27, 153.

Brunius begins with a comparison between Hiroshima mon amour and Last Year at Marienbad. While in Hiroshima the realities of divergent times and places is an important factor, Marienbad is a study of the timelessness of the mind's action. There is no other film about which so little has been said in so many words. Brunius suspects Resnais and Robbe-Grillet didn't agree that much on the interpretation of the film, but disagreement would be an encouragement in the right direction for spectators: they should find meaning in the film for themselves. Brunius accuses critics of reading the script and not dealing with the film: "Theirs are literary reactions to a printed script." He contends that Marienbad may be the first film, in which, to a large extent, content is form "and would not exist outside this particular form." He sees the film as the logical end-result of films in the tradition of The Cabinet of Dr. Caligari, Sherlock Jr., Un Chien Andalou, Citizen Kane and La Règle du jeu. Audaciously, he claims that Last Year at Marienbad is the greatest film ever made. He cites Resnais as noting that Albertazzi's Italian accent in French was meant to show that his narration was not an interior monologue. Brunius contends that the narrator does not know, himself, which scenes are dreams and which are memories of a lived past: "This uncertainty is essentially the subject of the film." He continues, suggesting that the dream segments may be A's, not X's. Multiple dreams justify the many costume changes and the breaks in continuity. Such breaks may point out a shift to another time, another memory, or the same thing imagined by the other character. Brunius denies any present-tense tyranny in the film. He sees the opening and closing scenes of the film as "past" scenes. After positing several possible "readings" of the film, Brunius decides on one that would see everything in Marienbad as a dream. All the mechanisms of the dream are there: disguise, displacement, condensation, dramatization.

He discusses recurrent dreams and the principle of false recognition in them. The language of the narrator, specifically his often repeated "once again," is a justification for the recurrent-dream theory. Brunius sees the frozen attitudes and postures of the characters as examples of remembered dream scenes. There are various endings presented within the film, most of them rejected, because they do not fit the narrator's desires. Brunius suggests meetings between X and A beyond "last year": they may have been two years ago at Marienbad or elsewhere. He notes that the script calls for M to be around fifty, old enough to be A's father. He deduces that the ambiguity surrounding the relationship between A and M is perhaps due to a covert suggestion of incest in that relationship, even when M has been transformed into a kind of brother figure. Rosmersholm, the play by Ibsen (unnamed in the script, clear in the film), involves the theme of incest. Brunius concludes by noting that the various games of matches, cards and dominoes echo the triangle situation of the three main characters, and the games, like the characters, remain ambiguous.

109 CHEVALLIER, JACQUES. "L'Immortelle." Image et Son, No. 218, (n.p.).
Chevallier calls L'Immortelle the first filmic attempt to capture a completely mental time.

110 COLEMAN, JOHN. "The Marienbad Game." New Statesman, 63, No. 1615 (February 23), 273.
Critical review of Last Year at Marienbad: "The droning of the narrative voice becomes gradually like an hallucination.... The characters are mannequins." Without offering any analysis of the film or of Robbe-Grillet's fiction, which he also attacks, Coleman concludes: "The queasy justification for such license relies, as the tedious novels of Mr. Robbe-Grillet rely, on one stretched insight: that much of our so-called thinking is a matter of acting-out and rehearsal.... I would suspect that a good part of its attraction lies in its utter permissiveness, in the entry it seems to offer into a chic game."

111 COLPI, HENRI. "On Last Year at Marienbad." New York Film Bulletin, 3, No. 2, (n.p.).
Colpi discusses his work with Resnais on the editing of the film.

112 COOK, ALTON. "Last Year at Marienbad." New York World Telegram and Sun (March 8), (n.p.). Reprinted in Film as Film: Critical Responses to Film Art. Edited by Joy Gould Boyum and Adrienne Scott. Boston: Allyn and Bacon, 1971, pp. 235-36.

Review of *Last Year at Marienbad*. Cook calls the film "a weird exercise in confusion." He compares the film with *Rashomon*. He faults the "bewildering" style of the film, and "the ideas hardly seem substantial enough to bear such prolonged and repetitive examination."

113 CROSBY, JOHN. "Far-Out Art." New York *Herald Tribune* (March 14), (n.p.).

Just words here, not even a review of *Last Year at Marienbad*: "The heroine looks a little like Jacqueline Kennedy and the whole movie reminded me strongly of Mrs. Kennedy showing off the White House. 'This is the Red Room. It's red.' That sort of dialogue."

114 CROWTHER, BOSLEY. "Esoteric Poetry." *New York Times*, Section 2 (March 11), p. X.

Last Year at Marienbad is very "far out," compared to films by Cocteau or Antonioni. Crowther notes that there are parallel symbols rather than explicit symbols in the film. He concludes that the film is "cinematically fresh and an elegant escape, like the poetry of Algernon Charles Swinburne or the novels of Marcel Proust.

115 _____. "*Last Year at Marienbad*." *New York Times* (March 8), (n.p.).

Praises the film for its puzzle aspects, for the black-and-white photography and the organ music, while lamenting the subtitles.

116 DREYFUS, DINA. "Cinéma et roman." *La Revue d'Esthétique*, 15, No. 1 (January-March), 75-84.

Discussion of Robbe-Grillet's fiction and *Last Year at Marienbad*, the common denominator being the theme of repetition. Dreyfus acknowledges some statements by Robbe-Grillet on film, then attacks him for his preoccupation with form, for his comparisons between the novel and film, and for his erroneous ideas about the cinematic image.

117 DURGNAT, RAYMOND. "A Conversation with Alain Resnais and Alain Robbe-Grillet." *Films and Filming* (February-March).

Translation of the Labarthe/Rivette interview from *Cahiers du Cinéma* (No. 123, September 1961).

118 _____. "*Last Year at Marienbad*." *Films and Filming*, 8, No. 6 (March), 30-31.

Durgnat plays allusion games. *Marienbad* recalls for Durgnat, in turn, *L'Avventura*, *Les Amants*, *Moderato Cantabile*, *Paris nous appartient*, *Le Monde du silence*, *The Paintings of Paul Delvaux*: all to imply either how much Durgnat knows or how much the film is derivative and not innovative. He sees the film as a game, with the Sacha

Pitoeff character as the key to understanding the film. Durgnat doesn't explain why. After all this non-analysis, Durgnat concludes by saying that Last Year at Marienbad is the year's most indispensable film.

119 FOX, JOAN. "The New Wave." Canadian Art, 19, No. 80 (July-August), 303-305. Reprinted in The Film. Edited by Andrew Sarris. Indianapolis and New York: Bobbs-Merrill, 1968, pp. 39-44.

Written at a time when the New Wave was at its height of popularity in France, Fox notes that the novel has declined, to be reincarnated in the cinema. "Film-goers must now learn to 'read' moving picture images as they once read the written word." Yet the masses remain unprepared for films like the "stream-of-consciousness" Last Year at Marienbad. In that film wishes and fantasies are as important as memories. Man is capable of an "irrational" free will. The ending, if taken literally, is seen as a significant breakthrough, from the unconscious into conscious life. Yet, he criticizes the film for its avoidance of social reality: "L'Année dernière à Marienbad captures the tone of fabulous boredom at what was the real Versailles. Yet it praises the grand luxe of the upper strata while avoiding their responsibility for the reactionaries and rebels of France."

*120 FUSCO, MARIO. "L'Année dernière à Marienbad." Tendances, No. 15 (February), pp. 64-83.

Unseen. Cited in Rybalka, p. 36 (See: 365).

121 GENETTE, GERARD. "Sur Robbe-Grillet." Tel Quel, No. 8 (Winter), pp. 34-44.

Genette notes that with Last Year at Marienbad Robbe-Grillet shifts his focus from the objective realism of his fiction to the imaginary. New references are the Surrealists, Lautréamont and Bioy Casares. Genette suggests that a re-reading of the novels reveals an irreality that was always there. Yet Marienbad can be seen as a "realist" film in contrast to more traditional films which are enclosed in a system of accepted conventions. Genette proposes a new analysis of Robbe-Grillet's earlier fiction, based on the "subjective realism" of Marienbad. Genette discusses Robbe-Grillet's literary transitions, of which he notes two types, both related to cinematography: (1) metamorphosis (soldier of the painting to soldier in the street in In the Labyrinth); the other (2), more abrupt, involves a sliding of focus from an object in one scene to another object in the next scene. Genette calls both kinds cinematic and related to analogy. He concludes with a discussion of natural analogues, artificial reproductions and repetition-and-variation in Robbe-Grillet's narration.

Ultimately, Robbe-Grillet's refusal of classical psychology leads him to fantasy pure and simple.

122 GILL, BRENDAN. "The Current Cinema: Dreamers." New Yorker (March 10), (n.p.).
Review of Last Year at Marienbad. Gill compares the film with James Joyce's Finnegan's Wake, especially in terms of the element of chance in both. "Radically unlike as they are, the movie and the novel have it in common that they are successful forays into unmapped country and that their success has nothing tempting about it."

123 HOLLAND, NORMAN H. "Film, Metafilm and Un-film." Hudson Review, 15, No. 3 (Autumn), 406-12.
Article on Last Year at Marienbad. Holland defines metafilm as (1) film moving toward more than film and (2) film that plays, toys, flirts with being film alone. He reviews all the unfavorable reviews Marienbad received, then suggests that the key image is games and play: the shuffled deck, dealt dominoes, the formal shooting-match, the Nim game. He explains the Nim game and how to win. Holland concludes that Marienbad is a "pure" film, which could not be anything but a film, not even a nouveau roman. He contrasts it with Hollywood's "impure un-films (adaptations)."

124 HOPE, FRANCIS. "Toys, Idle Toys." The Spectator, No. 6978 (March 23), p. 375.
Review of Last Year at Marienbad, based more on reading the script than on seeing the film. He dismisses the film ultimately as a "childish, nursery game."

125 JEAN, RAYMOND. "L'Année dernière à Marienbad." Cahiers du Sud, 49, No. 365 (February-March), 121-23.
Jean is deceived, not by the film's faults, but by its qualities. He criticizes the film as the weakest of Resnais' films and as an unfortunate step for Robbe-Grillet. The most formal elements of Marienbad remind him of the worst effects of Cocteau.

126 JOSA, SOLANGE. "Marienbad: une voie pour le cinéma futur? ou peut-être..." Esprit, 30, No. 1, 121-23.
Last Year at Marienbad is seen as a game, a game which undercuts the power of language and images, a game of art for art. The narrative voice affirms that to be alive is not to be able to immobilize oneself, which means the necessity of reaching out to others. Josa offers the usual interpretations: X invents the past; A is the only real character, all others finding voice in her; X and A are theatrical representations of Orpheus and Eurydice. "Or is Marienbad a prophetic film about man, finally god of the

earth in the future, no longer daring to confess his sufferings or anguish about death, so he walks about, graceful, useless, alone?" Josa concludes: "Marienbad is such a total film that a second version, a sequel, a copy, is unthinkable."

127 KAUFFMANN, STANLEY. "Movies: Torment and Time." New Republic, 146, No. 13 (March 26), 26-27.
The "torment" of the title refers to Bergman's Through a Glass Darkly; the "time" refers to Last Year at Marienbad. Kauffmann defines Resnais as no innovator, as one who follows in the tradition of Cocteau, Delluc, Dulac, Epstein and other filmmakers of the 1920's in France. After providing a brief synopsis of the film, Kauffmann concludes: "It is very interesting; it is not very moving.... The technique becomes the end instead of the means."

128 _____. "Room With a Déjà Vu." Show (May), pp. 30-31.
Kauffmann focuses on the break with chronology in Last Year at Marienbad. He notes that the other guests in the film (1) sometimes freeze motionless as the protagonists move among them, (2) sometimes behave normally and (3) sometimes are seen to speak but cannot be heard. Kauffmann compares Robbe-Grillet's novels with those of Kafka, concluding that Marienbad "is an imagist poem." Frustrated by the search for meaning and unhelped by comparisons with Chirico and Picasso, Kauffmann ends his review with a comparison between Resnais/Robbe-Grillet and Antonioni, a comparison favorable to Antonioni.

129 LABARTHE, ANDRÉ and JACQUES RIVETTE. "A Conversation with Alain Resnais and Alain Robbe-Grillet." New York Film Bulletin, 3, No. 2, 1-13.
Translation of their Cahiers du Cinéma interview on Last Year at Marienbad (No. 123, September 1961).

*130 LEIRENS, JEAN. "L'Année dernière à Marienbad." Revue Générale Belge (January), pp. 134-139.
Unseen. Cited in Besses, p. 88 (See: 377); French VII, 1964, #36544 (See: Source List).

131 LEUTRAT, JEAN-LOUIS. "En pays connu." Image et Son, No. 148 (February), (n.p.).
Leutrat compares Last Year at Marienbad with the work of Julien Gracq.

132 MACDONALD, DWIGHT. "Mystification at Marienbad." Esquire (June), pp. 49, 54, 56.
Macdonald admires the "sustained visual delight" of the film but objects to the lack of emotion. He suggests that it is the Finnegan's Wake of the movies. He further notes that the film is the answer to Eisenstein and Pudovkin, who

in 1928 advocated "an orchestral counterpoint of visual and aural images" and "the distinct non-synchronization of sound and picture." He suggests that Marienbad may be a parody of film, with all its "film hints that don't lead anywhere: the shadowy bulk of Hitchcock on the wall, the feather costume of A like von Sternberg, the organ music of the silent films."

133 MARION, DENIS. "Un rêve éveillé." Critique, No. 179 (April), pp. 329-38.

Last Year at Marienbad is different from anything else that preceded it for three reasons: (1) the ciné-roman published by Robbe-Grillet was also the scenario for Resnais with very few changes, whereas ordinarily a script goes through many changes and many steps in the shooting of a film, and so the ciné-roman can be seen as either a literary text transposed from the film or as the novelistic adaptation of a completed film; (2) with everything avant-garde about Last Year at Marienbad, the film's audience is much greater than the usual avant-garde audience; and (3) a new height of controversy has been reached between passion and boredom, between fanaticism for the film and outright indignation. Marion notes that the film is based on a dream, either a sleeping dream or a waking dream, as the title of the article implies. He uses Freudian terms to analyze the characters. He notes that most scenes take place inside the hotel, even the pistol-firing scenes, as unlikely as that seems. The garden only comes into play in the second quarter of the film, the bedroom only in the last quarter. The hotel represents the present: there are no windows and no door leading outside. It's a closed world. The garden is the privileged space for events that supposedly took place "last year": the ambiguity lies in discerning whether their meetings took place in a garden elsewhere or in this garden attached to this hotel. The hotel is related symbolically to A, the garden to X. This is not an ordinary garden, since it is totally empty, sculpted, suggestive of memory itself or, better yet, of a cemetery. Marion notes that the bedroom is related to the past (to X's recollections), to the present (the last dialogue between A and M) and to the imaginary (the suggested rape scenes, which, according to Robbe-Grillet, stem from the mind of A). The bedroom is also multivalent in its modulations of furniture, ornamentation, lighting, etc. Marion believes that what we see in the "simple" bedroom is probably true; what we see in the "stylized" bedroom is likely to be imaginary or the product of an hysterical point of view. He believes that the statue functions only to allow the four possible interpretations (a guest's, X's, A's, M's) of the statue. If we apply X's interpretation of the statue to his situation with A, we see that he doesn't really believe in the success of the argument he pursues with A. If we apply A's interpretation of the statue to her situation with X, we see that she is fascinated, even "seduced" by the arguments of X that she continues to negate and deny. Marion suggests that X is never really remembering as he tells his story: he is imagining and dreaming. It is only as dream that the glass can possibly break simultaneously in A's bedroom and in the bar. Thus, Last Year at Marienbad is the story of a fantasy that mistakes itself for a remembrance. In vague Freudian symbolism, the corridors and vestibules become for Marion feminine symbols. Lights are masculine symbols. The overly large rooms are symbolic of narcissism. The broken shoe is a symbol for the woman's fear (and guilt). The broken bracelet symbolizes the broken union between A and M. The balcony represents A's and M's life together. The importance of such symbolism, even though it's not overly evident in the film and even though it can't be maintained to extremes in an analysis of the film, is that it suggests for Marion that A is much more tempted by X's story and X is much more afraid of committing himself to his own story than either would have us believe on the surface.

134 MEKAS, JONAS. "Movie Journal." Village Voice (March 15), p. 13.

Mekas argues that Last Year at Marienbad is neither a great nor a revolutionary film. It uses devices introduced by the experimental cinema. Yet the film does produce the missing link between the commercial, dramatic film and the experimental, poetic cinema. Mekas mentions Maya Deren in particular as having pioneered these techniques fifteen years before Marienbad. Mekas also cites Stan Brakhage's Anticipation of the Night and Marie Menken's Arabesque. Mekas avows that he has a prejudice against words: "At best Marienbad could be called 'poetic' in terms of its being bad prose. I believe it was Robbe-Grillet himself who did worst to the film: he sentimentalized it with his commentary."

135 MILNER, MAX. "Marienbad: une voie pour le cinéma futur? ou peut-être...classicisme ou académisme?" Esprit, 30, No. 1, 145-47.

For a film so supposedly radical, Milner suggests that Last Year at Marienbad is exempt of surprises in its language. It is a filmic copy (classicism) of time-space interplay already explored by the nouveau roman. Milner is criticizing both the companion article by Marie-Claire Ropars-Wuilleumier and the film itself. He hopes that Marienbad will not be typical of a cinema for filmmakers, as the nouveau roman has introduced the "novelistic novel." He compares Resnais/Robbe-Grillet to Eisenstein and Max

Ophuls in terms of their incorporating all art forms in film, even suggesting that Marienbad might usher forth a Wagnerian Gesamtkunstwerk to come. "If Marienbad is not the ultimate masterpiece that too many critics have declared it to be, at least it can be excused its faults for being the first step toward the realization of that ultimate masterpiece."

136 MISHKIN, LEO. "Screen Review: Marienbad Novel, Baffling Import." New York Morning Telegraph (March 8), p. 2.

Mishkin was baffled by Last Year at Marienbad, and so he believes his readers should be too. He describes the look of the sets, gives surface portraits of the three main characters and concludes: "In any event, it is a film that breaks new frontiers and opens up new paths of exploration for the motion picture as an art form." Mostly nonsense.

137 MORANDINI, MORANDO. "Robbe-Grillet e Resnais nel laberinto di Marienbad." L'Osservatore Politico Letterario, 8, No. 1 (January), 113-16.

Review of Last Year at Marienbad, as it relates to "labyrinth" structures already present in Robbe-Grillet's fiction, which create the multiple possibilities of meaning in the film.

138 MORRISSETTE, BRUCE. "Theory and Practice in the Works of Robbe-Grillet." Modern Language Notes, 77, No. 3 (May), 257-67.

Most of this article has to do with reconciling supposed discrepancies between Robbe-Grillet's critical statements and his works, but there are some references to Robbe-Grillet's film activity. Morrissette suggests that the cinema reflects the modern view of reality in terms of objects and may influence the future novel. He affirms that Marienbad contains the "subjectivity" already inherent in the early novels of Robbe-Grillet. He thinks it fitting that this metamorphosis should come with a ciné-roman, for Robbe-Grillet claims the cinema is especially well adapted to the projection of images, real or false, of memories, anticipations or imaginations. Then Morrissette concludes with a caveat: "The constructions of an evolving art cannot be judged by obsolescent criteria."

*139 NOWELL-SMITH, GEOFFREY. "L'Année dernière à Marienbad." New Left Review, Nos. 13-14 (January-April), pp. 146-50.

Unseen. Cited in French VII, 1966, #51193 (See: Source List).

140 PARTRIDGE, BURGO. "Films: Making Full Use of the Medium." Time and Tide, 43, No. 9 (March 1), 28.

Mixed review of Last Year at Marienbad. To its credit, it offers an innovative use of flashbacks, according to Partridge, and it makes full use of the medium. To A and X, truth is subjective, but to M, the husband-lover, it is objective. Only M knows what the statue in the garden means. The match game is a mystery to X; it is a mathematical process to M. Partridge accuses Resnais and Robbe-Grillet of creating mystery for mystery's sake. The acting is seen as less dull than non-existent. "The film is suspiciously intellectual, snobbish, pretentious."

141 PINGAUD, BERNARD. "La Technique de la description dans le jeune roman d'aujourd'hui." Cahiers de l'Association Internationale des Etudes Françaises, No. 14 (March), pp. 172-77.

Article primarily on fiction, but with implications for film. Pingaud disagrees with Robbe-Grillet on the non-signifying language of the nouveau roman. He suggests that Robbe-Grillet's language in his fiction is that of tragedy, in the classical sense of that term. He concludes: "Perhaps we will see in the years to come that the real objective literature is the cinema."

142 POWELL, DILYS. "The Marienbad Mystery." The Sunday Times (February 25), p. 43.

Powell concentrates on repetitions in the film of Last Year at Marienbad, both verbal and visual. "Everything turns in on itself, and time, in this love-story, is a circle. That is why at a first look I thought the film simple to understand; all, I said, is explained if you accept it as a fantasy of after-life, a reunion of the dead.... Of course I was wrong."

143 QUIGLY, ISABEL. "Some time, Never." The Spectator, No. 6975 (March 2), p. 274.

Review of Last Year at Marienbad. Quigly contends that one's response to the film is a matter of temperament, not aesthetics. Overall, she is against the film. She calls it a "monstrous legpull." She notes that Robbe-Grillet contends that the work must take meaning from the spectator, and she sees this kind of "subjectivity" as dishonest. She classifies herself on the side of the "humans" ("temperament") and she dislikes the formal qualities of the film (aesthetics).

144 RESNAIS, ALAIN. "Trying to Understand My Own Film." Films and Filming, 8, No. 5 (February), 9-10.

Resnais relates what he believed when he made the film Last Year at Marienbad, what he was trying to do in the film, how he perceived the "story" of the film.

145 RESNAIS, ALAIN and ALAIN ROBBE-GRILLET. "Last Words on Last Year." Films and Filming, 8, No. 6 (March), 39-41.
Joint interview by the filmmakers, in which they discuss their differences in terms of the final film and in which they note how they would like the spectator to approach the film.

146 RHODE, ERIC. "Back to Byzantium." The Listener and BBC Television Review (March 8), (n.p.). Reprinted in Film as Film: Critical Responses to Film Art. Edited by Joy Gould Boyum and Adrienne Scott. Boston: Allyn and Bacon, 1971, pp. 239-46.
Rhode notes that Robbe-Grillet's critical statements about Last Year at Marienbad are "as good an excuse for critical anarchy as one could imagine." Rhode asks how such a coherent film could be so ambiguous. Most of the article is a contrast between naturalism and symbolism, focusing on Marienbad as a case example. He argues that the film is symbolist to such an extent that it has many of the characteristics of naturalism. Contrary to naturalism, Robbe-Grillet's time-frame is eternal, not chronological or sequential, and his protagonists, like the symbolist poets, live in isolation. "They are forced to dream some terrible vision in order to fulfill themselves." Yet, the script for the film is not symbolist. Though Robbe-Grillet may be a naturalist by temperament, Rhode suggests, Resnais is "a symbolist who is trying to create a cinema of pure form." Rhode concludes that Marienbad, in having failed to reconcile the doctrines of symbolism and naturalism, has also failed to make a significant advance in film. "It is a work of art, but of a minor order. Like most symbolist poetry it is obscure, hermetic, and precious. Its dream world denies the use of reason, of moral obligation, of all that is, in the last resort, human."

*147 ROBBE-GRILLET, ALAIN. "De Marienbad à L'Immortelle." Le Figaro Littéraire (September 1), p. 9.
Unseen. Cited in Heath, p. 124 (See: 454).

*148 _____. "Gedanken zu einem Film." WW, No. 17, p. 14.
Unseen. Cited in ZFRP, 1961-1962, #28468 (See: Source List).

149 _____. Last Year at Marienbad. Translated by Richard Howard. New York: Grove Press, 168 pp.
The English translation of Robbe-Grillet's ciné-roman.

150 ROUD, RICHARD. "Novel novel; Fable fable?" Sight and Sound, 31, No. 2 (Spring), 84-88.
The title of the article comes from a quote from Mary McCarthy, who answers the question "Is it still possible to

write novels?" with "certainly not, yet, and perhaps, tentatively no." Roud explores some film-literature parallels: Defoe corresponds to the primitives of the cinema; Fielding, Dickens correspond to Griffith and the American cinema of the 1920's; Balzac, Dostoyevsky, to Stroheim and Pabst; Zola and the Goncourt brothers to the Italian neo-realist movement; Henry James to Antonioni. Roud then discusses the "breakthrough" novels of the 1920's, novels which returned to forms preceding the novel: Joyce returned to epic in Ulysses, Kafka returned to fable and allegory in The Castle. Others turned to non-novelistic forms: here Roud mentions Robbe-Grillet as having turned to the world of the painter. He discusses Last Year at Marienbad, noting that it is difficult to identify with characters like A and X. The plot is deliberately thin, events or incidents are lacking, and no explanations are given for character behavior or motivation. Roud suggests that Marienbad has gone further than any other film toward the fable form: "It pleads for the emotional." Roud says of the fable form: "It recognizes the irrational elements in life: the importance of coincidence, chance, luck. Thus, more life-like and more real than literature which goes under the name of realism. The fable frees the filmmaker from the obligations of storytelling, just as painters were allowed by the invention of the camera to be free of reproducing reality." Roud calls Marienbad the "completely integrated work of art," and he concludes: "Just as thematic material in music or subject matter in painting never dominates the work as a whole, so Resnais and Robbe-Grillet have never sacrificed to their plot the other elements which make up a film."

*151 SALACHAS, GILBERT. "L'Année dernière à Marienbad." Télécine (May), (n.p.).
Unseen. Cited in Prédal, p. 183 (See: 362).

152 TAYLOR, JOHN RUSSELL. "Last Year at Marienbad." The Times Literary Supplement (February 9), (n.p.). Reprinted in Film as Film: Critical Responses to Film Art. Edited by Joy Gould Boyum and Adrienne Scott. Boston: Allyn and Bacon, 1971, pp. 246-48.
Taylor believes that Marienbad is in some ways less of a film than an intellectual trap. "Certainly it is a trap if the spectator goes at it with the intellect, wanting to know what it means and determined to work out one explanation which will fit all the facts...." He suggests that there is some semi-Ouspenskian spiral of time at work in the film. He suggests several symbolic and mythical interpretations of the film, the most interesting of which is that the film could be a metaphysical commentary on the last two reels of Vertigo, and the Hitchcock silhouette by the elevator could be a deliberate "cryptogrammatic pointer."

153 THIRARD, P.-L. "Un film de Maurice Burnan?" Positif, No. 44 (March), pp. 44-47.

Thirard notes the various critics' confusion about the film Last Year at Marienbad. They can only agree on one thing, according to Thirard: the film's boredom. The formal qualities of Marienbad seem added on, not integral or necessary. They are decorations. The film lacks internal coherence, and Thirard ends up wishing that Resnais would devote himself to the forever-unfinished Harry Dickson film and the filmic treatment of detective fiction in comic-strip fashion rather than dealing with the nouveau roman style of Robbe-Grillet.

154 TILLIETTE, XAVIER. "Les Inconnus de Marienbad." Etudes, 312, No. 1 (January), 79-87.

Tilliette begins by quoting Goethe to "immortalize" Last Year at Marienbad. He notes that the confusion between the authors as to the ultimate meaning of the film should serve as an example to critics: they should feel confused too. He puts the film in a tradition with the films of Welles, Carné, Visconti and Bergman. He then contrasts the styles of Marguerite Duras (lyrical, animated, passionate) and Robbe-Grillet (authoritative, minute, precise, mannequin-like) to contrast Hiroshima mon amour with Last Year at Marienbad. He concludes that tribute must be paid to Resnais for having synthesized and translated both styles so effectively. Tilliette suggests that Marienbad is a film that bypasses the critics to become the film of the spectator. He notes that Robbe-Grillet saw the film as the "story of a persuasion," while Resnais saw it as the "refusal of the past" by the "Ariane of wounded love." Finally, he relates the film to Mallarmé's "ceramics" in literature.

*155 TISSERAND, J.-P. "De Marienbad à L'Immortelle Robbe-Grillet renouvelle son écriture cinématographique." Le Figaro Littéraire, No. 854 (September 1), p. 9.

Unseen. Cited in French VII, 1963, #30940 (See: Source List).

156 UYTTERHOEVEN, PIERRE. "Entretien avec Alain Robbe-Grillet." Image et Son, No. 148 (February), (n.p.).

Interview with Robbe-Grillet on Last Year at Marienbad and L'Immortelle.

*157 VAN SCHENDAL, MICHEL. "Les Vestiges de Marienbad." Situations, 4, No. 2 (July), 45-48.

Unseen. Cited in French VII, 1965, #2341 (See: Source List).

158 VERHESEN, FERNAND. "Du roman au poème." Synthèses, No. 194 (July), pp. 348-53.

Verhesen notes that Stendhal's style is similar to that of Robbe-Grillet, Nathalie Sarraute and Claude Simon. Brief mention of Last Year at Marienbad to explain Robbe-Grillet's genesis and also to explain the style of the new novel.

159 VIATTE, AUGUSTE. "L'Année dernière à Marienbad." La Revue de l'Université de Laval, Québec, 16, No. 9 (May), 819-24.

The ciné-roman is explained as the merger of techniques of the nouveau roman and what, since around 1928, has been called the "avant garde" cinema. He notes Robbe-Grillet's refusal to name the characters in Last Year at Marienbad, the unnatural poses of the actors in the film, and the camera angles which accentuate the "dehumanization" by focusing on objects while keeping people on the periphery. He makes analogies between Marienbad and Sartre's Huis Clos. He points out the lack of story, the alternate replies of "follow me, please" and "leave me, I beg you." Then, inexplicably, he talks about the powers of hypnosis in audio-visual methods, and he mentions Hitler in the same breath as Robbe-Grillet.

160 WUILLEUMIER, MARIE-CLAIRE: "Marienbad: une voie pour le cinéma futur?" Esprit, 30, No. 1, 135-42.

Marienbad is not just a film to be seen from several spectator points of view. It is also a changing work in itself, a mobile, a construct in constant transformation. The most striking thing about the film is the possibility of so many interpretations and the impossibility of one single interpretation. Seemingly, there are two meetings between X and A, one "last year" and one in an undefined present. But the verb tenses of the narrative voice-over open the possibility of three or more meetings, by alternating between the present tense, the past tense (completed, finite) and the imperfect tense (past but ongoing, habitual, indefinite). There is a strong interplay between the theatrical play and the X-A relationship. The scene in the play at the beginning of the film has become itself a scene played out between X and A, and we see coming to life what we had seen put on stage, while we hear a part of the play that we have seen played out between X and A. The whole film, then, becomes a series of echoes, which prompts a non-realist reading, a neo-realist reading, a Surrealist reading, all of them being possible. One can "read" the film by its music alone or by the accents of the voices and their tonality or by the different degrees of light-exposure of the images. She likens the film to a painting without a subject, a symphony no longer ordered by melody, a poem freed to communicate only the rhythm of its words. Marienbad opens the path toward a new cinema, at the same time that it exposes the limits of that new cinema in terms of audience comprehension and response.

161 ZUNSER, JESSE. "Last Year at Marienbad." Cue (March 10), (n.p.).
Zunser quotes Resnais as having said: "If we'd chosen to use a detective story,...it might have added up to almost the same film." Zunser sees the film as being both brilliant and banal, soaringly poetic and tiresomely talky, mature and sophomoric, "dramatically as dizzying and monotonously repetitious as a carousel."

1963

162 AIGRISSE, GILBERTE. "Esthétiques comparées de deux films 'psychanalytiques' récents: L'Année dernière à Marienbad, Les Dimanches de Ville-d'Avray." Action et Pensée, 39, No. 4 (December), 97-112.
Comparison between Last Year at Marienbad, in which time is indeterminate and characters' psychological past or present motivation lacking, and Les Dimanches de Ville-d'Avray, in which the main theme is memory between fixed and overlapping times, as they apply to the relationship between an adult and a youngster.

163 AMES, VAN METER. "The New in the Novel." Journal of Aesthetics and Art Criticism, 21, No. 3 (Spring), 243-50.
Survey from a perspective of philosophy and social humanism of the nouveau roman in France, with special attention paid to Claude Mauriac, Nathalie Sarraute, Michel Butor, Marguerite Duras and Robbe-Grillet. A very brief discussion of Hiroshima mon amour and Last Year at Marienbad.

*164 ANON. "Alain Robbe-Grillet." Vogue, No. 141 (January 1), p. 124.
Unseen. Cited in Schuster, p. 324 (See: Source List).

165 ANON. "Berlin Tries to Justify Its Film Festival." The Times, No. 55741 (July 1), p. 14.
Review of L'Immortelle.

166 ANON. "Book of the Film." The Times Literary Supplement (September 27), (n.p.).
Discussion of the ciné-roman, comparing Last Year at Marienbad (because it was written prior to filming) favorably to L'Immortelle ("written" after the film). The author finds the latter wordy, too detailed, cumbersome, complaining that even a surface reading of the book of L'Immortelle takes three or four times as long as watching the film.

167 ANON. "Edinburgh Cinema: Triumphant Words." The Observer, No. 8983 (September 1), p. 21.
Review of L'Immortelle.

*168 ANON. "L'Immortelle vu par l'ouvreuse." Cinéma 63, No. 76, pp. 84-85.
Unseen. Cited in Gardies, p. 187 (See: 440).

*169 ANON. On Robbe-Grillet. Cinema Universitario, No. 19, p. 22.
Unseen. Cited in BFI Lib. Ref. (See: Source List).

*170 ANON. On Robbe-Grillet. Young Film, No. 2, p. 8.
Unseen. Cited in BFI Lib. Ref. (See: Source List). Article on Robbe-Grillet's direction of L'Immortelle.

171 ANON. "Recent Developments in Film Technique." The Times, No. 55641 (March 5), p. 15.
Brief sketch on Last Year at Marienbad.

*172 AYFRE, AMÉDÉE. "L'Année dernière à Marienbad." Cinéforum, No. 24 (April), (n.p.).
Unseen. Cited in Prédal, p. 183 (See: 362).

173 BELLOUR, RAYMOND. "Un cinéma réel." Artsept, No. 1 (January-March), pp. 5-27.
References to Robbe-Grillet, especially to Last Year at Marienbad. Other articles on Marienbad by Geneviève Rodis-Lewis, Paul Leutrat, Jean-Louis Leutrat, and a letter from Michel Leiris.

174 BLOCH-MICHEL, JEAN. "L'Image," in his Le Présent de l'indicatif. Essai sur le nouveau roman. Paris: Gallimard, pp. 77-106.
This is Chapter Three of Bloch-Michel's book. In the chapter, he discusses film's influence on literature, noting that filmic or visual images have replaced traditionally literary images in the nouveau roman. In terms of the time-frame presented by such images, Bloch-Michel is in accord with Robbe-Grillet as well as with his own thesis: the tense and mood are present indicative.

*175 COLLET, JEAN. "Le Cinéma fossile." Signes du Temps, No. 5 (May), pp. 32-33.
Unseen. Cited in French VII, 1964, #43926 (See: Source List). Critical review of L'Immortelle.

*176 CORTE, ANTONIO. "L'Immortale, su misura." La Fiera Letteraria, 18, No. 16 (April 21), 5.
Unseen. Cited in French VII, 1964, #36533 (See: Source List). Critical review of L'Immortelle.

177 COWIE, PETER. Antonioni-Bergman-Resnais. London: Tantivy Press, 158 pp.
Section on Last Year at Marienbad (144-53).

178 DONIOL-VALCROZE, JACQUES. "Istanbul nous appartient." Cahiers du Cinéma, 34, No. 38 (May), 54-57.

Article on L'Immortelle, one of the few to praise the film when it first came out, and written by one of the editors at Cahiers (except for him, unanimously against Robbe-Grillet at the time), who also played the role of the protagonist in the film. His real-life wife Françoise Brion played the role of the woman L. or Lale in the film. Doniol-Valcroze insists that there is no "subject" to the film; rather, there is a "motif" which he summarizes. The structure of the film is radical in that it is the first real attempt in film to portray mental time, according to Doniol-Valcroze. Thus, the film is about a man in front of a window thinking about a woman he has loved, whether or not she ever existed. The acting of N, the professor (Doniol-Valcroze's role), is, accordingly, deliberately stiff and that of the woman deliberately animated and lively, then progressively immobile (since she was, for Robbe-Grillet, unreal). Doniol-Valcroze points out that the critics who were the most severe with Last Year at Marienbad attacked L'Immortelle in the name of Marienbad: Robbe-Grillet's film had somehow validated Resnais' film. He concludes by noting the radical innovations of the musical sound-track in the film, quoting Maurice Le Roux, who suggests that since Hiroshima mon amour and especially with L'Immortelle the cinema had reached the level of musical theater, of new opera, of film-opera: "It's really an audio-visual art of meditation whose structure is musical."

*179 _____. "Jacques Doniol-Valcroze parle de L'Immortelle." Cinéma 63, No. 77, pp. 13-15.

Unseen. Cited in Gardies, p. 187 (See: 440).

*180 DORT, BERNARD. "Un cinéma de la description." Artsept, No. 2 (April-June), pp. 125-30.

181 DURGNAT, RAYMOND. Nouvelle Vague: The First Decade. Loughton, Essex: Motion Monographs, 90 pp.

References to Last Year at Marienbad.

182 EGLY, MAX. "Repère No. 2: L'Année dernière à Marienbad," in Regards neufs sur le cinéma. Edited by Max Egly and Jacques Chevallier. Paris: Seuil, pp. 241-43.

Egly affirms that all films prior to Last Year at Marienbad were more or less tied to the narrative structures of the novel, the theater, or journalism. With Marienbad the spectator cannot distinguish between the screenwriter and the director, and the spectator must create any meaning that the film has. The film's ordering of images is no longer chronological, but rather psychological, and so one can no longer speak of sequences in this film. To exaggerate his point, Egly states that the ordering of the images given by the filmmakers is no longer indispensable, is no longer the only ordering, and the spectator is invited to re-order the film visually as well as psychologically. Marienbad is a film that can be analyzed as a film or as an art object, a painting or statue. Marienbad questions our notions of realism at the same time that it proposes a new realism of the imaginary.

183 FISSON, PIERRE. "Moi, Robbe-Grillet." Le Figaro Littéraire, No. 879 (February 23), p. 3.
Presentation of Fisson's interviews with several people on Robbe-Grillet's novels and Last Year at Marienbad. Robbe-Grillet is also interviewed. He notes that he is aware of critical reactions to his work, and he discusses his film activity, including L'Immortelle as well as Marienbad.

184 GAUTHIER, GUY. "L'Immortelle." Image et Son, No. 163 (June), pp. 33-34.
Gauthier suggests that each image in the film is a mental one, so that only a few frames in the entire film can be called "objective" frames. He notes the "literary" style of the film, the dehumanized, physiological looks or descriptions. He notes the lack of emotions or tension in this "neutral" film: "Cold composition, interminable freeze-frames, voices as expressive as alarm clocks, and a stiffness of gestures make of us spectators, in the full sense of the word, and not participants." Gauthier insists that it is impossible to speak of Brechtian distanciation devices in connection with the film, because the film doesn't incite us to think. He adds that there is a problem in portraying mental space, as opposed to physical space, because mental space knows no boundaries, no limits; so, the film presents a labyrinth of geometrically false spaces, silhouettes within the frames, a pan on a bridge with the same couple shown several times. He concludes that the film cannot exist apart from its style, since there is no physical reality portrayed within.

185 GRAHAM, PETER. "The Face of '63: No. 4 - France." Films and Filming, 9, No. 8 (May), 13-22.
Graham discusses the decline of the New Wave, with special attention to Truffaut, Godard, Chabrol and the Cahiers critics-turned-filmmakers, to their defense of their films, their in-jokes and allusions. One passing reference to Robbe-Grillet as a new director with L'Immortelle.

186 LUCHTING, WOLFGANG A. "Hiroshima mon amour, Time, and Proust." Journal of Aesthetics and Art Criticism, 21, No. 3 (Spring), 299-313.

Fairly detailed analysis of Hiroshima mon amour in terms of its time constructs, not just in the tradition of Proust but other writers as well who've experimented with time, such as Thomas Mann, Lawrence Durrell and Robert Musil. Last Year at Marienbad is referred to several times, both in terms of its own time structure and as an aid to seeing the time structure in Hiroshima mon amour.

*187 MAURIAC, CLAUDE. "L'Immortelle d'Alain Robbe-Grillet." Le Figaro Littéraire, No. 884 (March 30), p. 20.
Unseen. Cited in Besses, p. 88 (See: 377).

188 MORRISSETTE, BRUCE. Les Romans de Robbe-Grillet. Preface by Roland Barthes. Paris: Minuit, 308 pp.
Two chapters of this very important work concern Robbe-Grillet's film activity: Chapter Six: "Monsieur X sur le double circuit" (on Last Year at Marienbad) and Chapter Seven: "Une voie pour le nouveau cinéma: L'Immortelle." Morrissette traces the history of the ciné-roman, noting Robbe-Grillet's unique contribution to it. He refutes what he sees as false analogies between film and literature, arguing for the specificity of each. Morrissette traces cinematic devices in Robbe-Grillet's novels, such as the use of dissolves in La Jalousie. He then presents a fascinating analysis of the style of Robbe-Grillet's ciné-roman for Marienbad, noting the duality between the stylized commentary of the narrator and X in the film and Robbe-Grillet's "neutral" style: a duality which never appears in the film. In the film everything that Robbe-Grillet had indicated in his "neutral" style (descriptions of settings, of movements, gestures and action) is transformed by Resnais' camera into a style equivalent to the music and the spoken dialogue. Morrissette surveys the various interpretations of the film by critics like Roger Tailleur, Claude Ollier, François Weyergans, Bernard Pingaud and Gerard Bonnot; then, typical of Morrissette's unique mixture of the scholarly and the speculative, he presents an even more allegorical reading of the film, substantiated by outside reading, to show that A is a suggestible subject under the effects of hypnosis towards persuasion. That hypnotic effect in the film creates in the spectator a sense of déjà vu, making the spectator a "victim" as well of X's persuasive story. In his analysis of L'Immortelle, Morrissette remains much closer to the cinematic text, analyzing what he terms the "objective subjectivity" in the film. He suggests that the film can't be seen as from one single character's point of view nor can it be seen as chronological or linear. He notes that N is called André Varais in the text, a reference to André VS of Les Gommes, an example of Robbe-Grillet's increasing use of intertextuality. He also notes that L was called A in the first

draft of the film. Morrissette breaks the film into nine sections: thematic prelude; the meeting; the reunion; the episodes of love; the vigil of N at the cemetery; the quest for the lost L; the accident, the death of L; an inquiry of posthumous jealousy; and the death of N. Both of these chapters comprise the most important writing in English on either film.

189 MOWCOWITZ, GENE. "L'Immortelle." Variety (May 8), (n.p.).
Comparison of Last Year at Marienbad with L'Immortelle, to the advantage of the former. After providing a plot summary of L'Immortelle, Moscowitz criticizes the acting of Jacques Doniol-Valcroze (N) and Françoise Brion (L) in the film. He notes that Robbe-Grillet lacks the "glacial perfection" in technique of Resnais.

190 OXENHANDLER, NEIL. "Marienbad Revisited." Film Quarterly, 17, No. 1 (Fall), 30-35.
He contends that the criticism of Last Year at Marienbad has been too reductionist, providing no "key" for viewing the film. He disagrees with Jacques Brunius that X must be dreaming, and he summarizes the criticism of Bruce Morrissette, Claude Ollier and François Weyergans. He notes that it is possible that Marienbad and Hiroshima mon amour both take place in a mental institution. He points out differences between Resnais and Robbe-Grillet: Resnais wants to analyze character, wants to believe something did happen at Marienbad; Robbe-Grillet says no and points instead to "emotional states," saying that these can't be linked rationally. Oxenhandler discusses three kinds of connections to be made in the film: emotional, formal and literal. As an example of the emotional, he notes the bedroom scenes evoked in the bar. For formal: the light versus dark motifs, the fast versus slow motion of the photography. For literal: the out-of-phase or achronological aspects of the film. He notes that the film fails for him precisely where Robbe-Grillet says it should succeed: it doesn't move him. There is an ultimate rejection of the film on "humanist" grounds: "It isn't possible for me to care whether these two sleek mannequins get together or not."

191 PECHTER, WILLIAM S. "Last Night at Marienbad." Kenyon Review, 25, No. 2 (Spring), 337-43. Reprinted in his Twenty-Four Times a Second. New York: Harper and Row, 1971, pp. 59-76.
Pechter notes the trailer to the film, the special issue of the New York Film Bulletin devoted to the film, the wild popularity of the Nim game within the film, sold after the film, concluding that all this merchandising doesn't help one cope with the film itself. He notes: "Why not this form for the work of art of the future; beginning with its own review, culminating in a bibliography; an encumbrance

at both ends?" He notes the trend of the judgmental prelude and explanatory coda in the film and other modern works, suggesting that the producers have spared no expense to save us from having to decide what we think. He viewed the film with an "impassive, numb neutrality," relating his response to the problems of achieving an unaided response to the modern work of art, with so much media hype surrounding it. Pechter begs the question: to what end? Even if all the various symbolic interpretations of the film of Last Year at Marienbad add up, then to what end, since the film contains all meanings and reveals none. Contrary to what Robbe-Grillet has said about all images in the film being in the present tense, Pechter affirms that Marienbad exists more firmly in the past tense than any other film he knows of. He opposes conceptual thinking and visual thinking: "It is common for this conceptual thinking to be accompanied by the loss of image, even exterior image, as when one stares blankly into space, eyes focused out on some inanimate object; in such a mental state, visual images operate only on the level of distraction." Finally, he opposes beauty and knowledge, Marienbad serving the former. He notes that the ultimate value of the film may be in its artistic self-defeat.

192 PLEYNET, MARCELLIN. "La Peinture de Robert Rauschenberg et l'actualité." Tel Quel, No. 13 (Spring), pp. 68-69.

A very prophetic article, since Robbe-Grillet would collaborate with Rauschenberg on a book entitled Traces suspectes en surface in 1975-1976. Pleynet discusses Rauschenberg's history, from his beginnings at Black Mountain College, to his "combine-paintings" in 1961, making use of the most banal and everyday objects (coke bottles, ties, chairs, ladders, etc.). Making use of Rauschenberg's everyday objects, Robbe-Grillet has transformed André Breton's dictum for Surrealism that "beauty will be convulsive or it will not be" to "the everyday world will be convulsive or it will not be." Pleynet sees in the Robbe-Grillet of 1963 one who reproduces objects, not from the physical presence of the objects themselves, but from the images of those objects. Pleynet concludes with Rauschenberg, the painter of the Imaginary, whose objective collages offer no subject but what is given by the spectator, whose powers to create meaning in the work are at least as great as those of the artist. Here, Pleynet compares the work of Rauschenberg with Robbe-Grillet's L'Immortelle. Pleynet concludes with a statement by Rauschenberg: "The proof is that for me the past changes constantly while the future remains the same."

193 ROBBE-GRILLET, ALAIN. "Comment mesurer l'inventeur de mesures?" L'Express, No. 627 (June 20), pp. 44-45.

Discussion of the limits on the artist, the struggle in his works against conventions, with references to his film activity.

194 _____. "L'Année dernière à Marienbad," in Regards neufs sur le cinéma. Edited by Max Egly and Jacques Chevallier. Paris: Seuil, pp. 44-46.

Reprint of Robbe-Grillet's introduction to the ciné-roman for Last Year at Marienbad, noting that the art of film derives from its play with forms, how the project for Marienbad came about, what he admired in the work of Resnais, and how he foresaw the film, from its synopsis to its structures.

195 _____. "La Littérature, Aujourd'hui - VI." Tel Quel, No. 14 (Summer), pp. 39-45.

Interview with Robbe-Grillet in a series. Discussion of Robbe-Grillet's prose as mental works devoid of time or chronology. Robbe-Grillet discusses Last Year at Marienbad, saying that the film takes place in an eternal present which makes any recourse to memory impossible; so, the world of the film is sufficient unto itself. It is a universe which decomposes in its very construction. Robbe-Grillet notes that in the modern narrative work, time is stripped of its temporality.

196 _____. "L'Immortelle: 1 à 27." La Nouvelle Revue Française, No. 11 (May), pp. 946-61.

Printed excerpts from Robbe-Grillet's shooting script and notes for the first twenty-seven sequences of the film of L'Immortelle.

197 _____. L'Immortelle. Paris: Minuit, 210 pp., 40 photos.

The published ciné-roman for the film. The introduction is especially fascinating, since Robbe-Grillet therein defines the ciné-roman, noting that it is to the finished film what the libretto is to the opera, noting also his indications for the acting styles of the male and female leads in the film, which suggests that the woman is in the imagination of the male lead only, and that the male protagonist that we see is but a projection of the unseen camera-narrator, who is the real N, watching a stiff projection of himself. Reading the ciné-roman is the best introduction I know of to Robbe-Grillet's fiction, since his "neutral" style is here so explanatory. For instance, each time that a main character is about to turn toward the camera, there is an indication for a cut in the film, suggesting that the mutual look between camera-voyeur-narrator and a character, even the projection of self, is impossible, because a voyeur cannot bear to be looked at.

198 _____. "Temps et description dans le récit d'aujourd'hui," in his Pour un nouveau roman. Paris: Gallimard, pp. 155-69.

Written in 1963, this is Robbe-Grillet's most important statement on the cinema up until the making of Trans-Europ-Express. The text incorporates comparisons between literature and film, his novels and his films, the ciné-roman and what had become clear to him theoretically as a result of having made L'Immortelle. He refutes the idea that the descriptive new novels are merely aborted films. Film shows immediately what fiction describes in many pages. He insists on the movement of his description rather than the thing described. He emphasizes the attraction of the cinema on the new novelists as stemming from the audio-visual possibilities, the chance to operate simultaneously on two levels, the visual and the aural. He emphasizes the soundtrack's importance for him, and he stresses the imaginary aspect of the film image as being all-important: the chance not just to deal with the true and the false, but also with the make-believe. He insists on the present tense of the film image, a present with ambiguity. The true, the false and the make-believe have become the subject of all modern works. "Thus seen, the image...prevents belief at the same time that it affirms itself, just as description prevents one from seeing what is being described."

199 SOLLERS, PHILIPPE. "Le Rêve en plein jour." La Nouvelle Revue Française, No. 11 (May), pp. 904-11.

Sollers suggests that Robbe-Grillet's L'Immortelle represents a continuation of Robbe-Grillet's formal research in the novel and that, via the film image, there is even less visibility in his film than in his novels. Imagination is the main character in all of Robbe-Grillet's works. This imagination is simultaneously the author's and that of one who looks on, one who observes the action. The "one who looks on" sees what the author imagines just as the author is kept from seeing what the "one who looks on" imagines. Sollers notes three modes in the film: realist, psychic and imaginary. On the realist plane, a man meets an enigmatic woman, looks for her, loses her, finds her again, and so on. On the psychic plane, it's a question of an hallucination which leads to self-suggestion and suicide. On the imaginary plane, the film is the story of a vampire, with hints of necrophilia, unexplained apparitions and disappearances. Sollers makes an analogy between L'Immortelle and Freud's analysis of Jenson's Gradiva, in which there is also a realistic presentation of the delirium and dreams of an obsessed person in an eternal Pompei. Sollers discusses the editing and camera work, which often involve either optical tricks, which permit the appearance of an object where it really isn't or couldn't be, or an "ancient chemical process" aimed at producing the form of a body after its destruction. He sees the "one who looks on" figure in the film as symbolic and that figure's turning away from the window repeatedly toward the interior of the room as a figurative inward-turning. He notes that the dream, the erotic images, the "morbid" suggestions, all are heightened by the fact that they take place in broad daylight. L'Année dernière à Marienbad creates a mental universe outside of everyday reality; L'Immortelle is more effective, because its mental universe is created within external (and diurnal) reality. He suggests that Robbe-Grillet's writing is like an arabesque. This arabesque is complemented in the film by the Arab music. Sollers concludes by placing Robbe-Grillet in a direct line with the Surrealists.

200 STOLTZFUS, BEN. "Alain Robbe-Grillet and Surrealism." Modern Language Notes, 78, No. 3 (May), 271-77.
References within this article to Last Year at Marienbad, as it relates to Surrealism.

201 THIRARD, P.-L. "Ce cinéma intellectuel...." Positif, Nos. 54-55 (Summer), pp. 123-25.
An attack on Le Procès de Jeanne d'Arc, Les Abysses and Robbe-Grillet's L'Immortelle as being too intellectual and too elitist. He notes that Les Gommes was Robbe-Grillet's best novel and only good novel. He suggests that L'Immortelle lacks internal logic.

1964

202 ALTER, JEAN V. "Alain Robbe-Grillet and the Cinematographic Style." Modern Language Journal, 48, No. 6 (October), 363-66.
Last Year at Marienbad and L'Immortelle provide two different concepts of the ciné-roman. L'Immortelle-book appears as a simple off-print of L'Immortelle-film, since the initial literary description was modified as the film was being shot, enriched by the inventions of the director and finally adapted from a technical language to the literary style. Robbe-Grillet the filmmaker predominates. With Marienbad it was Robbe-Grillet the writer. As such, the ciné-roman of Last Year at Marienbad may be considered as an autonomous literary work, without consideration for Resnais' film. Contrary to the more literary scenarios of Sartre or Marguerite Duras, Robbe-Grillet's scenario is very sophisticated in cinematic terms. Camera indications allow for literary cutting, short paragraphs and associative linking of paragraphs. Alter notes two traits of the cinema-novel: psychological contrasts and speed. "Speed" indications such as "close-up of A," "View of the drawing-room"

and "Traveling of the garden" allow for a rapid transition from one image to another as well as allowing for images to be evoked without any accompanying description. Robbe-Grillet's subject matter is suited to the technical style: "The story of a persuasion, which is essentially a conflict of wills, can use very well a rapid movement of scenes where the accelerated exchange of images replaces successfully the verbal exchanges of a novel." Alter sees the spoken text of the film as Robbe-Grillet's compensation for the free play of the images. He notes that perspective has gone from multiple in Les Gommes to dual in Le Voyeur to a single character in La Jalousie and a "unilateral creative imagination" in Dans le labyrinthe, corresponding, thus, to the "perspective of a single camera which records the internal or external vision of a single person." Marienbad represents a return to the multiple perspectives of Les Gommes. Alter notes a "magic lantern effect" in Marienbad: the scenes seem to be static, without internal movement, although they succeed each other very rapidly, which is explained by Alter as stemming from mainly mental images, which have a tendency to solidify in our mind, even when they refer to a moving object. Associated with this "magic lantern effect" is the theater effect. As in Racine's tragedies, there is hardly any real action in Marienbad, but rather a conflict of wills. Thus, Marienbad is closer to classical theater than to the cinema. "If there is a stylistic link between Robbe-Grillet's novels and Marienbad, it is expressed in the anti-cinematic trends: the static nature of images, the importance of mental images. On the other hand, the two aspects of novels which seemed close to the motion picture technique, chosisme and single perspective, are abandoned in the scenario and replaced by new means which define the originality of the work: speed and duality of sound and images. Marienbad's success results from the combination of these two approaches." Alter concludes that Robbe-Grillet is more a psychologist than a creator of new forms in the novel.

203 ASHMORE, JEROME. "Symbolism in Marienbad." Kansas City University Review, 30, No. 3 (March), 225-33.

Ashmore considers Robbe-Grillet a chosiste but accepts the invitation to interpret Last Year at Marienbad. According to Ashmore, Resnais and Robbe-Grillet extend such invitations as a trap. Nevertheless, he sees the film as a construct of symbols. He calls the film a refined presentation of modern existentialism. He presents a series of naive affirmations about Marienbad portraying modern man cast adrift in his society. All is reduced, then, to the theme of alienation. Typical of his bland and ridiculous symbolism: "The Male tries, fails, and does not understand. The Female waits. Trying and waiting do not blend."

*204 BANN, STEPHEN. "Robbe-Grillet and Marienbad." Cambridge Review, 85, No. 2074 (May 2), 390-91.
Unseen. Cited in French XX, 1973, #100598 (See: Source List).

*205 BENMUSSA, SIMONE. "Alain Robbe-Grillet parle de la télévision." L'Express (October 19-25), pp. 72-73.
Unseen. Cited in Rybalka, p. 34 (See: 365).

206 BERNAL, OLGA. Alain Robbe-Grillet; Le Roman de l'absence. Paris: Gallimard, 257 pp.
Not very helpful in terms of Robbe-Grillet's film activity, but there are references to Robbe-Grillet's images being cinematographic and like modern painting. In the third section ("Réalisme relatif: les modalités du regard"), Bernal compares the images of Last Year at Marienbad with those of Robbe-Grillet's earlier novels.

207 GOLDMANN, LUCIEN. "Nouveau roman et réalité," in his Pour une sociologie du roman. Paris: Gallimard, pp. 279-333.
After a long introductory contrast between Robbe-Grillet and Nathalie Sarraute, Goldmann studies Last Year at Marienbad (pp. 319-324). He notes that hope and anguish coexist in the film, that nothing could ever happen in the baroque hotel of the film, that those who lose at games have been suppressed from the film. He suggests that nothing can prove conclusively whether or not X and A met "last year," not any photograph, not a broken shoe nor any shared memory. Goldmann notes that X and A leave the closed world of the chateau out of "hope" for an ill-defined world (the garden) where they can be themselves. His study of L'Immortelle (pp. 325-33), in conjunction with Anne Olivier (See: 208), sets aside the technical aspects of the film and focuses only on the content. He sees the "story" of the film as a continuation of the subject of all of Robbe-Grillet's previous novels and of Marienbad as well: the relationship between the human subject, the dehumanized world of objects and the possibilities for hope. He notes that Lale symbolizes the imaginary, the real and the unreal, all at the same time, which allows the male protagonist to affirm himself and to hope. He suggests that guilt surrounding responsibility for Lale's death pushes the narrator to reproduce the car accident which kills him. He breaks the film into three parts and finds it significant that suicide appears in Robbe-Grillet's work for the first time and equates that fact with the appearance of suicide in Sartre's Les Séquestrés d'Altona.

*208 GOLDMANN, LUCIEN and ANNE OLIVIER. "L'Immortelle est de retour." France-Observateur, No. 751 (September 24), pp. 15-16.
Unseen. Cited in Besses, p. 88 (See: 377).

209 JANVIER, LUDOVIC. "Alain Robbe-Grillet et le couple fascination-liberté," in his Une parole exigeante: le nouveau roman. Paris: Minuit, pp. 111-45.

Janvier notes that the ciné-roman serves as a memory-aid, allowing the reader to remember and "fix" in his/her memory what the film expresses in a very special and rapid way. He compares Last Year at Marienbad with Dans le labyrinthe, noting that immobility reinforces the "fatal" nature of labyrinths. He suggests that "persuasion" may be the theme of L'Immortelle as well as Marienbad. He catalogues the various "punishments," the tendency toward sado-masochism, the outcome of repressed obsessions. He sees rape fantasies in both films.

210 McDONNELL, THOMAS P. "Recording Camera." Commonweal, 81, No. 13 (December 18), 430-31.

Ostensibly a review of Robbe-Grillet's novel Les Gommes at the time of its first publication in English (as The Erasers), eleven years after its publication in France, yet there are comparisons with film: "Any film, for instance, which simply shows pieces of furniture uncluttered with the inner worlds of those who use them must necessarily come closer to the structure of the real world than any novel could possibly indicate." He suggests that several viewings of Last Year at Marienbad would be good "detection training" for reading Robbe-Grillet's novels.

211 MICHA, RENÉ. "Le Nouveau Cinéma." Les Temps Modernes, No. 214 (March), pp. 1717-28.

Throughout his article, Micha questions what is meant by "experimental" film, basing his questions on the choices of films for the Experimental Film Festival at Knokke. He notes that with Marguerite Duras certain modes of vision, of story-telling and expression appear in several art forms at the same time and that film plays the role of synthesizer for these various forms. He suggests that many films which would come under the category of commercial cinema qualify for "experimental" status, perhaps much more so than some of the films that won prizes at Knokke. In this respect, Micha mentions Last Year at Marienbad and L'Immortelle, as well as Resnais' Muriel and Fellini's 8 1/2. The rest of the article is a glorified plot summary of some American underground films.

212 MORRISSETTE, BRUCE. "Une voie pour le nouveau cinéma." Critique, No. 204 (March), pp. 411-33.

This is Morrissette's perceptive study of L'Immortelle, taken from the chapter in his book Les Romans de Robbe-Grillet (See: 188).

213 PEVEL, HENRI. "Résonances mallarméennes du nouveau roman." Médiations, No. 7 (Spring), pp. 95-113.
Pevel uses Mallarmé's poetry, especially his structures of "ambiguity," the simultaneous negations and affirmations, as a basis of studying the nouveau roman, here typified by the film Last Year at Marienbad.

214 STOLTZFUS, BEN. "Camus et Robbe-Grillet: La Connivence tragique de L'Etranger et du Voyeur." La Revue des Lettres Modernes, No. 94, pp. 153-66.
Brief mention of Last Year at Marienbad.

215 _____. Alain Robbe-Grillet and the New French Novel. Carbondale: Southern Illinois University Press, 166 pp.
In his chapter "This Year at Marienbad--Film or Novel" (pp. 102-21), Stoltzfus compares Robbe-Grillet with Eisenstein in terms of the relation between compelled spectator and projected film character. He notes the differences between the script and film of Last Year at Marienbad. Somewhat inexplicably, he then proceeds to give "humanist" readings to the film: "Marienbad, like his previous novels, is a demonstration, an example of what can happen to those who dehumanize the world about them." He denies Resnais' imagery as "nothing more than the traditional love triangle" and compares Marienbad with both La Jalousie and Robert Montgomery's Lady in the Lake in terms of "subjective" camera-narration. There is a long analysis of the dream mechanism in Freudian terms. Stoltzfus digresses to compare Robbe-Grillet with Sartre, to trace the development of American fiction between the wars, to insist on Hemingway, Sartre, Camus and Faulkner, extending the arguments of Claude-Edmonde Magny in L'Age du roman américain. An eclectic and very existentialist view of Robbe-Grillet, comfortable with fiction and its traditions but sketchy and overly-simplistic about film. At the end of the chapter entitled "Surrealism and Its Image" (pp. 122-34), Stoltzfus focuses on the use of l'amour fou in Last Year at Marienbad.

216 TAYLOR, JOHN RUSSELL. "The New Wave," in his Cinema Eye, Cinema Ear. New York: Hill and Wang, pp. 200-29.
Pages 224-28 deal with Last Year at Marienbad. Taylor suggests that the film is a series of elaborate art photographs and concludes that the film is a trap.

1965

*217 ANDERSCH, ALFRED. Die Blindheit des Kunstwerks und andere Aufsätze. Frankfurt: Suhrkamp, (n.p.).
Unseen. Cited in French VII, 1966, #45564 (See: Source List). Sections on Robbe-Grillet, Resnais, Chabrol, Godard, Sartre and Vigo.

218 ANON. "Entretien avec Alain Robbe-Grillet." Art et Essai, No. 6, p. 5.
Interview with Robbe-Grillet, in which he explains his ideas on the cinema, referring to Last Year at Marienbad and L'Immortelle.

219 ANON. "Les Bruits de la ville." Le Nouvel Observateur, No. 47 (October 6-12), pp. 24-25.
Survey references to Robbe-Grillet, Resnais, Raymond Queneau and Romain Gary.

*220 ANON. "Table ronde," in Formalisme et Signification/Cahiers Internationaux de Symbolisme, Nos. 9-10, pp. 97-125.
These pages are concerned with L'Immortelle with the sub-heading, "A propos des oeuvres littéraires et cinématographiques du nouveau roman."

221 BLOCH-MICHEL, JEAN. "Gadgets littéraires." Preuves, 15, No. 178 (December), 74-79.
Discussion of the influence of the cinema in Robbe-Grillet and Michel Butor. Bloch-Michel believes that both are attempting a kind of cinema-literature, and he concludes that Robbe-Grillet's La Maison de rendez-vous is more a script than a novel.

*222 BRENNER, JACQUES. Journal de la vie littéraire: 1962-1964. Paris: Gallimard, pp. 153-63.
Unseen. Cited in Fraizer, p. 37 (See: 475). Brenner treats time in La Jalousie and Last Year at Marienbad.

*223 BRION, MARCEL. "Alain Robbe-Grillet, un romancier réalisateur de film." Biblio, 38, No. 8 (October), 3-7.
Unseen. Cited in French VII, 1966, #51174 (See: Source List).

224 DAVIS, DORIS McGINTY. "Le Voyeur et L'Année dernière à Marienbad." French Review, 38, No. 4 (February), 477-84.
Davis notes that the cinema fits Robbe-Grillet's peculiar form of description. She compares a scene from Madame Bovary of Flaubert (the seduction scene between Rodolphe and Emma) with the seduction scene from Last Year at Marienbad. What is a moral judgment in Flaubert becomes a physical observation in Robbe-Grillet. She analyzes cinematic techniques in Le Voyeur, concluding that the old system of ethics has been replaced by a new ethic based on observation and the visual sense.

225 NO ENTRY.

*226 EVANS, CALVIN. "Cinematography and Robbe-Grillet's Jealousy," in Nine Essays in Modern Literature. Edited by Donald Stanford. Baton Rouge: Louisiana State University Press, pp. 117-28.

*227 HUGUENIN, JEAN-RENÉ. Une autre jeunesse. Paris: Seuil, 125 pp.
Unseen. Cited in French VII, 1966, #45591 (See: Source List). On the novel, Aragon, Butor, Gracq, Guillemin, F. Mauriac, Maurras, Resnais, Robbe-Grillet, Sarraute and Simon.

*228 JACOB, GILLES. "La Certitude de l'ambiguité," in his Le Cinéma moderne. Lyon: Serdoc, (n.p.).
Unseen. Cited in Gardies, p. 187 (See: 440).

229 KAEL, PAULINE. "The Come-Dressed-As-The-Sick-Soul-of-Europe Parties: La Notte, Last Year at Marienbad, La Dolce Vita," in her I Lost It at the Movies. Boston and Toronto: Little, Brown and Company, pp. 179-96.
Kael suggests that these films are so introverted and so interior that one doesn't know whether there's something new and deep in them or whether they're simply empty. Kael's title suggests the latter, of course. The alienation of the characters in Marienbad and in the other films is meaningless, an empty pose. She calls these figures cardboard intellectuals, the middle-class view of sterile artists. Referring to Marienbad, "the high-fashion experimental film" and the "snow job in the ice palace," she calls the prose "thick and malted" and feels the musical soundtrack is like High Mass. She concludes by suggesting that all these films have as their source Renoir's The Rules of the Game, and how different his "party" was.

230 MAGNAN, JEAN-MARIE. "Perdre le témoin." Cahiers du Sud, 59, No. 381 (February-March), 121-24.
Magnan discusses the voice-over narration in Last Year at Marienbad. Tension is created between the voice that guides and A who hesitates and retreats from that voice. The images struggle against this voice in vain. In this sense the whole film may take place in the past and may be as old as the play put on in the film. More than Marienbad, L'Immortelle proposes the ephemeral, the stripping of reality, furtive connections, memory lapses, intrusions of the imaginary. Against the pure, irrational flow of images, the narrator keeps trying to return to a more geometric pattern, a more abstract view of everything. This tension creates the sudden "nudity" and washing away of certain shots. The death of L is telescoped and may have taken place in the very first shots of the film: her long cries, the sound of brakes and shattered glass. The success of

L'Immortelle lies partly in Robbe-Grillet's tampering less, writing less and polishing less than in Marienbad. The appearances of M are always telescoped by the barking dogs, who just bark and seem to be there as if by magic or hallucination. N dies of a memory, killed by an obsession. All the subjective visions and constant switching of point of view render reality suspect. "Whereas in the novels the one who looks is invisible, in the cinema the vision is situated, attached to someone specific, to avoid too much confusion."

231 MAZARS, PIERRE. "Surréalisme et cinéma contemporain, prolongements et convergences," in Etudes Cinématographiques (Surréalisme et Cinéma, II), Nos. 40-42 (Summer), pp. 177-82.
Brief mention of Last Year at Marienbad.

232 MIESCH, JEAN. Robbe-Grillet. Paris: Editions Universitaires, 122 pp.
Four chapters of the book concern the cinema: 5--Cinéma et roman (39-53); 6--L'Année dernière à Marienbad (55-60); 7--L'Immortelle (61-66); and 8--Le ciné-roman (67-69). Miesch notes that favorable circumstances surrounding the New Wave were in part responsible for Duras, Resnais and Robbe-Grillet to collaborate and make films together. But by the time of L'Immortelle and Muriel (1963), circumstances were no longer favorable. He notes the critical reaction to Robbe-Grillet's novels as "aborted films," a reaction which was in part justified when Robbe-Grillet began making films. He quotes Resnais as having said that he would always be for silent films in any silent vs. sound debate. Miesch sees Marienbad as a "literary" film and L'Immortelle as a "musical" film. He notes Robbe-Grillet's three objections to most critics' attacks on L'Immortelle. Those attacks were based on (1) the lack of "natural" acting, (2) the impossibility of distinguishing between the real and the imaginary, and (3) the tendency of everything to transform into a "post-card" look. Miesch sees L'Immortelle as the synthesis between the novel La Jalousie (quest) and the film Last Year at Marienbad (seduction). He notes that the fluidity of the visuals in Marienbad is replaced by a desired rigidity in the visuals in L'Immortelle, which reinforces the comic aspects of the film. He cites the last image of the film, that of L laughing silently on the boat, as pertaining to the comic nature of the film. He notes that the ciné-roman is different from the scenarios published in L'Avant-scène du Cinéma, in that those scenarios are based on the sequence, while the ciné-roman is based on the individual shot, each one being described. He concludes that the ciné-roman is highly practical, a compensation for the small towns in France where L'Immortelle would never play and as a Proustian madeleine for someone who had actually seen the film.

233 MIZRACHI, FRANÇOIS. "Thèmes surréalistes dans l'oeuvre d'Alain Resnais." Etudes Cinématographiques (Surréalisme et Cinéma, II), Nos. 40-42 (Summer), pp. 199-208.
Resnais' various tributes to André Breton are noted and references are made to the period look and such Surrealist themes as l'amour fou in Last Year at Marienbad.

234 MORRISSETTE, BRUCE. Alain Robbe-Grillet. New York: Columbia University Press, 48 pp.
Morrissette notes that Last Year at Marienbad was the prolongation and outcome of Robbe-Grillet's formal research and stylistic devices in his novels. He notes the similarity between Marienbad and Finnegan's Wake in terms of the circular re-entry in both. "In this sense, nothing 'exists' outside the film itself, last year is this year." Any perspectives into another time or space belong to the imaginary. Morrissette reiterates his notion that A may be a highly suggestible person who is hypnotized and thus persuaded by X. Or we may see the film as "another materialization of the creative process, similar to that of In the Labyrinth, in which X is a sort of author or creative artist who forges a new truth or reality from the raw materials of his imagination. Marienbad would then be 'his' novel." Morrissette notes the various interior duplications and camera distortions in the film. He relates the prelude shots of L'Immortelle with the multiple inner parentheses of Raymond Roussel's Nouvelles Impressions d'Afrique. He notes the mixture of "old" and "new" scenes, creating the mixture of "real" and "imaginary" in the film. The plot is closer to ordinary experience than that of Marienbad and there are no camera devices to indicate the unreal scenes, for Robbe-Grillet believes the cinema can "give images of mental content without identifying the scenes as such." Morrissette thinks that Doniol-Valcroze's deliberately stiff acting should turn the viewer's attention away from N and toward L or toward whatever N is looking at. This kind of acting is a means of subjectifying the narration while keeping the third-person mode. Morrissette then chronicles the metamorphosis of objects and the doubling of character in the film, to show that L'Immortelle also continues Robbe-Grillet's former research, at the same time that it represents a new cinema which will deal with "created" subjective truth.

*235 PINGAUD, BERNARD. "L'Aquarium." Inventaire, pp. 190-202.
Unseen. Cited in Klapp, 1965-1966, p. 51 (See: Source List).

236 ROBBE-GRILLET, ALAIN. For a New Novel: Essays on Fiction. Translated by Richard Howard. New York: Grove Press, 175 pp.

This is the English translation of Robbe-Grillet's Pour un nouveau roman (Paris: Gallimard, 1963).

237 SAINT-PHALLE, THÉRÈSE DE. "La Littérature envahit le cinéma." Le Figaro Littéraire, 20, No. 1013 (September 16-22), 3.
Surface discussion of several writers who have gotten involved in the cinema: Robbe-Grillet, Beckett, Ionesco and Duras.

*238 SICLIER, JACQUES. "Film und Roman im Dialog," in Französische Kultur: Documente. Koln: Documente, (n.p.), pp. 47-56.
Unseen. Cited in French VII, 1965, #40186 (See: Source List). Discussion of Robbe-Grillet, Resnais, Duras, Varda, Prévert, Renoir, Cocteau, Bresson, Aurenche and Bost, the relationship between scriptwriter and director and between both and literature.

1966

239 ALTER, JEAN V. "Les Ciné-romans," in his La Vision du monde d'Alain Robbe-Grillet. Structures et significations. Geneva: Droz, pp. 50-64.
Discussion of Last Year at Marienbad and L'Immortelle, the differences between them as ciné-romans and as films.

240 ANON. "French Film Directors Busy." The Times, No. 56778 (November 2), p. 16.
On Robbe-Grillet, Bresson and Truffaut. Mention of Robbe-Grillet's Trans-Europ-Express.

241 ANON. "Oeuvres en cours." La Quinzaine Littéraire, No. 13 (October 1-15), p. 7.
Mention of Robbe-Grillet at work on Trans-Europ-Express.

242 ANON. On Robbe-Grillet. Film (West Germany), No. 1 (January), p. 22.
An account of Robbe-Grillet's 1966 Berlin speech on his attitude toward film, its relationship to literature, to his novels and to his career.

243 ANON. "Questions aux cinéastes." Cahiers du Cinéma, No. 185 (December), pp. 112-24.
Questionnaire for filmmakers on the relationship between film and literature. Those responding were Jean Aurel, Henning Carlsen, André Delvaux, Jacques Doniol-Valcroze, Samuel Fuller, Jean-Luc Godard, Marcel Hanoun, Ado Kyrou, Luc Moullet, Marcel Moussy, Jean-Daniel Pollet, Eric Rohmer, Josef von Sternberg, Jean-Marie Straub and Carlos Vilardebo. Of interest here are the answers of André Delvaux, who compares Last Year at Marienbad with Proust,

while insisting on the specificity of film and literature, suggesting that Robbe-Grillet making L'Immortelle becomes a tribute to Resnais for having made Marienbad, and Jacques Doniol-Valcroze, especially his response to question #8, in which he discusses the merits of L'Immortelle as a ciné-roman.

244 ANON. "Questions aux romanciers." Cahiers du Cinéma, No. 185 (December), pp. 84-105.
Questionnaire for novelists on the relationship between film and literature. Those responding were Alfred Andersch, Marcel Arland, Jean-Louis Baudry, Erskine Caldwell, Italo Calvino, John Dos Passos, Lawrence Durrell, Jean-Pierre Faye, Romain Gary, Aidan Higgins, Walter Hollerer, Pierre Jean Jouve, Alfred Kern, Pierre Klossowski, J. M. G. Le Clézio, François Nourissier, Claude Ollier, André Pieyre de Mandiargues, Dominique Rolin, Edoardo Sanguinetti, William Saroyan, Nathalie Sarraute, Georges Simenon, Claude Simon and William Styron. Of interest here are Claude Simon's answers, especially as they relate to the similarities and differences between film and literature, with special focus on Robbe-Grillet as an example.

245 ANON. "Questions aux romanciers ayant écrit pour le cinéma." Cahiers du Cinéma, No. 185 (December), pp. 106-11.
Questionnaire for novelists who have also been screenwriters. Those responding were Jean-Louis Bory, Michel Cournot, Paule Delsol, Pierre Gascar, Claude Mauriac, Robbe-Grillet, Philippe Sollers and Jean Thibaudeau. Robbe-Grillet "declines" to answer, just as Godard had done in the questionnaire for filmmakers. Perhaps part of declining for Robbe-Grillet was that he was asked as a novelist who had also written for the cinema, but not as a filmmaker.

246 ANON. "Une certaine platitude." Le Nouvel Observateur, No. 110 (December 21-27), p. 37.
On Robbe-Grillet as filmmaker in the process of making Trans-Europ-Express.

*247 BLOCH-MICHEL, JEAN. "L'Ecole du regard' et il cinema." Tempo Presente, 11, No. 7 (July), 20-35.
Unseen. Cited in French VII, 1968, #64910 (See: Source List).

248 CAPELLE, ANNE. "France-Europe-Express." Arts (December 28), pp. 44-46.
Review of Trans-Europ-Express as a parody.

249 _____. "Marie-France Pisier." Arts-Loisirs, No. 66 (December 28), pp. 44-46.
Review of Trans-Europ-Express.

250 ______. "Robbe-Grillet prend le train." Arts-Loisirs, No. 45 (August 3-9), pp. 38-41.
Interview with Robbe-Grillet on the making of Trans-Europ-Express and on the role that Robbe-Grillet plays in the film, that of the filmmaker making up his film. Clearly, Robbe-Grillet is playing Jean the filmmaker and not his real-life self in the film.

251 CHAPSAL, MADELEINE. "Books: Who is Robbe-Grillet?" The Reporter (July 14), pp. 54-57.
Chapsal acknowledges the public resistance to a Robbe-Grillet novel, comparing him with Robert Pinget and Lewis Carroll, suggesting that Robbe-Grillet has fulfilled in literature André Bazin's dictum for the cinema: to "substitute for the world around us the world of our desires." Taking the first sentence of four Robbe-Grillet novels, Chapsal attempts an introduction to Robbe-Grillet's use of the imagination as a total justification for writing. There is only passing mention of Last Year at Marienbad and L'Immortelle. The article is really a defense of Robbe-Grillet's La Maison de rendez-vous from anticipated attacks.

252 FAYE, JEAN-PIERRE. "Les Aventures du récitatif." Cahiers du Cinéma, No. 185 (December), pp. 14-25.
Historical survey of the transmutations of the récit, from Don Quixote to Robbe-Grillet in 1966. Robbe-Grillet is mentioned but not discussed.

253 GLATZER, ROBERT. "Trans-Europ-Express." West Side News (May 23), p. 6.
Glatzer calls the film a game of advanced Botticelli, concluding that "ultimately the story is just not strong enough to sustain things." He compares Robbe-Grillet unfavorably with Fellini.

254 GOLLUB, JUDITH PODSELVER. "Nouveau Roman et Nouveau Cinéma." Ph.D. dissertation, UCLA, 174 pp.
Traces the critical reaction to Robbe-Grillet's chosiste novels as "proto-films". Gollub sees Last Year at Marienbad as the first true nouveau roman, because it abolishes time, the narrative and sense. "Only in the guise of a spectacle could the aims of the new novel be fulfilled." She explores the specificity of each medium, then draws parallels, noting that both writers and filmmakers were emulating creators in the musical and graphic arts in rejecting all meaning outside the art form and concentrating on the invention of new forms. She suggests that these efforts take on a formal freedom that Sartre called terrorism.

*255 GRAMIGNA, GIULIANO. "La Macchina iconografica di Alain Robbe-Grillet." La Fiera Letteraria, 41, Nos. 33-34 (September 1), 15.

Unseen. Cited in French VII, 1967, #58045 (See: Source List).

256 HOBSON, HAROLD. "L'Immortelle." Christian Science Monitor (August 12), p. 66.
Nonsensical review based vaguely on a retold plot summary of L'Immortelle.

257 LATIL-LE DANTEC, MIREILLE. "Alain Robbe-Grillet, héraut de l'imaginaire." Etudes, No. 324 (March), pp. 371-87.
Primarily an analysis of La Maison de rendez-vous, there is reference to Last Year at Marienbad, in terms of the novel's synthesis of some of the film's concerns.

258 MARDORÉ, MICHEL. "La Moustache de Roussel et de Robbe-Grillet." Cahiers du Cinéma, No. 181 (August), pp. 66-67.
Review of Paul Vecchiali's film Les Ruses du diable from the aspect of playing with surfaces, of using popular clichés and popular myths in the same way that Roussel did and Robbe-Grillet does.

259 METZ, CHRISTIAN. "Le Cinéma moderne et la narrativité." Cahiers du Cinéma, No. 185 (December), pp. 43-68.
Definition of "modern" in film: (1) death of the spectacle? No. All of these concerns are posited as questions and are rhetorical, since Metz responds in the negative each time. Metz is attacking the Cinéma 62 people (Michel Mardoré, Pierre Billard, Marcel Martin, René Gilson). Metz finds many exceptions to their categories. In #5 ("a fundamental realism?"), L'Immortelle is used as an example of film being the most subjective of all the arts. Inferred here is a critique of cinéma vérité. In #6 ("a cinema of rules?"), Metz discusses the "literary" New Wave, mentioning the films of Resnais, Varda, Marker, Gatti and Colpi. By extension, the films of Robbe-Grillet would fit here too. Metz notes that these films are characterized by open-ended questions and ambiguities: did Alphonse in Muriel send a letter twenty years ago to Hélène or not? Was there a "last year" at Marienbad or not? Was the amnesiac the husband or not in Une aussi longue absence? Resnais and Godard are seen as the two great poles of modern film, Resnais for his "meticulously indirect realism" and Godard for his "generously disjunctive realism." The last half of Metz's article presents a semiological approach, as opposed to the "historical" approach of the first half, in which he explains his now-famous grande syntagmatique, an explanation of film grammar in terms of the various kinds of sequences.

260 MORRISSETTE, BRUCE. "Last Year at Istanbul." Film Quarterly, 20, No. 2 (Winter), 38-42.

Morrissette discusses Resnais' tampering with Robbe-Grillet's script in Last Year at Marienbad: baroque camera effects, deliberately over-exposed "white" scenes to denote heightened emotion and playing with time and Resnais' ending: the heroine's "apparent acceptance of the hero's advances, as she repeatedly opens her arms to him, instead of the near-rape called for in Robbe-Grillet's original scenario." With L'Immortelle Morrissette underlines the fictional structures apparent in both Robbe-Grillet's novels and films: multiple ambiguities, circular scenes, doubling, objectified subjectivity (projections of fears or desires) and memory repetitions. He notes that Robbe-Grillet admired James M. Cain's The Postman Always Rings Twice, because it was built upon a false repetition of two seemingly identical automobile accidents but with ironically different consequences. Morrissette then discusses the comic effect in Robbe-Grillet and his use of games and game structures. He breaks L'Immortelle into three sections: the entanglement, the search for the woman, the double crash and ambiguous ending. He notes that the flat acting of Doniol-Valcroze as the professor is an approximation of the je-néant or "absent I" technique of narration in Robbe-Grillet's novels, citing La Jalousie in this regard. He praises the film for the new levels of subjectivity achieved, precisely because nothing is objectively deformed. "Without unusual camera angles or lighting, without photographic manipulation, without recourse to the fantastic decor of the expressionist or surrealist film, he is able to make us feel a more intense subjectivity than that of The Cabinet of Dr. Caligari or Un Chien Andalou."

261 PINGAUD, BERNARD. "Nouveau roman et nouveau cinéma." Cahiers du Cinéma, No. 185 (December), pp. 26-40.

Analysis of the early Robbe-Grillet novels in light of Robbe-Grillet's theoretical statements in Pour un nouveau roman, to show the basic differences between novel and film in terms of narration. Discussion of Robbe-Grillet's description of objects, his obsessed narrators, his use of the present-tense time frame. Analysis of purely mental or subjective films: Rashomon, Last Year at Marienbad, L'Immortelle and Agnes Varda's L'Opéra Mouffe. In the theoretical statements, Pingaud is guilty of too many obvious clichés: "The cinematic image can never be words. Cinematic images cannot be transformed into verbal discourse. The film image tells what it shows, and it shows; it does not speak." Ultimately, for Pingaud, literature is involved with meaning, cinema with the senses. There is an inverse proportion between the clarity of the film and its artifice, which explains the many interpretations of Marienbad. He suggests that Marienbad is not a "mental universe," as its authors affirm, but rather pure theatrical spectacle, the height of exaggerated and deliberate artifice. He contrasts Resnais' Muriel (the ultimate "real" film, in a tradition of cinéma verité) with Robbe-Grillet's L'Immortelle with its double play on the real and the imaginary. About L'Immortelle, Pingaud affirms: "Either the story is plausible and it is made to seem absurd with the use of popular conventions like post-card exoticism, false eroticism, etc. or the story is imaginary and we can't accept it as such, since we always remain outside of it."

262 RHODE, ERIC. "Alain Resnais," in his Tower of Babel: Speculations on the Cinema. Philadelphia and New York: Chilton Books, pp. 137-58.

Rhode affirms that Robbe-Grillet, despite his "avant-garde trappings," is a naturalistic writer whose naturalism is simply taken to an extreme. Robbe-Grillet's script for Last Year at Marienbad only becomes truly symbolist in Resnais' treatment. The bedroom in the film allows the possibility of love, murder and rape, in any combination, or perhaps not at all. Part of the garden represents the possible meeting of X and A the previous year. The salons are for male challenges. Rhode suggests that M is perhaps X's double. The long shot of the hotel and its surrounding estates is, for Rhode, the "absolute--the ideal of the imagination, Xanadu itself, the perfect work of art." Marienbad is, then, an "artifice of eternity." The film, however, is not convincing in terms of its impure violent deeds. "The broken tumbler, the woman A lying dishevelled on her bed, appear more as embarrassing accidents than as imitations of some barely suppressed horror. And the guests' normality is more an attempt to conceal petulance at being caught in an eternal recurrence, rather than dark cruelty." In the film, to seem controls to be. He relates the content of the film to court tales with codes of courtesy. The "year and a day" wait occurs in fairy tales but also in La Princesse de Clèves, "the most realist of romances." For Rhode, even the match games are reminiscent of medieval jousts.

263 RICARDOU, JEAN. "Page, film, récit." Cahiers du Cinéma, No. 185 (December), pp. 71-74.

Using Claude Brémond's "le message narratif" as the basis for his article, Ricardou explores narrative devices in Robbe-Grillet's La Jalousie, calling it the "pure novel of pagination." He details the differences between camera description and literary description. While the camera is totally independent of what it shows, the panorama of literary description tends to limit the number of objects described: example, the fixed scenes in Last Year at Marienbad: the polarization of animated stones and petrified people. This double opposition is possible because of the specific attributes of the camera. According to Brémond, the fiction is independent of the narration. Thus, there may be new differences but not innovations between the media. A novel can be new in relation to other novels, not in relation to films. Likewise, a film can only be innovative in terms of prior cinema. He (Ricardou) criticizes Valery and Breton for their naive assumptions that photographs could replace descriptions in literature. By extension, there is a critique of roman-films or ciné-romans. Ricardou maintains the specificity of each medium. The argument is insightful and thorough as far as it goes. Yet, Robbe-Grillet, the special practitioner of the ciné-roman, can also maintain the specificity of both media, thus invalidating Ricardou's argument somewhat.

264 SICLIER, JACQUES and CLAUDE GAUTEUR. "Cinéma dans le cinéma." Image et Son, No. 200 (December), pp. 50-94.
The New Wave is covered in pages 67-91. The emphasis of the article is on films which contain films or filmmakers within them, thus pointing to a "cinema of cinephiles." Robbe-Grillet's Trans-Europ-Express is mentioned as such a film.

1967

*265 ANON. Filmography of Alain Robbe-Grillet. Art et Essai, No. 19 (February), p. 11.

*266 ANON. Interview with Robbe-Grillet. Film (Poland), No. 950, p. 11. (BFI Ref. Lib.).
Interview with Robbe-Grillet on the making of Trans-Europ-Express.

*267 ANON. On Robbe-Grillet. Filmcritica, 183, No. 4 (November-December), 551-56.
Unseen. Cited in BFI Ref. Lib. (See: Source List). Summary of Robbe-Grillet's film activity, with special focus on Trans-Europ-Express.

268 ANON. "Page and Screen." The Times Literary Supplement, No. 3390 (February 16), p. 127.
On Robbe-Grillet, his ciné-romans and his films, from the perspective of the special Cahiers du Cinéma issue (#185, 1966) entitled "Problèmes du récit."

269 ANON. "Some New French Films." The Times, No. 56846 (January 23), p. 14.
Surface review of three films, one of which is Robbe-Grillet's Trans-Europ-Express.

*270 ANON. "Trans-Europ-Express." L'Evènement, No. 12 (January), p. 70.
Unseen. Cited in French VII, 1968, #64015 (See: Source List).

271 ANZIEU, DIDIER. "Trans-Europ-Express ou les jeux de la création cinématographique selon Robbe-Grillet." Les Temps Modernes, 22, No. 250 (March), 1713-22.
Anzieu calls the film a trick film. The spectator has a multiple-choice of the film he/she wants to see. Anzieu proposes several reading levels for the film. It can be seen as a detective film. In this context, he notes all the intrigues, the false starts, the novelist-as-detective. He notes the book Transes in the "film" within the film, which has a hole in the middle for a concealed revolver. Anzieu suggests that the hole (like the hole in Le Voyeur) might be a metaphor for the viewer. Still on this level of reading, the film can also be seen as a parody of the detective film. Elias is a bungler, sent on wild goose chases, duped by a prostitute: the anti-hero caught up in the world of puns. Anzieu cites the pun on the word l'Anvers (Antwerp and "l'envers") as indicative of the parody. He proposes a second reading level of the film as myth, noting that Elias' name is a compound of the Biblical Joas and Racine's Eliacin (from Athalie, in which play Racine changed the name of Joas to Eliacin). Elias is, then, the new Adam, in search of the Abbot Petitjean, tempted by Eva (sin) and tested by the unseen powers (God). He proposes finally that the film be seen as a metaphor for the film-making process itself. Anzieu disagrees with comparisons made by other critics between Trans-Europ-Express and La Maison de rendez-vous.

*272 BARONCELLI, JEAN DE. "Trans-Europ-Express." Le Monde, No. 6859 (January 31), p. 12.
Unseen. Cited in French VII, 1968, #63990 (See: Source List).

273 BERTIN, CELIA. "Romanciers-cinéastes." La Revue de Paris, 74, No. 4 (April), 146-49.
Bertin traces the development of Robbe-Grillet and Marguerite Duras as novelists who both wrote scenarios for Resnais and then became filmmakers themselves. Specifically, she focuses on Duras' La Musica and Robbe-Grillet's Trans-Europ-Express.

274 BILLARD, PIERRE. "Drogue, humour et Trans-Europ-Express." L'Express, No. 814 (January 23-29), pp. 28-30.
Billard begins by noting that Robbe-Grillet knows that every fiction is the novel of a trickster. But he denounces himself/declares himself as a jokester in order to invite us

to participate in his game. Billard explains Robbe-Grillet's sense of perspective as an attack on depth: his images reflect the flat world of the billboard, the cartoon, stereotyped human relations that are dominated by overwhelming mythologies. Billard traces the various levels of "game" in Trans-Europ-Express. One is the game of errors. Billard notes the deliberate contradictions, the deliberate false identities, the deliberate undercutting of the narrative. Example: Elias kills Eva because she stole his key for the locker where he had left the drugs. But when Elias left the drugs at the locker, he forgot the key in the door. This key, which he never had, and which someone somehow stole from him, now reappears in his possession at the same time that the policeman, to whom Eva had given the key, continues to look for it. Another level of game in the film is the game of lost scenario. Here Billard suggests that the whole film may be the dream of the actor Trintignant, transposed into a world of film clichés and stereotypes. Another level of game is the game of who's who. Elias isn't introduced as a gangster, but as a film actor named Trintignant. On the other hand, the actor indicated as a bartender is a real bartender playing the role of the stereotyped bartender. The film is about running drugs, but there are no drugs, only flour. Elias doesn't rape Eva, but he pays her to pretend she's being raped. The customs officers are gangsters. Billard pays tribute to Robbe-Grillet for noting the rise in the level of violence in modern society, the tendency toward a nickle-arcade society where the gods, the ideals and goals, even the language, all change meanings and values. He concludes that whereas Godard feels this society as a wound, Robbe-Grillet assimilates it, finding nourishment and creative inspiration from it.

275 BOISDEFFRE, PIERRE DE. La Cafetière est sur la table ou contre le "Nouveau Roman." Paris: Editions de la Table Ronde, 155 pp.

No critic is more violently opposed to Robbe-Grillet than Boisdeffre. Two chapters from the book concern Robbe-Grillet's film activity: "Faute d'un regard, une caméra" (101-108) and "Impuissance des mots, fascination des images" (109-14). He portrays Robbe-Grillet as a kind of pervert, a freak recluse from life, tired of thinking up plots, or maybe they're too complicated for him, so he stays at the level of "snapshots." Boisdeffre compares the new novel with the Chinese Cultural Revolution: burning books and forcing a taste on the public. Thus, Robbe-Grillet is a "profiteer." He concludes that Robbe-Grillet should be making films, not writing novels.

276 BONTEMPS, JACQUES. "Le Cahier des autres." Cahiers du Cinéma, No. 188 (March), p. 6.
Bontemps quotes Pierre Bourgeade attacking Robbe-Grillet for Trans-Europ-Express, for being too intellectual to grasp the mysteries of the real Trans-Europe Express train or the Orient Express or any train. The eroticism of the film is forced and ludicrous. "Eroticism implies boldness, rage and risk, all of which is lacking in Trans-Europ-Express."

277 _____. "Le Cahier des autres." Cahiers du Cinéma, No. 191 (June), pp. 4-5.
Brief mention of Robbe-Grillet and Trans-Europ-Express.

278 BORY, JEAN-LOUIS. "Les Pirouettes de Robby et Grilletto." Le Nouvel Observateur, No. 115 (January 25-31), pp. 44-45.
Critical review of Trans-Europ-Express and the "games" in the film.

279 BOURGEADE, PIERRE. "Trans-familial Express." La Quinzaine Littéraire, No. 22 (February 15-28), p. 28.
Bourgeade attacks Robbe-Grillet for being too intellectual to make a film about trains or to deal with eroticism.

280 BROCHIER, J.-J. "Robbe-Grillet: 'mes romans, mes films et mes ciné-romans'; entretien avec J.-J. Brochier." La Magazine Littéraire, No. 6 (April), pp. 10-20.
Interesting interview, in which Robbe-Grillet explains the shift in his writing ciné-romans, from the preconceived Last Year at Marienbad, written before the film, to L'Immortelle, worked on during and after the film, to Trans-Europ-Express, which involved less writing prior to shooting, more participation from the actors and crew: a shift from writing to filming, which explains the fact that Robbe-Grillet never finished the ciné-roman for Trans-Europ-Express. Robbe-Grillet summarizes his career to date, noting that novel, film-novel and film are complementary activities for him.

281 BROOKS, PETER. "A la carte." Partisan Review, 34, No. 1 (Winter), 128-31.
Robbe-Grillet's novels were very timely in that they coincided with a whole new current of criticism in France. Thus, some of the best French critics have undertaken extended analyses of Robbe-Grillet's fiction: Roland Barthes, Bernard Pingaud, Philippe Sollers, Jean Ricardou, Gerard Genette. If Robbe-Grillet has sought to destroy the "romantic heart of things," there is a sense in which he is constantly fascinated by the romanticism of surfaces, a preoccupation especially noticeable in the films of Last Year at Marienbad and L'Immortelle. Brooks concludes that

Robbe-Grillet's fiction never gets beyond collage: it remains overly bound to the artificiality and the banality of the material.

282 BURCH, NOEL. "Comment s'articule l'espace-temps." Cahiers du Cinéma, No. 188 (March), pp. 40-45.

Burch begins by defining découpage in French: (1) the last stage of the scenario or script, the stage at which all camera indications are added; (2) the cutting up of narrative descriptions into images. A third meaning exists only in French, that of final cut, the last stage of editing of the finished film. He presents his notion of film as a succession of découpages in space (within the film) and découpages in time (both within the film and in the editing). If one gets away from the idea of "invisible" cutting, then a whole network of editing possibilities emerges. In terms of the non-measurability of both the flashback and the flashforward, they are identical. At least, Burch notes that Robbe-Grillet uses both organically and identically. Burch proposes new rules for editing, based on fifteen possibilities, a series of five temporal and three spatial. If one adds the possible changes of angle and proximity, the number of possible cuts is infinite. He then suggests the case of open linkage, in which the spectator can never orient himself or herself. Last Year at Marienbad is a film like this, especially in its use of ellipses and indefinite (scripted) flashbacks.

283 _____. "Réflexions sur le sujet: I. Sujets de fiction." Cahiers du Cinéma, No. 196 (December), pp. 52-59.

Burch describes Robbe-Grillet's fiction as "written film" and studies some of the cinematic techniques in the novels, then focuses on Last Year at Marienbad to analyze Robbe-Grillet's distinctions between subject and form.

284 _____. "Vers un cinéma dialectique: III. De l'usage structurel du son." Cahiers du Cinéma, No. 193 (September), pp. 50-55.

Burch analyzes the structural use of sound in the films of Jacques Rivette, Agnes Varda and Robbe-Grillet: specifically, in terms of Robbe-Grillet, how sound projects the narrative, serves as counterpoint to the image and allows for a new restructuring of the image (composition, editing) because of its independence of the image.

285 _____. "Vers un cinéma dialectique. I. Répertoire des structures simples." Cahiers du Cinéma, No. 191 (June), pp. 54-60.

Burch uses the films of Robbe-Grillet, Abel Gance, Resnais, Chris Marker, Jacques Tati and Agnes Varda in this article. He discusses the parameters of découpage. He praises Resnais for his ability to alternate shots of long duration with shots of short duration. He notes that Resnais is one of the few filmmakers to understand the duration-readability relationship as a dialectic. Burch speaks of photographic parameters, such as the differences between focus and out-of-focus shots. These create contrast and tonality. He uses the contrast between inside and outside in Last Year at Marienbad as an example. Marienbad is mentioned again in terms of the time dialectic within the film, the way in which sequences and sometimes shot-sequences interplay with other sequences to create a constant tension between past, present and future. The film is also cited for its dialectic of setting: baroque versus normal sets. Burch discusses the "itinerant" structures in Robbe-Grillet's Trans-Europ-Express and the dialectic of scenes involving non-professionals with scenes involving professional actors. He concludes that the explanation of structure equals dialectic, for structures are inevitably perceived as dialectical.

286 CAPDENAC, MICHEL. "Le Jeu de l'aventure, du mythe et de l'amour." Les Lettres Françaises (January 26), p. 18.
Interview with Robbe-Grillet on Trans-Europ-Express, concerning the "game" structures in the film, the playing with myth and Robbe-Grillet's notion of having transferred society's eroticism to the film.

287 CHAPSAL, MADELEINE. "Robbe-Grillet." La Quinzaine Littéraire, No. 22 (February 15-28), p. 29.
Brief review of Trans-Europ-Express.

288 CHEVASSU, FRANÇOIS. "Trans-Europ-Express." Image et Son, No. 203 (March), pp. 111-14.
Calls the film mediocre and pretentious. We shouldn't succumb to an intellectual terrorism which would force us to see Robbe-Grillet's film as important in any way, Chevassu concludes. Everything is in the scenario; little is left for light, for pace, for acting, for editing, for the economic conditions of filming, for the choice between color and black-and-white, between scope and the normal format. He suggests that Robbe-Grillet is still ignorant when it comes to cinematography. Point by point, Chevassu attacks the film's music, its use of parody, its eroticism and its exploration of the imaginary.

289 COLEMAN, JOHN. "Transition." New Statesman, 73, No. 1885 (April 28), 592.
Brief reviews of Peter Watkins' Privilege and Robbe-Grillet's L'Immortelle, the latter noted as important for its coming prior to the first BBC showing of the film in England. Coleman notes that he loathed Last Year at

Marienbad. He only disliked L'Immortelle. He objects primarily to the "strangeness" of the film.

*290 COLLET, JEAN. "Trans-Europ-Express, d'Alain Robbe-Grillet: Les Voies de garage de l'intelligence." Signes du Temps, No. 3 (March), pp. 31-32.
Unseen. Cited in French VII, 1968, #64000 (See: Source List).

291 COMOLLI, JEAN-LOUIS. "Le Cahier des autres." Cahiers du Cinéma, No. 188 (March), pp. 4-5.
Article is subtitled "Le Sexe et les jambes." Comolli reproduces a letter of indignation from Juliette Berto, who played the part of a woman in Godard's Two or Three Things that I Know About Her, who wouldn't say: "My sex is between my legs." The Cahiers people had compared her with Robbe-Grillet's prudery in Trans-Europ-Express. She writes indignantly that she rejects Robbe-Grillet totally.

292 COOPER, R. W. "Sinister Aspects of a Love Affair." The Times (May 2), (n.p.).
Cooper seems to be saying that Robbe-Grillet is a victim of his prior occupation (novelist) in this absurd review of L'Immortelle. As one of the leading writers of the new novel, Robbe-Grillet should be expected to do experimental things in film. Cooper notes that Robbe-Grillet told him that the film had been rejected by French critics, because he was a writer, just as his first novels had been condemned because he began his career as an engineer.

293 DENT, ALAN. "Ravishing Guesswork." The Illustrated London News, 250, No. 6666 (May 6), 30-31.
Review of L'Immortelle as a puzzle-film with multiple possibilities for interpretation.

294 DEWEY, LANGDON. "Trans-Europ-Express." Filmfacts, No. 50 (Winter), pp. 31-32.
Brief synopsis of the film.

*295 DONIOL-VALCROZE, JACQUES. "Un cinéma moderne." La Nef, 24, No. 29 (January-March), 107-14.
Unseen. Cited in French XX, 1969, #72268 (See: Source List). On Robbe-Grillet, Godard, Resnais, Rivette and Renoir.

296 DUPEYRON, GEORGES. "Le Cinéma." Europe, Nos. 456-57 (April-May), pp. 328-32.
On Godard and Robbe-Grillet, specifically, a review of Trans-Europ-Express.

*297 FOSBERG, M. W. "A Fly at the Spa: L'Année dernière à Marienbad." Theoria, No. 28, pp. 13-23.
Unseen. Cited in French XX, 1969, #71033 (See: Source List).

298 GEDULD, HARRY M. Filmmakers on Film-Making. Bloomington and London: Indiana University Press, 302 pp.
Contains reprints of Resnais' "Trying to Understand My Own Film" (155-64) and Resnais' and Robbe-Grillet's "Last Words on Last Year" (164-75).

299 GIBBS, PATRICK. "Beautiful Enigma." The Daily Telegraph, No. 34837 (April 28), p. 16.
Gibbs praises the look of L'Immortelle, although he doesn't know what it means.

300 JACOB, GILLES. "Trans-Europ-Express d'Alain Robbe-Grillet." Cinéma 67, No. 114 (March), pp. 56-69.
Extremely thorough and interesting reading of the film. He notes that Robbe-Grillet can do so much with a non-story, a pretext. Robbe-Grillet reveals himself as creator and actor, leaving all scenes and half-scenes in the film. Jacob emphasizes the ambiguity of Robbe-Grillet's films, an ambiguity that can only come from a logic of delirium, not from common sense. Jacob presents a possible reading of the film: Robbe-Grillet is the real drug-runner (drugs are hidden in his tape recorder) and Trintignant is simply Trintignant, an actor. He notes oppositions in the film: Robbe-Grillet as narrator-actor is filmed with a forward mobile camera, while Robbe-Grillet the author-filmmaker is shot from a backward mobile camera. The film is like a deck of cards which the spectator is invited to shuffle in terms of scenes. Jacob notes the dreamed scenes, the broken ("conditional") scenes, sequences of recapitulation, repeated or imaginary scenes, associative scenes, short and "hallucinatory" editing, negative images (the bee-keeper who goes to "black" in order to die), repetitions or refusals to choose, old-movie parody scenes (à la Feuillade). When Robbe-Grillet within the film is caught at an impasse in the narrative, he switches routes, via Trintignant, leading to the same scenes as before but by different routes. Robbe-Grillet is less a profiteer of the erotic or sadistic than one who shows all the bombardment and sadism of society's media (notes, films, commercials, magazines, cartoons). Jacob notes the different time frames operating simultaneously in the film: Jean (Robbe-Grillet) and Trintignant both going to Antwerp, then, while Robbe-Grillet is still on the train, Trintignant is making a return trip to Paris; then, Trintignant returns to Antwerp on the same train as Robbe-Grillet, thus catching up with him. The title of the film and the whole film are based on

a series of generative puns. The Abbot Petitjean may be a possible allusion to the real pseudonym of Petitjean in the Ben Barka affair in France. Anvers becomes "envers," Elias becomes Alias, the anagram also including "asile." Jacob salutes Robbe-Grillet for his use of Samy Halfon (his film producer) and Jerome Lindon (his boss at Minuit) within the film. Finally, he salutes Robbe-Grillet for leaving the work "open" with its unfinished look.

301 LAWSON, JOHN HOWARD. "Violence," in his Film: The Creative Process, revised edition. New York: Hill and Wang, pp. 230-42.
Pages 237-39 deal with Last Year at Marienbad. Lawson notes that there is no motivation behind the characters' actions, no dividing line between dream and reality nor between past and present. He points out the differences between Robbe-Grillet's script and Resnais' execution: specifically, the suppression of a shooting and a rape scene. "Resnais has conceived the final development, not in terms of 'growing fantasies,' but as an escape from a world of stifling illusion." Finally, he contrasts Last Year at Marienbad with Godard's A bout de souffle.

*302 MARCABRU, PIERRE. "Robbe-Grillet: Un express qui nous mène en bateau." Arts-Loisirs, No. 70 (January 25-31), pp. 24-25.
Unseen. Cited in French VII, 1969, #71040 (See: Source List).

303 MARMORI, GIANCARLO. "Pop." Atlas (May), pp. 53-56.
On Trans-Europ-Express. Marmori begins with Didier Anzieu's psychoanalytical interpretations of Robbe-Grillet's novels and films as being full of oedipal symbols. Marmori notes that Robbe-Grillet calls the sadism in his works "pop": fully conscious of itself and merely counterfeiting the depth and darkness of the unconscious..."from the eroticism of pornographic literature to the exoticism of James Bond and Modesty Blaise, from comic strips to Playboy magazine." Marmori jokes that Trans-Europ-Express is loaded with Freudian symbols to spite psychiatrists in the audience, from the name of the cafe ("Océan") as a symbol of the Mother to the trains which are phallic. Marmori studies Robbe-Grillet's use of "intellectual" women to play erotic roles: Françoise Brion in L'Immortelle, Marie-France Pisier (she got her law degree the day shooting was finished) in Trans-Europ-Express. "It is noticeable in his films, then, that the leading actress is always somewhat 'unsuited' for the role assigned to her--almost as if she were playing it against her will." Marmori notes the use of "La Traviata" of Verdi in Trans-Europ-Express during the rape scene to make the scene funny, more "pop." "Robbe-Grillet's art is

characterized by a peculiarly glassy and pallid look at the world of men and things. It is an art punctuated by resentments and treacherous impatience, at times horrifying and at other times achieving a comic effect by a kind of acrobatic intellectual distance. Robbe-Grillet is evolving, little by little, from the turbid and unconscious sadism of his early manner to a cultural consciousness reflected in his parodistic 'pop' works." Curiously, Marmori announces Robbe-Grillet's next film as L'Homme qui meurt (The Dying Man), when in fact it was called L'Homme qui ment (The Man Who Lies).

*304 MAURIAC, CLAUDE. "Trans-Europ-Express d'Alain Robbe-Grillet." Le Figaro Littéraire, No. 1084 (January 26), p. 16.
Unseen. Cited in French VII, 1968, #64009 (See: Source List).

*305 MONNIER, JEAN-PIERRE. "Les Nouveaux Maitres," in his L'Age ingrat du roman. Neuchatel: Bacconière, pp. 69-93.
Unseen. Cited in Fraizer, p. 101, #232 (See: 475). Many references to Last Year at Marienbad.

306 MORRISSETTE, BRUCE. "The Evolution of Narrative Viewpoint in Robbe-Grillet." Novel: A Forum on Fiction, 1, No. 1 (Fall), 24-33.
One of the most interesting and still "unresolved" aspects of fictional structure remains that of narrative viewpoint. The abandonment of "justified" viewpoint and of the "omniscient" narrator leads to a new kind of omniscience in which the reader is placed at the often moving narrational center. Parallel with this, Morrissette notes the emerging "cinema of interior truth" (Raymond Borde's term), and he cites as examples Hiroshima mon amour and Last Year at Marienbad. In a sixth category of narrative viewpoint, Morrissette discusses point of view in Marienbad and L'Immortelle. He relates both films to the novels of Robbe-Grillet's middle period: specifically, to Le Voyeur and La Jalousie. "Thus, mental content, which is primarily visual, becomes a natural narrative mode for the cinema, which can show the characters' imaginings while retaining the same degree of 'realism' in the decor and photography as that used in the 'normal' scenes, if indeed any scenes may be thought of as existing apart from the characters' perceptions."

307 MOSCOWITZ, GENE. "Trans-Europ-Express." Variety (January 18), p. 6.
He calls Last Year at Marienbad "hermetic," L'Immortelle "static," and Trans-Europ-Express a "fairly amusing tidbit." He thinks the erotic scenes in the latter are forced. "This is mainly for specialized usage abroad on its tricky if familiar treatment."

308 NARBONI, JEAN. "La Maldonne des sleepings." Cahiers du Cinéma, No. 188 (March), pp. 65-66.
On Trans-Europ-Express. Narboni notes that one of the most striking characteristics of "modernist" works is the move away from the finished work and toward the artist within his own work, affirming his own doubts, questioning even the very construction or form of his work (or hers, as the case may be), a form that permits his entry. Such expressed doubts in the filmic process take the form of whether to film this or that, before or after, in front or behind, in freeze-frame or in movement, in close-up or long shot. Narboni thinks Godard's Two or Three Things that I Know About Her reveals these hesitations and choices extremely well, so that each frame seems the result of having first gained victory over doubt; in Trans-Europ-Express Robbe-Grillet seems to be creating on the spot, demystifying the idea of the finished work. Yet, Narboni doubts the "authenticity" of the work. There is no victory over doubt with this "creator," but rather a coquettish complacency with the idea of doubt itself. When Robbe-Grillet decides in front of the camera simply to suppress certain images or scenes, Narboni feels little evidence of constraint, of doubt, of any hard-gained lucidity. Robbe-Grillet's "maybe," his "it seems that," his question marks seem authoritarian, satisfied in themselves.

*309 PIATIER, JACQUELINE. "Entretien avec Alain Robbe-Grillet à propos de Trans-Europ-Express: 'On a tendance en France à refuser du sérieux à tout ce qui amuse.'" Le Monde, No. 6854 (January 25), p. 14.
Unseen. Cited in French VII, 1968, #64002 (See: Source List). Interview with Robbe-Grillet on Trans-Europ-Express.

*310 PICON, GAETON. "Les Formes de l'esprit: Cinéma et littérature." Le Monde, No. 6893 (March 11), p. 13.
Unseen. Cited in French VII, 1968, #65011 (See: Source List).

311 PINGAUD, BERNARD and PIERRE SAMSON. Alain Resnais ou la création au cinéma, special issue of Cahiers de l'Arc, No. 31 (Winter), (n.p.).
Many references to Last Year at Marienbad.

312 POWELL, DILYS. "Indignation About What?" The Sunday Times, No. 7509 (April 30), p. 50.
Hostile review of Trans-Europ-Express.

312 ROBBE-GRILLET, ALAIN. "Brèves réflexions sur le fait de décrire une scène de cinéma. Antinomie du film et du roman." La Revue d'Esthétique, No. 20, pp. 131-38.

An extremely important statement in terms of Robbe-Grillet's middle period as a filmmaker. A footnote says this article forms part of a chapter from the ciné-roman for Trans-Europ-Express. The ciné-roman was never finished. Robbe-Grillet notes that literary descriptions of objects, scenes, gestures, decors and settings are radically different from both the real objects and from the representation of such objects in images (drawings, photography, film). He adds that in writing his novels he has never studied a real object or image of an object to guide him in describing that object. Yet there are many descriptions of images in his novels and in many modern novels (the photo enlargement in Les Gommes, the film poster in Le Voyeur, the cover-page with a popular illustration in La Maison de rendez-vous, the "Défaite de Reichenfels" image in Dans le labyrinthe). None of these images described exist in reality. "We must recognize the fact that the written phrase represents a radical denial of our everyday tangible world." He notes that his procedure is the reverse when making a film: he only likes natural locations, which guide him in the shooting (choice of photographic angles, lenses, editing, camera movement). The real Trans-Europe train served as a basis for his film. He notes that Trans-Europ-Express differs from Marienbad and L'Immortelle in that no completed script for the actors or scenario for the crew was ever written. The film was meant to remain from start to finish in a state of "mobile structure in permanent metamorphosis." The film was mapped for four weeks of shooting, four months of editing. The "scenario" remained throughout the shooting full of "maybe" and "either this or that," full of suppositions and conditional indications. "It's boring work, very difficult work, to transcribe shot by shot the final version of a film like this. For similar reasons, I've never wanted to film any of my novels."

314 _____. "Propos de cinéastes." La Revue d'Esthétique, 20, Nos. 2-3 (April-September), (n.p.).

Contains a long article by Jean Mitry and brief statements by Robbe-Grillet, Resnais, Godard and Bresson.

315 SONTAG, SUSAN. "Resnais' Muriel," in her Against Interpretation and Other Essays. New York: Delta, pp. 232-41.

She suggests that Muriel tries to do what both Hiroshima mon amour and Last Year at Marienbad did. She notes that all three films have as a common theme the search for an inexpressible past. She emphasizes the abstractness of memory in Marienbad.

316 STOLTZFUS, BEN. "Robbe-Grillet, L'Immortelle and the Novel: Reality, Nothingness and Imagination." L'Esprit Créateur, 7, No. 2 (Summer), 123-34.

Stoltzfus cites the labyrinthine streets of Les Gommes, using the novels to explain some of the structures in the film of L'Immortelle. The jealous husband and the "jalousies" of the novel are duplicated in the film. He compares the deaths in the novels to the imagined deaths of Lale in L'Immortelle. He notes that "Leila" in Arabic means "soul-mate." Randomly, Stoltzfus seems to want to paraphrase psychologically or symbolically images from the film, taken out of context, out of their image-clusters. Many naive statements: "We are not told that N is sad but it is easy now to infer that he is suffering. In other words, we are seeing a pictorial equivalent of sorrow." He concludes with the idea of creation in these works as a symbolic reading level. Robbe-Grillet's characters' tendency to anthropomorphize leads them to murder, violence and mental disorders. Thus, all images in L'Immortelle are "contaminated" by the vision of N. Stoltzfus accuses Robbe-Grillet of heavy-handedness and overplaying in L'Immortelle.

317 TAYLOR, JOHN RUSSELL. "Bresson Masterpiece Among New Paris Films." The Times, No. 56907 (April 5), p. 10.
Mention of new films by Bresson, Chabrol, Demy, Duras, Godard, Malle and Trans-Europ-Express of Robbe-Grillet.

318 TESSIER, MAX. "Trans-Europ-Express." Jeune Cinéma, No. 21 (March), pp. 38-39.
Calls Trans-Europ-Express less a film than a "writing on film," physically on the film surface. He accuses Robbe-Grillet of a lack of imagination, complaining that the film is such an intellectual game. He compares it with La Maison de rendez-vous, both of them being too "cerebral" to be effective.

319 THIRARD, PAUL-LOUIS. "Trans-Europ-Express." Positif, No. 83 (April), p. 59.
Thirard complains that the film is lots of noise for nothing. He calls it pseudo-Pirandello and suggests that the so-called "erotic" scenes of the film are not erotic at all.

320 TOWARNICKI, FRÉDÉRIC DE. "L'Homme qui ment: Procès verbal." Cinéma 67, No. 121, pp. 57-64.
Excellent background article to viewing L'Homme qui ment, including interviews with Robbe-Grillet and some of the crew, arranged in the form of testimony. The setting for the film is noted as the chateau of the Baroness von Czobel. The unique qualities of a Robbe-Grillet film necessitate a new critique. Here proposed is the method of the "procès verbal," or witness-stand, as though the film were being treated as a trial, seen by various witnesses. Robbe-Grillet notes that the film has some affinity with

L'Immortelle and is an advance upon the structural innovations of Trans-Europ-Express, especially in terms of discontinuity and humor as working concepts. What it shares with L'Immortelle is its oneiric quality. Robbe-Grillet notes the various myths at work in the film, from Boris Goudounov to Don Juan, emphasizing that the Don Juan of Kierkegaard was both an usurper and a seducer. Quoting Kierkegaard: "It is only interesting to seduce a woman if she is in love with another man. There must be someone to compete with and to replace." He notes the dialectic between the real and the imaginary, between inventing oneself and being invented by others, between being alone and being with one's double (of course, invented). Robbe-Grillet reports that there were 4000 shots in Trans-Europ-Express, 800 in L'Immortelle, and around 1200 in L'Homme qui ment. Trintignant as the absent man (representing both himself and the missing Jean Robin) is the link between the lesbian women. He defines their lesbianism by his absence. When Trintignant is interviewed, he notes that the scenes were played out with distancing in the acting, primarily through the use of humor, but that there was even distancing involved in the humor, from itself. He notes that Robbe-Grillet's dialogue would be excellent on stage: "simple, direct, efficient." He adds that there is always a counterpoint in the film between humor and distance. Catherine Robbe-Grillet notes that of 32,000 meters of film, only 2700 were kept for editing. Her role was as a cartoon character, her acting necessarily excessive, stereotyped and heavy-handed. She compares La Maison de rendez-vous with Trans-Europ-Express in terms of both suggesting the lack of "depth" in our civilization. She adds that the film could have been called "The Imposter," "The Usurper" or "The Seducer," and she reports that the actresses began living as they lived in the film during the course of shooting. The Czech producer Marencin reports that he worked with Robbe-Grillet because he had previously translated Last Year at Marienbad and L'Immortelle into Czech. He imposed two conditions on Robbe-Grillet: the film had to be shot at least partially in Czechoslovakia and the film couldn't be critical of Czechoslovakia.

321 TYLER, PARKER. "The Lady Called 'A'; or if Jules and Jim Had Only Lived at Marienbad," in his The Three Faces of the Film. South Brunswick and New York: A. S. Barnes; London: Thomas Yoseloff, pp. 75-80.

Last Year at Marienbad is not the most artistic film ever made, but it is the most self-consciously artistic film ever made. Tyler suggests that the published ciné-roman, contrary to what Robbe-Grillet says, offers an adequate substitute for the film. "For sublime unconsciously promoted chic, well-behaved and tastefully well-behaved to the point of painfulness and boredom, the Resnais-Robbe-Grillet film is the perfect item.... The reality of *Last Year at Marienbad* is that one never needs to be reminded that this is a *film*. It reeks of being a film. It could not possibly get away with pretending to be anything else."

322 UPDIKE, JOHN. "Grove is My Press, and Avant My Garde." *New Yorker*, 43, No. 37 (November 4), 223-28.
Updike states that Robbe-Grillet's fiction is almost exclusively cinematic. *La Maison de rendez-vous* is not so much written as scripted: "The full syntax of splicing, blurring, stop-action, enlargement, panning and fade-out is employed; the book lacks only camera tracks and a union member operating the dolly."

323 WILSON, DAVID. "London Film Festival." *The Guardian*, No. 37747 (November 18), p. 5.
Review of Godard and Robbe-Grillet.

324 _____. "New Films." *The Guardian*, No. 35572 (April 28), p. 9.
Review of Robbe-Grillet's *L'Immortelle*.

1968

325 ADLER, RENATA. "Screen: A Twist on the Gangster Genre." *New York Times* (May 13), p. 52.
Calls *Trans-Europ-Express* a "little parody of the old New Wave crime eroticism movies" and notes some in-jokes in the film.

326 ANON. "Indispensable Sources for a Study of Robbe-Grillet's Films." *Kinema* (Alain Robbe-Grillet). Edited by Martin Parnell. No. 1 (June), pp. 43-44.
Critical bibliography for Robbe-Grillet's films.

327 ANON. "*L'Homme qui ment*." *L'Avant-scène du Cinéma*, No. 82 (June), pp. 59-60.
Synopsis of the film, with quotes from Robbe-Grillet, credits for the film and a bio-filmography.

*328 ANON. "Les Mystères du dernier Robbe-Grillet." *Paris-Match*, No. 990 (March 30), p. 127.
Unseen. Cited in *French VII*, 1969, #71044 (*See*: Source List). Review of *The Man Who Lies*.

329 ANON. "*Trans-Europ-Express*." *Cue* (May 18), (n.p.).
Notes that the film has the combined styles of Hitchcock, Resnais and Godard. "There are some convincing scenes of eroticism, fine acting moments by Trintignant and pretty

Marie-France Pisier, and good visual work. But for every absorbing sequence, there is a fatiguing counterpart."

330 ANON. "Trans-Europ-Express." Filmfacts, 11, No. 13 (August 1), 193-95.
Synopsis of the film with credits and excerpts from selected reviews.

331 ANON. "Trans-Europ-Express." Time (June 7), (n.p.).
"There is fun, in fact, for everyone, except those who like real thrills in their thrillers."

*332 ARMES, ROY. "Alain Robbe-Grillet and Modern Cinema." Kinema (Alain Robbe-Grillet), No. 1 (June), pp. 9-40.
Unseen. Cited in French XX, 1975, #A10877 (See: Source List).

333 _____. "In the Labyrinth: L'Année dernière à Marienbad," in his The Cinema of Alain Resnais. London: A. Zwemmer; New York: A. S. Barnes, pp. 88-114.
Traces the meeting of Resnais and Robbe-Grillet and the steps leading up to making the film. "Of all his feature films, this is the one to which Resnais contributed least in the scripting stage." Armes details the various memories (steps) toward "persuasion" in the film: the evocation of the statue, a conversation with friends, an incident of walking in the gardens with a broken heel. At this point, X is uncertain, followed by contradictory events and a breakdown in linear chronology. Armes emphasizes the collaboration in terms of form, not content. Robbe-Grillet's script predominantly traces X's vision, while Resnais' film introduces the possibility of A's visions. "The images belong to her principally, representing her thoughts and her relation to the man." In opposition to Resnais' characters, who are obsessed with the past, Robbe-Grillet's characters are void, stripped of their past. Armes notes that Resnais chose a foreign actor speaking French with a slight accent for the role of X to let the spectator realize that the inner monologue is not in the words but in the images. "Here again, as so often in this film, the technique is the very opposite of literary since it aims at replacing with images what is, in the conventional cinema, verbalised and hence robbed of its true ambiguity." Following Robbe-Grillet's lead, Armes suggests that the true meaning of the film lies in the movement of the description, not in the thing described. He notes that Resnais edits the film in such a way that "the same doorway constantly gives access to a new room and the garden is constantly changing, sometimes with paths and hedges, at others with pools and fountains, the same statue being found in a variety of places and occasionally absent from where it was before." Thus,

a spatial reality independent of our everyday reality is constructed in the film. Armes concludes that the film looks like a statue and sounds like an opera.

334 BABY, YVONNE. "L'Homme qui ment." Le Monde, No. 7219 (March 29), p. 12.
Brief review-synopsis of The Man Who Lies.

335 BERTIN, CELIA. "Deux romanciers, deux films." La Revue de Paris, 75, No. 5 (May), 141-44.
Brief mention of The Man Who Lies.

336 BEYLIE, CLAUDE. "L'Opéra du temps." Cinéma 68, No. 128 (August-September), pp. 44-45.
The focus of this article is on Resnais' Je t'aime je t'aime (1968) but with cross-references and allusions to his earlier films, including Last Year at Marienbad. Beylie notes that Marienbad is intimately related to myth: Sleeping Beauty, with a touch of Cinderella and the Blue Bird.

337 BILLARD, PIERRE. "Robbe-Grillet coupe la vérité en morceaux." L'Express, No. 876 (April 1-7), p. 63.
Review of The Man Who Lies. Billard notes that the "game," which was so controlled in L'Immortelle and so farcical in Trans-Europ-Express, here attains the rigidity of a chess game. He thinks it is Robbe-Grillet's best film for the highly masterful way that the film plays with narrative structures, with our expectations, with traditional film rules, not only in the images but on the sound-track as well. He also thinks that underneath the game is a kind of classical tragedy that is even more pertinent in today's scattered society: the tragedy of a man split by his lies and his inability to discern between truth and fiction.

*338 BOISDEFFRE, PIERRE DE. "Robbe-Grillet, le nouveau roman et le cinéma." A la Page, No. 54 (December), pp. 1786-96.
Unseen. Cited in French VII, 1969, #71025 (See: Source List).

339 BORY, JEAN-LOUIS. "L'Homme qui tue et l'homme qui parle." Le Nouvel Observateur, No. 177 (April 3-9), pp. 50-51.
Review of The Man Who Lies, emphasizing the differences between content and form, especially this form of endlessly retelling, restarting, restructuring all that's gone before.

340 CAPDENAC, MICHEL. "Beau comme un mensonge." Les Lettres Françaises, No. 1228 (April 3-10), p. 21.
Brief review of The Man Who Lies, emphasizing Robbe-Grillet's mixture of the true, the false and especially the make-believe in the film.

341 CAPELLE, ANNE. "Robbe-Grillet: mon dernier film." La Quinzaine Littéraire, No. 48 (April 1-15), pp. 24-25.
Interview with Robbe-Grillet about The Man Who Lies, emphasizing the structures of the film and their relation to myth-content.

342 CHARDÈRE, BERNARD. "L'Homme qui ment." Positif, No. 95 (May), p. 67.
Unfavorable review of The Man Who Lies.

343 CHEVALLIER, JACQUES. "L'Homme qui ment." Image et Son, No. 218 (June-July), pp. 122-25.
Article on The Man Who Lies. Subjective images "invade" the objective images (through editing), as, for example, the shots of the womens' hair intercut with the first shots of Boris resurrected from apparent death. Chevallier thinks that the verbal hesitations of Boris are reflected in the visual hesitations of Robbe-Grillet. He notes the various "games" in the film and concludes: "With less science but more poetry Bunuel gets to the frontiers beyond reality more easily."

*344 COHN, BERNARD. "L'Homme qui ment." Positif, No. 95, (n.p.).
Unseen. Cited in Gardies, p. 187 (See: 440).

345 CORBIN, LOUISE. "Trans-Europ-Express." Films in Review, 19, No. 6 (June-July), 377.
Unfavorable review of the film. "Alain Robbe-Grillet, who wrote the pretentious but meaningless piffle called Last Year at Marienbad, both wrote and directed this even more meaningless film." Corbin calls the film a satirization on New Wave satirizations on crime films. She thinks that many of these satirizations are merely pornography to excite sado-masochists.

*346 CORNAND, A. "L'Homme qui ment." Image et Son, Nos. 219-220, (n.p.).
Unseen. Cited in Gardies, p. 187 (See: 440). Review of The Man Who Lies.

347 DUBORG, MAURICE. "Le Roman-cinéma." Cinéma 68, No. 131 (December), pp. 54-69.
Not directly related to Robbe-Grillet's film activity, but interestingly analogous to Robbe-Grillet's refinement of the ciné-roman. Duborg's analysis covers the popular literature called "roman-cinéma" from 1915-1930, which allowed audiences to (1) relive the plots of films they had seen and (2) know the scenario of films one hoped to see.

*348 ENARD, JEAN-PIERRE. "L'Homme qui ment." Télé-ciné, 23, No. 145 (September), 12-19.

Unseen. Cited in French XX, 1973, #100602 (See: Source List). Review of The Man Who Lies.

*349 FABRIZZIO, CLAUDE. "Entretien. Alain Robbe-Grillet: quelques vérités sur L'Homme qui ment." Les Lettres Françaises, No. 1226 (March 20-26), pp. 18-19.
Unseen. Cited in French XX, 1970, #77512 (See: Source List). Interview with Robbe-Grillet on The Man Who Lies.

350 FERRINI, FRANCO. "Trans-Europ-Express." Cinema & Film, 2, Nos. 5-6, 213-16.
Synopsis of the film with a long description of the various "games" in the film and points of contrast with Robbe-Grillet's earlier films.

351 GILI, JEAN A. "L'Homme qui ment: le cinéma mensonge." Cinéma 68, No. 131 (December), pp. 135-36.
Notes the large gap between Robbe-Grillet's supposed intentions and his supposed achievements. Gili believes Resnais "saved" Last Year at Marienbad. Quotes Robbe-Grillet as saying that it's a film about narcissism and onanism. Michel Fano's excellent sound-track and Igor Luther's beautiful photography (grays were suppressed by a lab process, so that only blacks and whites remain) don't save the sterile concept behind the film. Gili finds Robbe-Grillet "locked" into a game of myth, making a film that is a total dehumanization.

352 GILLIATT, PENELOPE. "Current Cinema." New Yorker, No. 44 (May 18), pp. 152-53.
Unfavorable review of Trans-Europ-Express, noting that it is "one of those French intellectual games that comically doll up simple pulp-fiction stories with dark hints of something metaphysical going on." She is highly critical of the enigmatic nature of the film and concludes: "The glum thought strikes you that Robbe-Grillet is making a point about the difficulty of telling reality from fiction. Leaving aside children of three and three-quarters, I don't know any people except clever Frenchmen who find this a difficulty."

353 GLATZER, ROBERT. "Trans-Europ-Express." Chelsea Clinton News (May 23), (n.p.).
Unfavorable review of the film, suggesting that the producer, instead of acting in the film, should have rejected the script altogether.

354 HALE, WANDA. "Spy Thriller Plays It For Laughs." New York Daily News (May 13), p. 50.
Flattering review of Trans-Europ-Express as a spoof, noting the film within the film and the clichés used for humor.

355 HATCH, ROBERT. "Films." The Nation, 206, No. 23 (June 3), 742.

Mixed review of Trans-Europ-Express, in which Hatch calls Catherine Robbe-Grillet the daughter of Robbe-Grillet. Hatch concludes that the film is a picture about time-wasting designed to waste time attractively.

356 McCANN, BARRY. "Alain Robbe-Grillet." Film, No. 51 (Spring), pp. 22-27.

Begins with a retelling of the plot of Trans-Europ-Express. McCann justifies Robbe-Grillet's insertions and digressions in the film. The scenes all have reasons, "even the strange one where a parcel, carried by Elias, worries the filmmakers, who all agree that he should just throw it away. So he does--by three different methods, in rapid succession, one for each writer." He calls the film the easiest of all of Robbe-Grillet's films to follow. He defends the film against the censorship directed at the film's eroticism. The rape is agreed upon, so Marie-France Pisier is an actress in a double sense. He notes that England is the only country to have refused the film a certificate of entry. He cites Robbe-Grillet's notion that the twentieth century is superficial, whereas the nineteenth was philosophical. The film is about superficial surfaces and imagination. The train is a symbol for imagination, while the real world rushes by outside: thus, there is a critique of the filmmakers within the film too. Verdi's "La Traviata" was chosen to represent the bold gestures of the nineteenth century. Elias impersonates movie posters, a critique of the role of cinema in the twentieth century. The film is itself the world, then, which it creates as it goes along. Robbe-Grillet: "It is in the moment or it is nothing. As soon as it has disappeared it has not just gone into the past, it is no longer anything." In a similar vein, filmic descriptions of objects reveal their presence, while literary descriptions of objects destroy them. McCann alludes to Last Year at Marienbad, L'Immortelle and The Man Who Lies.

357 MEKAS, JONAS. "Movie Journal." Village Voice (May 23), (n.p.).

Laments the passage from literature to the cinema of good writers (Pasolini, Robbe-Grillet, Mailer), who make "naive" and "sloppy" films. He cites L'Immortelle and Trans-Europ-Express as examples.

358 MORRISSETTE, BRUCE. "Games and Game Structures in Robbe-Grillet." Yale French Studies, No. 41, pp. 159-67.

Analysis of the Nim game in Last Year at Marienbad, noting that it is not Chinese but German: "nimm" or "take-away." The Nim game is reflected/duplicated in the broken pieces of glass, the slippers, the photographs and the torn pieces of the letter. Morrissette cites the Oedipus myth and the structure of the Tarot cards in Les Gommes, the serial "games of resemblances" in Le Voyeur and La Jalousie. He also notes the games of wild-goose-chase in Trans-Europ-Express, the starts and retreats and new starts.

*359 _____. "Problèmes du roman cinématographique." Cahiers de l'Association Internationale des Etudes Françaises (May), (n.p.).
Unseen. Cited in Morrissette (See: Source List).

360 _____. "Trends in the New French Cinema." The American Society Legion of Honor Magazine, 39, No. 3, 153-72.
Traces theories of "pure" cinema in the 1920's from Henri Chomette to updated Jacques Brunius to Last Year at Marienbad and the last "object sequence" of Antonioni's Eclipse. He notes this direction in film narrative to show that the "real" loses its precise meaning: time in Méliès to time in Roussel to time in Resnais and Robbe-Grillet. He suggests the persistent influence of Surrealism, especially of Bunuel, and the impact of Italian neo-realism on the French New Wave. He points to Marienbad as having free structures of time and plot that would characterize the later Robbe-Grillet films. He summarizes L'Immortelle, offering that the end of the film might be compared with James M. Cain's The Postman Always Rings Twice. He notes parallels between the baroque, especially Corneille's plays, and the new cinema.

*361 NOGUEZ, DOMINIQUE. "L'Homme qui ment." Cahiers du Cinéma, Nos. 200-201, (n.p.).
Unseen. Cited in Gardies, p. 187 (See: 440). Review of The Man Who Lies.

362 PRÉDAL, RENÉ. "Resnais et le 'nouveau roman.'" Etudes Cinématographiques (Alain Resnais), Nos. 64-68. Paris: Minard, pp. 12-18.
Quotes from Resnais and Robbe-Grillet about working together and their intentions for Last Year at Marienbad. Other references to Marienbad are scattered throughout this excellent book on Resnais.

363 REISZ, KAREL and GAVIN MILLAR. "Last Year at Marienbad," in their The Technique of Film Editing, revised edition. New York: Hastings House, pp. 358-69.
They note that the traditional distinction between present and past, fact and fantasy, is gone. They quote Alfred Jarry to the effect that "perception is a true hallucination." They insist on Robbe-Grillet as co-author of the work: "It is not an accident that we quote the 'author'

rather than the 'director' of Marienbad. They decided to sign the film together, since they were equally responsible for its conception...." They note that Marienbad is a new novel in which it is more convenient to photograph the images than to describe them. They agree that the film's chronology is baffling, not only for spectators to reconstruct, but also for projectionists who have often put on the wrong reel and not known their mistake throughout the film.

364 ROBBE-GRILLET, ALAIN. "L'Homme qui ment." La Quinzaine Littéraire, No. 48, (n.p.).
Discussion of The Man Who Lies in terms of the Boris character, the serial nature of his narration, the implications in terms of myth.

365 RYBALKA, MICHEL. "Alain Robbe-Grillet: A Bibliography." West Coast Review, 3, No. 2 (Fall), 31-38.
Excellent bibliography, listing references to the novels and films as well as interviews Robbe-Grillet has given.

366 SARRIS, ANDREW. "Trans-Europ-Express." Village Voice (May 23), p. 43.
Semantics replace analysis here. Some plot summary advanced, then some jokes about Robbe-Grillet being a metteur-en-chaine ("director-of-chains") and being Alain Rope-Grillet. He notes that the film "demonstrates the limitations of self-conscious intelligence in the cinema."

367 SCHWARTZ, PAUL. "Anti-humanism in Art: Interview with Paul Schwartz." Studio, No. 175 (April), pp. 168-69.
Extremely important interview with Robbe-Grillet. Robbe-Grillet notes that it is not from any literary point of view that he takes an interest in the plastic arts. Whereas we look at a Rembrandt painting as if it were finished, in modern art as in modern film, the participation for the spectator is still in the "formative" state. Robbe-Grillet cites Marcel Duchamp, who insisted that the viewers made the painting, setting up a new rapport between the author and the spectator. He cites Lichtenstein and the use of the comic strip (flatness as form) as a reaction against lyrical abstraction. Robbe-Grillet sees this attack on depth as revolutionary, but when Lichtenstein states that this flatness (in terms of content) is the flatness we are all reduced to by the Vietnam war, then the experiment is doomed, because it's limited to a particular critique of society from a nineteenth-century humanist standpoint. In terms of film, Robbe-Grillet cites Godard. Godard uses red paint (flat) instead of blood (depth). That is revolutionary. But then Godard explains this flatness in terms of a humanist critique that Robbe-Grillet finds totally outmoded.

Robbe-Grillet cites the elimination of metaphors as something radical: for example, minimal art, an art without references. He announces that a new form of metaphor, not humanist, is coming.

368 STOLTZFUS, BEN. "Robbe-Grillet et le Bon Dieu." L'Esprit Créateur, 8, No. 4 (Winter), 302-11.

Traces the breakdown in the verisimilitude and relevance of the nineteenth-century novel in twentieth-century novels and films. "If this is true, then the 'new novel' must either be autobiographical, as Sarraute claims, or, as Robbe-Grillet asserts, purely imaginary." Stoltzfus defends Robbe-Grillet's novels and films as being rooted in reality. He notes that Robbe-Grillet represents a middle ground between Sartre's commitment of words to reality and the linguistic "hermeticism" of the Tel Quel group. Stoltzfus notes that in Trans-Europ-Express what seems true is false and what seems false is true. The gangster is not a gangster, the rape is not a rape and Elias says his name is Jean (the same name as Jean/Robbe-Grillet, the filmmaker within the film). In Trans-Europ-Express as well as in The Man Who Lies, there is an interdependence between the imagination of the author and the autonomy of his creations.

*369 THOMAIER, W. "Alain Robbe-Grillet." Sight and Sound, 37, No. 3 (Summer), p. 160.

Unseen. Cited in Schuster, p. 324 (See: Source List).

370 WARD, JOHN. "Alain Robbe-Grillet: the Novelist as Director." Sight and Sound, 37, No. 2 (Spring), 86-90.

Ward accuses Robbe-Grillet of applying chosiste principles from literature to film unsuccessfully in L'Immortelle: "The result was ponderous and repetitive, committing every fault that Alain Resnais should make, but somehow never does." He notes that Robbe-Grillet naturally turned to film, since "he had deprived the novel of nearly everything that makes it unique." He accuses Robbe-Grillet of lacking a film style of his own, unless it be the "popular fashion" style of Trans-Europ-Express. He notes the use of objective correlatives as in the novels to define Elias, objects to represent the emotional states and problems of his characters: all the ropes are symbols for Elias' "manacled and twisted sexuality," and the railway lines correspond to the "precariousness of his state and of an emotional life so delicately balanced that in a moment of extreme stress it topples over into murder." Ward believes that Godard's influence on Robbe-Grillet will be better than that of Resnais in the long run, for Resnais could only make him more literary; yet, he wishes Robbe-Grillet would get rid of the very elements of parody for which he admired Trans-Europ-Express.

371 ____. "L'Année dernière à Marienbad," in his Alain Resnais or the Theme of Time. New York: Doubleday, pp. 39-62.
Ward suggests a reconstruction of "last year," in which X and A did meet and have an affair, in which M kills A and X is left alone. The film is one long interior monologue by X. Since A is "dead," she does not really narrate. X only imagines or remembers how she would or did speak. In a footnote, Ward claims: "Resnais' and Robbe-Grillet's statements to the contrary are not relevant." He contrasts Robbe-Grillet with Bergson in terms of memory and suggests that Resnais applied a Bergsonian outlook in his film.

372 WILSON, DAVID. "Festivals 68." Sight and Sound, 37, No. 4 (Autumn), 177-78.
Survey of festivals at Berlin, Karlovy Vary, Pesaro and Venice. Chabrol's Les Biches is in the Robbe-Grillet vein: the young woman named "Why" is like A and other nameless Robbe-Grillet characters. Also, there are two bogus painters in the film named Robegue and Riais. Wilson gives an unfavorable review of The Man Who Lies: "L'Homme qui ment will be grist to the mill of those to whom Robbe-Grillet is a cinematic charlatan." He questions Robbe-Grillet's seriousness and authenticity.

373 WINSTEN, ARCHER. "Trans-Europ-Express at the Plaza." New York Post (May 13), p. 25.
Calling the film "pop fiction with wit," Winsten notes the games of hide-and-seek within the film, in which the creators acknowledge the games while obscuring the games by acting them out.

374 ZELTNER-NEUKOMM, GERDA. "Der literatische Hintergrund der Filmwerke von Resnais: Marguerite Duras, Alain Robbe-Grillet, Jean Cayrol." Schweizer Rundschau, No. 67, pp. 70-80.
Discussion of the "literary" cinema developed by Resnais through his collaboration and co-creation with leading novelists like Duras, Robbe-Grillet and Cayrol, emphasizing their original scripts as opposed to adaptations of novels.

1969

375 ANON. "Robbe-Grillet and Duras." Sight and Sound, 38, No. 3 (Summer), 129.
Discussion of Robbe-Grillet and Duras as novelists, as screenwriters for Resnais and as filmmakers, with reference to Duras' Destroy She Said and Robbe-Grillet's The Man Who Lies.

376 ARCHER, EUGENE. "Director of Enigmas: Alain Resnais," in The Emergence of Film Art. Edited by Lewis Jacobs. New York: Hopkinson and Blake, pp. 336-40.
Robbe-Grillet is mentioned as having written the script for Last Year at Marienbad and for having been puzzled by Resnais' "enigmatic" contradictions of everything he said about the film. Truffaut wrote of Resnais: "With Marienbad Resnais carried the cinema further than it had ever gone before without worrying about whether or not audiences would follow. If he were a novelist or a poet, this wouldn't matter--but in the cinema you're supposed to worry about your audience. Alain knows this, and that's why he seems so contradictory and mysterious. He's trying to hide his obsession with his art." Other than the Truffaut quote, there's not much to this article.

377 BESSES, ONA D. "A Bibliographic Essay on Alain Robbe-Grillet." Bulletin of Bibliography and Magazine Notes, 26, No. 2 (April-June), 52-59; 26, No. 3 (July-September), 87-88.
Excellent bibliography for sources pertaining to both the novels and the films.

378 BILLINGTON, MICHAEL. "Destroying a Myth." The Illustrated London News, 254, No. 6768 (April 19), 32.
Review of Trans-Europ-Express.

379 BISHOP, TOM and HELEN BISHOP. "The Man Who Lies: An Interview with Alain Robbe-Grillet," in Film Festival. New York: Grove Press, pp. 41-44, 87-89.
Extremely important interview with Robbe-Grillet. The title of the interview is interesting: it may refer to the film and its filmmaker or it may refer to Robbe-Grillet as "the man who lies." Either way, the material is important. Robbe-Grillet states that the title of the film is ironic, since Boris/Trintignant cannot lie, because there is no truth. "As there is no God there is no truth and as there is no truth exterior to Man, Man creates his own truth." He discusses the idea of "participation," affirming that his invitation to the viewer is not based on chance or arbitrary meanings in the film: it is not a "right you are if you think you are" proposition. He recounts the problems he encountered when he tried to collaborate with Nicolas Schoeffer, a designer who created cybernetic sculptures and mobiles, and Pierre Henry, the composer. "Schoeffer wanted to have the public intervene in the development of the opera--of the work--and I was completely opposed, because for me the work is open to the spectator. He must participate in it, must recreate it himself, but recreate it as it is." The Man Who Lies is as carefully put together as a film as La Maison de rendez-vous is as a novel, both having been done about the same time. The man who speaks in The

Man Who Lies is Don Juan, the Don Giovanni of the eighteenth century who was the first man to have "chosen" his own word against the word of God. Yet there is also a parody of the Don Juan myths. Trintignant crumbling under the handshake of Dr. Muller is exactly like Don Giovanni when the statue of the Commendatore shakes his hand. The three women are also taken from the Don Juan legends. Yet there is no attempt at a literal transposition of the myth. "From the very beginning of the film he (Boris) appears in an atmosphere which is as unrealistic as possible. He is neatly dressed in a suit and tie in the midst of a forest completely surrounded by the German Army in tattered uniforms." From that, Robbe-Grillet affirms that the modern novelist is one who affirms that there's nothing other than what he says, and so he is precisely in the situation of Don Juan, Trintignant and the spectator. Robbe-Grillet notes that the actor who plays Jean Robin "has the face of a young Kafka, this character whom he calls Jean and who in fact is himself." In the French version of the film they are dubbed by the same voice. He explains the ending of the film: Trintignant sees himself again pursued by his double and he returns to the forest where he will again be hunted by the same soldiers, but it is really the double that hunts him and he is himself in pursuit of his double "as if he were desperately trying to stick two halves together." The three women are only ghosts that he creates. And the characters in the cafe or inn are already telling the story, a little like ghosts. At the beginning of the film, Boris speaks intelligently, relating "almost believable things but without any conviction." Gradually, what he relates becomes increasingly deranged, increasingly hysterical, and yet at the same time he says it with more conviction and with a passion "as if it were really becoming true." There is an undercutting of the "stories" that Boris tells by the rapid movement of Trintignant's hands in telling them. Robbe-Grillet notes that the film was made for Trintignant, written as a vehicle for him to express his full range as an actor. About the women, Robbe-Grillet states that it is as though the three of them loved one another through a man who is absent. The game of blind-man's-bluff is ordered for the women at the same time that it is a rejection of the male. There are literary allusions to Boris Goudounov, the usurper czar who reigned after having assassinated a child that should have been the real czar. This Boris was pursued, psychologically, by the ghost of the czar he had killed and who finally triumphs. Robbe-Grillet admits that he is fascinated with mad kings: Boris Goudounov, Macbeth, Pirandello's Henry IV, Eric XIV of Strindberg. "The mad king is a character who is very disturbing in a metaphysical way, because what he says is true because he is the king and what he says is false since he is mad." Robbe-Grillet recounts some of the allusions in the film to his previous novels and films. Of the influence of Pirandello, Robbe-Grillet notes that when Trintignant is awakened by the father and the caretaker, the background noises are the noises of a theater, a real theater and the real sounds of a Pirandello play at the Théâtre de France. Further, he notes that contact with a film is always an erotic contact. He notes that the film opened in Czechoslovakia the day that Soviet troops invaded. Thus, the East German uniforms in the film, an obvious lie, had become the truth in real life. He concludes by discussing his use of cartoon caricatures. After all, "a cartoon makes no pretense at any depth. It is very interesting from this point of view."

380 BLUMENBERG, RICHARD MITCHELL. "The Manipulation of Time and Space in the Novels of Alain Robbe-Grillet and in the Narrative Films of Alain Resnais, with Particular Reference to _Last Year at Marienbad_." Ph.D. dissertation, Ohio University, 197 pp.

The title is indicative of the long and involved sentence structure; nevertheless, this is an interesting study of Robbe-Grillet's novels, Resnais' films and the convergence of the two in _Last Year at Marienbad_. Blumenberg defines "subjective" fiction as that in which description replaces action. He contrasts description, which involves spatial relationships, with narration, which involves temporal relationships. It is Robbe-Grillet's narration through description and his use of probability over fact that render time spatially in _Marienbad_. He notes that the opening shots of the film prefigure subsequent action rather than serving as exposition. Thus, the "story" of _Marienbad_ is not told so much as it is described through image juxtapositions, involving Eisenstein-like conflicts between shot elements. Blumenberg notes that the _ciné-roman_ borrows techniques from both the novel and the cinema: from the novel come (1) point of view; (2) symbolic imagery; (3) narrative rhythm; and (4) description. From the cinema come (1) image juxtapositions (montage); (2) photographic representation; (3) perceptual imagery; (4) visual description through shot composition; and (5) the inescapability of the present tense. He notes that the name given to the male protagonist, X, suggests not only his role as object but also the figurative position as center from which all interrelationships emanate. The fixed poses in the film emphasize memory over existence. Blumenberg sees the "persuasion" conflict between X and A as being significant, in that X first tries to convince A that they met at Marienbad. She resists. When he switches from Marienbad to last year, from space to time, he succeeds in implanting doubt and then convincing her.

381 BURCH, NOEL. *Praxis du Cinéma*. Paris: Gallimard, 172 pp.
Includes all of the articles originally published in *Cahiers du Cinéma*, with multiple references to Robbe-Grillet's innovative structures in terms of image-sound dialectics. Burch admits that he had originally dismissed Robbe-Grillet, only later to reappraise him as a filmmaker on a par with Resnais and Godard.

382 CANBY, VINCENT. "Screen: *L'Immortelle*: Love Story is Directed by Robbe-Grillet." *New York Times* (November 1), p. 39.
Accuses Françoise Brion of the blank look of a *Vogue* cover and suggests that the concept of the "perpetual present" in the film is a redundancy.

383 GABRIEL Y GALAN, JOSÉ-ANTONIO. "Los Espejos de Alain Robbe-Grillet: el *nouveau roman* al cine." *Revista de Occidente*, No. 72 (March), pp. 361-67.
Discussion of the relationship between the new novel and Robbe-Grillet's films, with emphasis on his films as extensions of his novels.

384 GOLLUB, JUDITH. "*Trans-Europ-Express*." *Film Quarterly*, 22, No. 3 (Spring), 40-44.
Points out Robbe-Grillet's concern with *how* to tell a story as opposed to the story itself as the basis for a critique of Robbe-Grillet. She believes his rejection of ulterior meaning to the work of art caused him to use close-ups of objects that play no thematic part in the "story" of the film and cuts from which no meaning can be derived. She gives no examples of either. She presumes much, speaking both for the spectator and for Robbe-Grillet, in both cases without documentation. She attacks *Trans-Europ-Express*, because it is not subjective enough, misunderstanding Robbe-Grillet's unique way of treating the subjective without tampering with the denotative or objective levels of the image. She criticizes the film for the "obsessive quality of man's eroticism," for the images as being too sexist.

385 GUARINO, ANN. "*L'Immortelle* Tells Haunting Love Story." New York *Daily News* (November 1), p. 26.
Positive review of the film through a rather mindless plot summary.

386 HASKELL, MOLLY. "Film: *L'Immortelle*." *Village Voice* (November 6), p. 50.
Reviews of both *L'Immortelle* and *Trans-Europ-Express*. "Both are pleasantly second-rate films which are made bearable not by Robbe-Grillet's intellectual scaffolding but by his quaint fondness for such exotic erotica as bars,

grillwork, black-lace underwear, white slave-trading and whore-houses." She concludes that the images flatten rather than shape reality.

387 MURPHY, BRIAN. "Trans-Europ-Express." Films and Filming, 15, No. 9 (June), 41-42.

Premise that Trans-Europ-Express is a film about the making of a film, a "mock gangster spy story about mock dope." Murphy cites the various trickery devices involved in mixing fact and fiction, noting that the story writes itself to such a point that when the filmmakers leave the train at the end of the film they see a newspaper article about events described in their fiction. "It is not, strictly speaking, a work of art: it is an absorbing essay about art. We react intellectually, not emotionally; we are interested, not moved."

388 PERRY, TED. "The Seventh Art as Sixth Sense." Educational Theatre Journal, 21, No. 1 (March), 28-35.

Fascinating article on filmmaking and Last Year at Marienbad, on the ontological relationship between objects in front of the camera and the image subsequently seen on the screen. He notes that the cinema experience is unique, not available prior to, or apart from, the cinema. Based on Jerome S. Bruner's "The Course of Cognitive Growth" (American Psychologist, 19, No. 1, 1964), Perry argues for several types of representations of the environment, processed and coded in our nervous system: enactive, iconic and symbolic. "Film creates new realities. It is a way of letting go of the environment in order to grasp it in a new way." He uses Marienbad as an example. The world presented in that film cannot be transposed into normal experience. He argues that those who find the film boring are threatened by the new reality, new perceptions and the fresh imagery of the environment offered in the film.

389 RICHARDSON, ROBERT. "Film and Modern Fiction," in his Literature and Film. Bloomington and London: Indiana University Press, pp. 79-90.

The last two pages of this chapter deal directly with Robbe-Grillet. He notes that Robbe-Grillet has used film's ability to capture detail and external surfaces to construct a new theory of fiction. This new theory, thus, distrusts psychology and character. "Robbe-Grillet has decided that objects and appearances alone have validity." Richardson ultimately dismisses Robbe-Grillet the filmmaker, noting that he has used film as a "way of legitimizing randomness" and that art should duplicate the real.

*390 ROBBE-GRILLET, ALAIN. "Et voilà pourquoi le cinéma est un art." Les Cahiers Littéraires de l'O.R.T.F., 7, No. 9 (February 2-15), 16-17.

Unseen. Cited in French XX, 1970, #78579 (See: Source List). Published interview on television by Robbe-Grillet.

391 ROUD, RICHARD. "Memories of Resnais." Sight and Sound, 38, No. 3 (Summer), 125-29, 162-63.
Interview with Resnais on the various influences upon him, culminating with questions about working with Robbe-Grillet and Duras. Resnais notes that he was impressed by La Jalousie and Dans le labyrinthe of Robbe-Grillet as possible film projects. "It seems to me that the kind of sumptuous mise-en-scène Robbe-Grillet is after needs a lot of money to be realized properly, with every detail perfect. But the conditions in which he is obliged to work don't allow him this luxury. It's a shame; in his books, every comma, every full stop is in its place, but he can't afford to make his films as visually perfect, as soigné."

392 SCOTT, NATHAN. Negative Capability. Studies in the New Literature and the Religious Situation. New Haven and London: Yale University Press, 173 pp.
Discussion of Last Year at Marienbad, especially pages 16-23. "It is Marienbad that first comes to mind when I begin to think of what is characteristically new and radical in the cinema of our time; it gives the age away, in the sense of presenting in itself a kind of summary of our period-style." He gives a plot summary for the film, then compares Robbe-Grillet's film-novel with the poetry of Charles Olson, the philosophy of British Linguistic Analysis, with the painting of Franz Kline and Mark Rothko and the music of John Cage.

393 STURROCK, JOHN. "Alain Robbe-Grillet," in his The French New Novel. London, New York and Toronto: Oxford University Press, pp. 170-235.
Long discussion of the novels with passing references to Last Year at Marienbad and L'Immortelle, but treated as though they were novels. Sturrock sees Robbe-Grillet as suffering from a "difficult writer" tag, and so he makes films to get accepted by the masses. "The fact that he has, in recent years, become more and more of a filmmaker and less and less of a writer, is indicative, no doubt, of his determination to situate himself more readily as being on the side of ordinary men and not a darling of the intellectuals." Sturrock is limited to thematic criticism, unable to explicate structures in Robbe-Grillet's films.

*394 TYGAL, S. "Alain Robbe-Grillet: Pour un cinéma d'essai." Les Lettres Françaises, No. 1301 (September 24), p. 16.
Unseen. Cited in French XX, 1971, #85827 (See: Source List). Interview with Robbe-Grillet about experimenting in the cinema, including Noel Burch and André Labarthe in the interview.

395 VELASCO, HORACIO G. "Semana Francesca." Hispano Americano, 55, No. 1420 (July 21), 54.
Review of Trans-Europ-Express.

*396 VIGH, ARPÁD. "Egyŭj irodalmi müfaj: A filmregény." Alföld, 20, No. 9, pp. 53-60.
Unseen. Cited in Fraizer, p. 263 (See: 475).

397 WINSTEN, ARCHER. "Reviewing Stand: L'Immortelle at Bleecker Cinema." New York Post (November 1), p. 19.
Plot summary with a confession: "I haven't the foggiest notion what it was about."

1970

*398 AMIEL, MIREILLE. "L'Eden et après." Ciněma 70, No. 144, (n.p.).
Unseen. Cited in Gardies, p. 187 (See: 440).

399 _____. "Un 'Maitre' persuasif." Ciněma 70, No. 149 (September-October), pp. 100-103.
Recounts reassessment of L'Eden et après, which she had passed over in an earlier review. Discussion of Robbe-Grillet's speech at Marly-le-Roi, his attack on Michel Mardoré and other critics, his questioning of Resnais and other "great" filmmakers, his calling François Truffaut and Françoise Sagan both inheritors of the nineteenth-century novel. "I am not interested in the objects that I describe, but in the movement of my description.... In a film, I am not interested in the plot, but in the structure of the plot." Robbe-Grillet noted in his speech that the same narrative content is shown twelve different times in the film, according to different structures. He discussed serialism, washed clean of ideological or affective content. "The characters have nothing to do with realism, they are only objects that refuse a personal interpretation, they are the elements of a structure." He said he dreamed of a film-opera, structured on the rapports between the music, the spoken text and the image. He noted that he was after an imaginary public but wouldn't be "castrated" by working just for those who know "how to read": reading France-Soir and reading James Joyce shouldn't be that different in a true "popular culture."

400 ANON. "L'Eden et après." Etude, No. 1836 (May 15), pp. 18-19.
Interview with Robbe-Grillet on L'Eden et après, the conception of the film and its serial structure.

401 ANON. On Robbe-Grillet. Film Cultura (Brazil), No. 150 (April-May), pp. 42-44.

General discussion of Robbe-Grillet and Resnais and of Last Year at Marienbad.

402 ANON. "Robbe-Grillet et après." Le Figaro Littéraire, No. 1249 (April 27-May 3), pp. 34-35.
Brief discussion of L'Eden et après as Robbe-Grillet's first color film, first film with a female protagonist and other ways in which the film differs from his previous films.

*403 ANON. "Robbe-Grillet, l'homme aux mirages." L'Express, No. 982 (May 4-10), p. 46.
Unseen. Cited in French XX, 1971, #85843 (See: Source List). Review of L'Eden et après.

404 ARMES, ROY. "Alain Robbe-Grillet," in his French Film. New York: Dutton (Studio Vista), pp. 148-51.
Calls Robbe-Grillet "the most original talent to emerge in the French cinema since Godard." Armes notes that what interests Robbe-Grillet in the cinema are the qualities that make a film unlike a novel: its power to fragment experience, to play on two senses of the viewer simultaneously, to "weld" past and present into a single flow of dissolving time altogether, and to make the most banal event appear magical and the most outlandish fiction real. Everything in a Robbe-Grillet film has been filtered through somebody's mind. Robbe-Grillet's work in film is an attempt to depict experience from within. Armes notes the exotic locations of the films, which, although they are authentic, serve as little more than tourist snapshots. He notes the imagery that freezes and repeats itself and the erotic imagery surrounding the women in Robbe-Grillet's films.

405 _____. "Chapter Seven: Film and Literature," in his French Cinema Since 1946. Volume Two: The Personal Style, second enlarged edition. London: A. Zwemmer; South Brunswick, New Jersey: A. S. Barnes, pp. 166-73.
The original publication of Armes' book in 1966 did not contain any extended reference to Robbe-Grillet. Indicative of the continuing critical malaise surrounding his film work is this "artificial" chapter called "Film and Literature," created primarily to deal with Robbe-Grillet. Armes suggests that L'Immortelle is less complex intellectually than Last Year at Marienbad but more erotic. After an excellent synopsis of L'Immortelle, Armes explores the aspects of the imaginary and the subjective point of view in the film. In Robbe-Grillet's words, the Turkish capital in the film is a mixture of Pierre Loti, the Blue Guide and the Arabian Nights. L is not presented as a real woman, but rather as a dream-image of a woman, half-whore and

half-goddess. The extremely stiff posture of Doniol-Valcroze is less interesting than the operatic mode of Marienbad. Good analysis of name-games and humor as a distancing device in Trans-Europ-Express. Armes notes that Robbe-Grillet has emphasized two properties of the film image in his films: the present tense and the mixture of reality and lie that comes from using real people and settings to tell a fictional story. In his willingness to present life at its most trivial level, Robbe-Grillet approaches pop culture and the fascination with the loud exterior of urban life: posters, ads, window displays, etc. Since his characters have neither a past nor a future, they can only engender mirror images, distortions and variations of themselves. Armes sees this as accounting for the "frozen" quality of the imagery: for instance, the narrator's hand forever reaching out to touch L's neck in L'Immortelle. He suggests that the structure of Robbe-Grillet's films is musical, a theme with variations and an ending that returns to the original starting point. Good filmography and bibliography.

406 BARONCELLI, JEAN DE. "L'Eden et après, d'Alain Robbe-Grillet." Le Monde, No. 7863 (April 25), p. 11.
Review of L'Eden et après.

407 BROCHIER, JEAN-JACQUES. "Deux activités parfaitement détachées l'une de l'autre." La Magazine Littéraire, No. 211 (June), pp. 14-16.
Discussion of L'Eden et après and Projet pour une Revolution a New York as film and novel.

408 CAMINADE, PIERRE. "La Condamnation de la métaphore par Robbe-Grillet," in his Image et métaphore, un problème de poétique contemporaine. Paris: Bordas, pp. 86-89.
Mostly based on Robbe-Grillet's novels and critical statements, the discussion of metaphor here is pertinent to the film activity as well.

409 CAPDENAC, MICHEL. "Paradis, parodie." Les Lettres Françaises, No. 1332 (April 29-May 5), p. 16.
Study of L'Eden et après, focusing on the "Eden" cafe and the "Eden" of Djerba as elements of parody on post-1968 students and their concerns.

410 CHALON, JEAN. "L'Eden selon Robbe-Grillet." Le Figaro Littéraire, No. 1247 (April 13-19), pp. 8-9.
Review of L'Eden et après.

411 COHEN, RICHARD. "The Man Who Lies." Womens' Wear Daily (April 14), p. 12.

Notes that the film resembles Last Year at Marienbad, since there is no "objective" truth to the narration. Like other reviewers, Cohen praises the performance of Trintignant and expresses doubts about the worth of the demands placed on the viewer by Robbe-Grillet.

*412 CRICK, P. "Trans-Europ-Express." Cinema (London), No. 5 (February), p. 21.
Unseen. Cited in Schuster, p. 324 (See: Source List).

413 GAY, PIERRE. "Nouveau Roman et cinéma nouveau." Cinéma 70, No. 148 (July-August), pp. 65-77.
Begins with an example of Godard on the rapports between film and literature having become interchangeable. Notes Robbe-Grillet and Pasolini as writer-filmmakers. Denies the need to rely on specificity of each medium to give each its independence and integrity. Gay criticizes Jean Ricardou, who, when he talks film, thinks literature. Especially criticized is the 1966 issue on "Problèmes du récit" in Cahiers du Cinéma (No. 185), because they treated the cinema as literature and because their questions were so phrased that the answers they received were stupid, ambiguous or inconclusive. Gay pays tribute to Resnais as a filmmaker and criticizes those who call his films "literary" films. The proof of Resnais' greatness is that Robbe-Grillet as a filmmaker can't come close to the beauty of Last Year at Marienbad in his own films. Gay criticizes The Man Who Lies and Duras' Destroy She Said as films so structured in the mental or subjective realm that they don't exist anymore. The cinema is seen as the future of the novel.

414 GREENSPUN, ROGER. "The Man Who Lies." New York Times (April 14), p. 53.
"If movies were thoughts, or dreams, or ideas about making movies, then Alain Robbe-Grillet might be a good filmmaker." He notes that the character playing the role of Jean Robin in The Man Who Lies is made to look like Kafka and concludes that Robbe-Grillet's imagination is less "engaging" than other directors' ordinary views of everyday life.

415 GRISOLLA, MICHEL. "L'Eden et après." Positif, No. 118 (Summer), p. 65.
Suggestion that this Robbe-Grillet film proves Resnais' old point about "Why make something simple when you can make it complicated?" Grisolla calls L'Eden et après Duchamp's "Nude Descending a Staircase" in living painting. He notes the Mondrian-like quality of the Cafe Eden in the film and concludes that the audience is far removed from Sade, Robbe-Grillet's idol.

416 GUARINO, ANN. "French Film is a Puzzle." New York Daily News (April 14), p. 56.
Review of The Man Who Lies, with everything but the last sentence being plot summary. "He contrives to tell a story of sorts in spite of his editing tricks, but one becomes bored with the effort of sorting out his facts."

417 HAHN, OTTO. "Interview sur la théorie." VH 101, No. 2 (Summer), pp. 93-101.
Interview with Robbe-Grillet on his film theory and on L'Eden et après.

418 HEATH, STEPHEN. "Towards Reading Robbe-Grillet." Granta, 75, No. 3 (February), 15-16.
Primarily focused on literature, the article notes that the second Robbe-Grillet, the "subjective" Robbe-Grillet, begins with the introduction to the ciné-roman for Last Year at Marienbad.

*419 H. ERDÉLYI, ILDIKO. "Alain Robbe-Grillet. Utveszto cimü regényének értelmezése." Alföld, 21, No. 10, 79-81.
Unseen. Cited in Fraizer, p. 263 (See: 475).

420 HERRIDGE, FRANCES. "The Man Who Lies." New York Post (April 14), p. 59.
Calls the film a "portrait of a schizophrenic" and notes that the truth of the film is in the eyes of the beholder, since there is no "objective" truth.

*421 JACOB, GILLES. "Robbe-Grillet, un art au présent." Cinéma 70, No. 145 (September-October), (n.p.).
Unseen. Cited in Gardies, p. 187 (See: 440).

*422 LANGLOIS, GÉRARD. "Entretien. L'Eden et après ou les Mille et Une Nuits d'Alain Robbe-Grillet." Les Lettres Françaises, No. 1330 (April 15-21), pp. 15-16.
Unseen. Cited in French XX, 1971, #85837 (See: Source List). Interview with Robbe-Grillet on L'Eden et après.

*423 LEIRENS, JEAN. "Bunuel, Petri, Robbe-Grillet." Revue Générale: Perspectives Européennes des Sciences Humaines, No. 9, pp. 139-43.
Unseen. Cited in French XX, 1971, #87279 (See: Source List).

*424 MARTIN, MARCEL. "L'Eden et après." Cinéma Pratique, No. 99, (n.p.).
Unseen. Cited in Gardies, p. 187 (See: 440).

*425 METZ, CHRISTIAN. "Le Vraisemblable." Communications, No. 11, (n.p.).
Unseen. Cited in Gardies, p. 186 (See: 440).

*426 _____. "La Théorie." V.H. 101, No. 2, (n.p.)
Unseen. Cited in Gardies, p. 186 (See: 440). Includes an interview with Robbe-Grillet.

427 PURDY, STROTHER B. "Gertrude Stein at Marienbad." Publications of the Modern Language Association, 85, No. 5 (October), 1096-1105.
Stein's repetitions are not effective in words but would be effective in film. Quoting Stein: "I was doing what the cinema was doing. In a cinema picture no two pictures are exactly alike--each one is just that much different from the one before." Stein ignored the difference between the rapidity of the film image's projection and the slow pace of her repetitions. Robbe-Grillet repeats images and words in multiple series as Stein did with words alone. Both Stein and Robbe-Grillet insist on hero-narrators, on readers who participate in the creative process. Both are interested in detective fiction. Both attacked plot and character in the traditional novel. Both treat time the same way as the time of composition. Stein's three principles of composition: (1) continuous present, (2) beginning again and (3) using everything. Purdy compares the treatment of objects in both and concludes that Robbe-Grillet is saved by his "humanism," citing the fallacy of Stein in Tender Buttons, that of eliminating people and making objects the protagonists.

428 ROBBE-GRILLET, ALAIN. "Lettre à Cinéma 70." Cinéma 70, No. 149 (September-October), pp. 100-102.
Robbe-Grillet justifies his attack on contemporary society (what Cinéma 70 had praised Bunuel's Tristana for, while neglecting Robbe-Grillet's L'Eden et après in the same issue) as an attack on that society's discourse or language. Robbe-Grillet notes that such attacks can be done in a very facile way, the proof being that Bunuel's film, in the last analysis, offends nobody.

429 ROPARS-WUILLEUMIER, MARIE-CLAIRE. De la littérature au cinéma. Paris: Armand Colin, 240 pp.
The entire book is an insightful study of the relationships between film and literature, extremely applicable to a study of Robbe-Grillet. Specifically, Chapter Five ("Alain Resnais: de l'écriture à la lecture") is helpful in terms of the collaborative form of "adaptation," using the ciné-roman to complement the film (Last Year at Marienbad). Chapter Six ("Nouveau roman et cinéma: influences et convergences") begins with Robbe-Grillet and ends with Godard. Especially significant is the subsection entitled "Le Mythe du cinéma chez Alain Robbe-Grillet" (165-70). Ropars-Wuilleumier traces the development of an optical and descriptive vocabulary in Robbe-Grillet's fiction in the

late 1950's, leading up to his filmmaking. His refusal to assign meaning to objects could only lead to film, where objects can be presented as objects, with presence as opposed to meaning. She suggests that since 1956 film has been refining its specificity as a medium by exploring time, by developing subjective camera and sound counterpoints (voice-over narration, syncopated editing, etc.). She notes that as early as 1963 Robbe-Grillet was emphasizing the role of the sound-track in film, a role important in that it brought an end to previous comparisons between film and literature in his work, which had been made as though all his films were silent. She believes that Robbe-Grillet's concept of the cinema is a limited one. Progressively, his films become more and more complex in their "circular puzzle" format. His images become burdened with parodic, fantastic and mythic overtones, to signal the imaginary aspect of these images. Thus, ironically, Robbe-Grillet's films have returned full-circle on themselves to fiction. She compares Boris of The Man Who Lies with the narrator of Jean Cayrol's Les Corps étrangers, who re-begins his "stories" throughout the novel. She believes that Robbe-Grillet's films fail because of his lack of familiarity with what is truly cinematic "writing." The book contains some important quotes, documents, excerpts of shooting scripts and other exchanges at the back in the "Annex" section.

430 _____. L'Ecran de la mémoire. Paris: Seuil, 237 pp.
References to Robbe-Grillet throughout this extremely valuable study, especially in "L'Année dernière à Marienbad" (114-20), and in "Réflexions sur les possibilités actuelles de l'expression cinématographique" (223-40).

431 WISNIEWSKI, LEON. "Marly et après." Cinéma 70, No. 149 (September-October), pp. 104-108.
Parody on In the Labyrinth, the same language used for explaining the "privileged hallucination" of the spectator at Marly-le-Roi before the talk and film of Robbe-Grillet as in the novel. Instead of dealing with the content of Robbe-Grillet's talk, Wisniewski describes all the objects at Marly from the point of view of the "absent-I" narrator.

*432 ZIMMER, JACQUES. "L'Eden et après." Saison Cinématographique, (n.p.).
Unseen. Cited in Gardies, p. 187 (See: 440).

1971

433 ANON. "Incontro con Alain Robbe-Grillet." Rivista del Cinematografo, No. 2 (February), pp. 84-85.
Interview with Robbe-Grillet on L'Eden et après.

434 BELMANS, JACQUES. "Robbe-Grillet ou l'univers dérisoire de la dérision." Synthèses, Nos. 295-296 (January-February), pp. 90-94.

One of the few really articulate negative critiques of Robbe-Grillet. Mentions Curzio Malaparte, André Malraux, Marcel Pagnol, Jean Giono, Pier Paolo Pasolini, Jean Cocteau, Sacha Guitry and Chris Marker as other writer-filmmakers. All these changed their style to fit the new medium. Belmans attacks Robbe-Grillet for doing the same things in film that he did in his novels. Belmans attacks the in-jokes of the films, the puzzle-film format, the sexual obsessions of the later films. He accuses Robbe-Grillet of a total lack of sincerity in the films, whose only merit is the sound-track. He wishes Michel Fano, the talented musician and pioneer of all the innovative sound-tracks in Robbe-Grillet's films, would put his talent to better use for a less "sterile" filmmaker.

435 CAEN, MICHEL. "L'Eden et après." Zoom, No. 3, (n.p.).

Calls L'Eden et après the best of Robbe-Grillet's films. "It may be the only authentically erotic French film ever made, in that it speaks directly to our nervous system."

*436 CHASSEGUET-SMIRGEL, JANINE. "A propos de L'Année dernière à Marienbad," in Pour une psychanalyse de l'art et de la créativité. Paris: Payot, (n.p.).

Unseen. Cited in French XX, 1972, #88256 (See: Source List).

437 CLEMENTS, ROBERT J. "European Literary Scene." Saturday Review (March 13), p. 28.

Ostensibly a review of Project for a Revolution in New York, Clements' article extends to the ciné-roman as well. His contention is that Project is even more cinematic than the book version of Last Year at Marienbad. He cites examples of flashbacks, flashforwards, dissolves, zooms, blur focus, etc.

438 FRENKEL, LISE. "Cinéma et psychanalyse." Cinéma 71, No. 154 (March), pp. 73-93.

Discussion of symbolism and psychoanalytical readings of Robbe-Grillet and Resnais (Last Year at Marienbad), Godard, Polanski, Antonioni and Bunuel.

439 ____. "Cinéma et psychanalyse." Cinéma 71, No. 155 (April), pp. 58-75.

Preparing a book (Ph.D. dissertation) on Robbe-Grillet, Frenkel discusses symbolism, focusing on the "real" versus the "imaginary" in Robbe-Grillet, especially in L'Eden et après.

440 GARDIES, ANDRÉ. Alain Robbe-Grillet. Paris: Seghers (Cinéastes d'aujourd'hui), 188 pp.

The absolutely indispensable book on Robbe-Grillet in terms of his film activity. Gardies notes the various structural considerations in Robbe-Grillet's film activity: verisimilitude, formalism, the organization of film by its structures, the present-tense imagery, the distancing devices, the humor and comic mode, eroticism and the dialectic between continuity and discontinuity. With the exception of Last Year at Marienbad and up to/including L'Eden et après, there are individual analyses of all of Robbe-Grillet's films, focusing on the fixed images in L'Immortelle, the sado-erotic scenes in Trans-Europ-Express, the complex sound-track in L'Homme qui ment, the serial arrangement (emphasizing the colors and the painting) in L'Eden et après. A special section is devoted to ludic games of puns, repetitions, situations and farces in the films. The second half of the work includes documents and extracts of interviews with Robbe-Grillet and a critical panorama on the films as well as some interviews with individual actors and technicians on the films. Excellent bibliography and filmography.

441 GOLDMANN, ANNIE. "L'Année dernière à Marienbad et L'Immortelle," in her Cinéma et société moderne: Le Cinéma de 1958 a 1968: Godard-Antonioni-Resnais-Robbe-Grillet. Paris: Anthropos, pp. 227-37.

Consideration of Last Year at Marienbad as Robbe-Grillet's film in terms of studying his later films. Goldmann argues that, far from switching from literature to film as an extension of the école du regard, Robbe-Grillet turned to film for the possibilities of playing with the real and the imaginary. Marienbad appears as the apparent triumph of the imaginary; L'Immortelle is the victory of reality, and Trans-Europ-Express is an attempt to reconcile the two. She breaks Marienbad into two "universes": the world of the garden, associated with X, and the world of the chateau, associated with A. The chateau's decor is rich but false, and the only thing left to do in this chateau is to play games, games that M always wins. X brings a new game: as he describes "last year" (the past), A assumes the postures of his narration in the present. The broken glass is the turning point, the point at which she begins to accept his versions of the past and play his "game" at Marienbad. Goldmann sees L'Immortelle as having three parts: (1) Leila denies the reality of everything; (2) the search for her in the real world, a world which denies her existence; (3) the death of Leila and the attempt of the narrator to reconcile the other two parts: her statements about the world with the real world's statements about her. Both her death and that of the narrator are real for Goldmann, signifying the victory of the real over the imaginary. With Trans-Europ-Express there is an attempt to create an imaginary world which draws upon the real world instead of being in conflict with it. Goldmann notes that Robbe-Grillet's imaginary is not the evasive imaginary of the Romantics nor the irrational imaginary of the Surrealists, but an autonomous sector with its own reality, its own laws, its own parallel existence alongside reality.

442 LECUYER, MAURICE. "Robbe-Grillet's La Jalousie and a Parallel in the Graphic Arts." Hartford Studies in Literature, No. 3, pp. 19-38.

A comparison of the dynamics of the Robbe-Grillet novel with those of the contemporary cartoon.

443 MERCIER, VIVIAN. "Alain Robbe-Grillet: Description and Narration," in his The New Novel from Queneau to Pinget. New York: Farrar, Straus and Giroux, pp. 165-214.

Mercier believes that Robbe-Grillet uses cinematographic techniques in his novels and discusses Last Year at Marienbad as the culmination of such techniques. After discussing Marienbad, L'Immortelle and Trans-Europ-Express, Mercier studies Robbe-Grillet's La Maison de rendez-vous, noting that the novel was "contaminated" by Robbe-Grillet's film experience.

*444 METZ, CHRISTIAN. "L'Analyse de l'image." Communications, No. 15, (n.p.).

Unseen. Cited in Gardies, p. 186 (See: 440).

445 MORRISSETTE, BRUCE. Les Romans de Robbe-Grillet. Paris: Minuit, 309 pp.

This is the revised version of Morrissette's 1963 book of the same title. Nothing is changed from that first edition. Added chapters include a study of La Maison de rendez-vous and Project for a Revolution in New York, emphasizing intertextuality between Robbe-Grillet's novels and films in both, and an explanation of the Nim game in Last Year at Marienbad.

446 _____. "Robbe-Grillet's Project for a Revolution in New York." The American Society Legion of Honor Magazine, No. 42, pp. 73-88.

Notes the growing role of themes from present-day society in Robbe-Grillet's films and novels, and that this is Robbe-Grillet's first novel in five years. There is more and more co-existence between the comic and the serious in Robbe-Grillet's work. L'Eden et après "presents for the first time what may properly be termed a thematic use of socio-political reality." Morrissette notes that the students in the film are portrayed more in terms of their "sardonic psycho-dramas" than in terms of any true revolutionary action.

447 RICARDOU, JEAN. "Esquisse d'une théorie des générateurs," in Positions et oppositions sur le roman contemporain (Actes et Colloques, No. 8). Paris: Klincksieck, pp. 143-50.
Excellent introduction to the use of generative theory, which becomes so important in Robbe-Grillet's color films. Ricardou presents a long analysis of anagram transformations and color generators in Claude Simon's La Bataille de Pharsale and in his own La Prise de Constantinople, with other examples from Robbe-Grillet's Le Voyeur.

448 ROBBE-GRILLET, ALAIN. The Immortal One. Translated by A. M. Sheridan Smith. London: Calder and Boyars, 173 pp., 20 photos.
The English translation of Robbe-Grillet's ciné-roman for L'Immortelle.

1972

449 ARECCO, S. "La Finzione di romanzo nel ultimo Robbe-Grillet." Filmcritica, 23, No. 224 (April-May), 183-86.
Study of intertextuality between Robbe-Grillet's novel Project for a Revolution in New York and his film L'Eden et après, both done in 1970.

450 CHATEAU, DOMINIQUE. "Propositions pour une théorie du film. I." Ça, 1, No. 1, 78-95.
Long and difficult reading, but ultimately rewarding as an alternative to Metz's film theory. Based on Chomsky's linguistics, Chateau's article is a critique of Metz, specifically of his grande syntagmatique, proposing instead the meticulous categorization of film narrative advanced by Noel Burch. Robbe-Grillet's films are cited as examples of films whose internal logic has little relationship with established sequential codes (Metz). "The conception of Alain Robbe-Grillet opposes that of Christian Metz as serial thought opposes structuralist thought." The implication here is that Metz's theory is based on binary oppositions, dialectics involving oppositions of two, while Robbe-Grillet's serialism admits of all the possibilities in between.

451 CISMARU, ALFRED. "Ten Years Ago at Marienbad." South Atlantic Bulletin, 37, No. 1 (January), 74.
Abstract of Cismaru's paper delivered to the South Atlantic conference in late 1971. Analysis of Robbe-Grillet's shift from the novel to film from a retrospect of ten years, focusing on Last Year at Marienbad and its abolition of

normal fictional boundaries and suggesting "total psychological" freedom.

452 CLOUZOT, CLAIRE. Le Cinéma français depuis la Nouvelle Vague. Paris: Fernand Nathan, 204 pp.

The best "history" of French film for the period covering the years 1959-1972. References to Robbe-Grillet especially in the second chapter: "Le groupe 'Rive Gauche'. Le cinéma des auteurs." (46-81). Robbe-Grillet is considered in a class with other "Left-Bank" and intellectual filmmakers like Resnais, Agnes Varda, Chris Marker, Marguerite Duras, Henri Colpi, Jean Cayrol and Armand Gatti. Analysis of his films extends from Last Year at Marienbad to L'Eden et après.

453 GARDIES, ANDRÉ. "Nouveau Roman et cinéma: une expérience décisive," in Nouveau Roman: hier, aujourd'hui (Colloque de Cerisy: I. Problèmes Généraux). Paris: Editions 10/18, pp. 185-99.

Gardies claims that it was not Robbe-Grillet's fictional technique (meticulous description) that led to his filmmaking, but rather a questioning of narrative structures that he could explore in both media simultaneously. His argument rests on the specificity of both media, while allowing for intertextuality between them. Gardies insists on the differences between the ciné-roman and the novel. He describes the shifts in point of view in La Maison de rendez-vous and contrasts those shifts with the function of time as the time of projection in L'Immortelle. The absence of gimmicks in the film (lack of dissolves, lap dissolves, blur focus, irises, etc.) is a proclamation of the omnipotence of the present tense of the image. There is a circular movement of the people and objects in the film, since time remains indeterminate, other than this present tense of the time of projection. The proof of the specificity of the two media is in the unsuccessful adaptations of Marguerite Duras' Moderato Cantabile and Robbe-Grillet's Les Gommes, in which the original novels, what made them the striking novels that they are, are lost in the resultant films. Gardies suggests an affinity, as opposed to adaptation, between La Jalousie and L'Immortelle. In the novel the tension derives from the presence of the narrating voice and the absence of the narrator, while this tension in the film is resolved with the stiff and neutral presence of the on-screen Doniol-Valcroze. Robbe-Grillet is quoted as saying: "The struggles with language are interior. The cinema is this continual struggle with an exterior matter that resists." After L'Immortelle, Robbe-Grillet writes less and less in the preparation of a film. This rejection of scripted film-writing signals a new interdependence between film and literature. Gardies sees three distinctions between the new novel and the new cinema: (1) the struggle against the effect of the "real"; (2) the presence of a sound-track, even in the original conception of a film; and (3) the collective nature of film. It is easy for literature to proclaim itself as literature and not as reality; it is more difficult for the cinema to say a table is a film-table rather than a "real" table. Likewise, most analyses comparing literature and film speak of film as if it were still silent, forgetting the possibilities and importance of the sound-track. In literature dialogue and description cannot be simultaneous; in film, they can. With Robbe-Grillet the image and the sound-track interact in a dialectical relationship. In The Man Who Lies, while the opening credits roll, the plausibility of those visuals of Trintignant running through a forest and being chased by real soldiers is undercut by the sound-track, which becomes progressively louder and louder. The collaboration between Robbe-Grillet and Michel Fano points out the collective nature of film, as opposed to the solitary work of the writer. With less writing prior to filming, more freedom is possible in the actual filming. One consequence of this change is a more mobile camera in Robbe-Grillet's later films. It is in the editing stage that Robbe-Grillet rediscovers the solitude of the writer; thus, the editing operates in a dialectical relationship with the filming, just as the sound-track and image-track form a dialectic. Gardies notes the intertextuality between Project for a Revolution in New York and L'Eden et après. In the discussion following the presentation of his article, Gardies notes that the simultaneous quality of contradiction between the sound-track and the image-track (the voice of Boris in The Man Who Lies says that the cafe was empty, while the image shows the cafe full of people) allows a comic effect prevalent in all of Robbe-Grillet's films. Robbe-Grillet adds in this discussion that he no longer writes ciné-romans, because, as Bruce Morrissette pointed out, they have a literary quality of their own. Thus, their function as a memory-aid to the film, according to Robbe-Grillet, was obscured.

454 HEATH, STEPHEN. "Alain Robbe-Grillet," in his The Nouveau Roman: A Study in the Practice of Writing. London: Elek; Philadelphia: Temple University Press, pp. 67-152.

An exhaustive study of Robbe-Grillet's novels, with copious footnotes and several references to Robbe-Grillet's film activity and the ciné-romans.

455 JOST, FRANÇOIS. "Variations sur quelque thèmes." Ça, 1, No. 1, pp. 63-77.

The emergence of Jost as one of the most perceptive young film critics in France today begins here in this excellent structuralist study of The Man Who Lies. Jost evokes the critical malaise surrounding a film like The Man Who Lies, suggesting that when critics can't make empirical sense of the film, they opt for binary oppositions: dream versus lie, fiction versus reality, the possible versus the impossible, the lived versus the oneiric. Jost suggests that the "true" meaning of the film lies in the infinite gamut of structures between those binary opposites. In the first reel of the film, the spectator is given all the locales, all the sounds, which will then "generate" and resound throughout the film. There is, then, an accumulation of repetitions, restatements and contradictions. The film involves an inversion of the traditional flashback by which a director tells a past event in the present. Here what is present is related by Trintignant to be, as though, past. When Laura is shown blindfolded, touching the portrait of Jean Robin in the game of blind-man's-bluff, Boris is heard to begin speaking of Jean Robin. The narrator becomes the receiver of the visual message, taking the place of the spectator. At the same time, Boris reinitiates as sender of the narrative message, even addressing the spectator as "you" in the manner of Michel Butor in La Modification. Jost distinguishes between themes that are elementary preparation (or micro-diegetic) and those that are relational preparation (or macro-diegetic). The latter set up relationships, clusters, image-juxtapositions. They "give" meaning. The former establish discourse. Jost suggests that the fragments of verbal discourse that we hear from Boris or from the men at the Inn contain generators, keys to future fabricated stories: the word prison, for example, will generate several "versions" from Boris. From such elementary preparatory themes, certain meta-themes like betrayal and oppression emerge. In the various accounts, all characters are shown to be variously hero and traitor. Jost explains how Boris loses the narrative thread, enmeshed as he sometimes is as the receiver of the narrative message, how the image-track temporarily subsumes his voice-over discourse, then how, with the death of Laura's father, Boris reasserts himself as the sender of the narrative message.

456 KAWIN, BRUCE. "From Combray to Marienbad," in his Telling It Again and Again: Repetition in Literature and Film. Ithaca and London: Cornell University Press, pp. 84-90.

Relates Robbe-Grillet to Proust, contrasting them. Robbe-Grillet's characters are passive, as un-self-conscious and as definitively self-centered as the lens of a camera. Plot summary of Last Year at Marienbad with the conclusion: "Whether what X made her remember was true or false is irrelevant in a world of surfaces, where any image is equally valid, and less important than the fact that this inability to remember is essential to A's totally present-centered existence." Kawin sees the perpetual present as making all recourse to memory impossible.

457 LEENHARDT, JACQUES. "Nouveau Roman et société," in Nouveau Roman: hier, aujourd'hui (Colloques de Cerisy: I. Problèmes Généraux). Paris: Editions 10/18, pp. 155-70.

Analysis of La Jalousie and Last Year at Marienbad from a sociological standpoint and extending the research of Lucien Goldmann, with many quotes from Robbe-Grillet's Pour un nouveau roman to justify this sociological approach. The sickness of the people at Marienbad is related to the morbid character of the 1950's, specifically the fall of the Fourth Republic in France in 1957-58. Robbe-Grillet is seen in light of the decomposition of a decadent bourgeois society. Leenhardt analyzes Robbe-Grillet's descriptions: (1) superficial description, which detaches objects from human beings in order to render the objects in their full presence at the same time that such a rendering destroys any idea of "depth" in the description; and (2) recurrent description, by which the reader is tricked, having felt that he/she understood a scene, only to find the scene negated or doubled or otherwise changed. This kind of description gets maximum use in The Man Who Lies. In the discussion that followed the presentation, Robbe-Grillet defends Leenhardt while criticizing Lucien Goldmann, because his approach, supposedly sociological, was really thematic and reductionist.

458 MEADES, JONATHAN. "Alain Robbe-Grillet: The Immortal One." Books and Bookmen, 17, No. 4 (January), 54, 56.

An insightful look at L'Immortelle-book as a film-novel. Meades sees Robbe-Grillet as one who protects his practice with his theory, one who tickles the academics and the chasers of the esoteric, one who is a good novelist but a bad filmmaker. Meades walks a tightrope between L'Immortelle-book and L'Immortelle-film, between both the book and film and Last Year at Marienbad. Film scripts are similar to an artist's working drawings or a novelist's notes. They are like arrows pointing to the finished work. A scenario, since it is unlikely to be filmed more than once, differs from the script for a play or the libretto for an opera, which may be performed and reinterpreted for centuries. Meades contends that L'Immortelle is a static film, yet "anyone who reads the script without having seen the film will find themselves well lost." Meades concludes that Robbe-Grillet's short-comings are as a director, not as a screenwriter.

459 MORRISSETTE, BRUCE. "Robbe-Grillet No. 1, 2,...X," in Nouveau Roman: hier, aujourd'hui (Colloque de Cerisy: II. Pratique). Paris: Editions 10/18, pp. 119-33.

Morrissette retraces the critical impasse that had existed in the early 1960's between critics who contended Robbe-Grillet was a chosiste (objective pole) and those who saw him as a symbolist or a practitioner of objective correlatives (subjective pole). There is a possibility of an infinite number of interpretations of Robbe-Grillet, once one lets go of the notion of binary oppositions (either-or situations) and admits the possibility of triadic structures (three leads to infinity). He suggests that Robbe-Grillet is like a Calder with his narrative mobiles in L'Eden et après, and he revises his own "Monsieur X sur le double circuit," replacing "double" with an infinite number. In the discussion that followed, Jean Ricardou noted that Morrissette's "para-literary" methods were dangerously metaphorical. Robbe-Grillet defended Morrissette, noting that criticism of his work functioned for him as a sign, not of what to follow, but of what to abandon.

460 _____. "Topology and the French Nouveau Roman." Boundary 2, 1, No. 1 (Fall), 45-58.

Separation of the critics into two classes, those from the "human sciences" (like Roland Barthes) and those "philological sociologists" (like Lucien Goldmann). Morrissette notes that other critics, notably Jean Ricardou, have extended their analyses, not outside the text, but back into the text, studying puns, anagrams, syllabic transfers and semantic interchanges in writers like Claude Simon and Robbe-Grillet. Morrissette has used analogies from mathematics and geometry to study Robbe-Grillet's novels and films: circles, spirals, figures of eight, Y and T forms, labyrinth boxes and corridors. He sees such structures at work in films like Last Year at Marienbad and Trans-Europ-Express. The newer novels seem to invite analogies from a domain beyond or different from simple two- or three-dimensional geometry. This domain may be called fictional topology. "Topology represents the primary intellectual operation capable of revealing the modalities of surfaces, volumes, boundaries, contiguities, holes, and above all the notions of inside and outside, with the attendant ideas of insertion, penetration, containment, emergence, and the like." He then studies the structure of the "hole" in Robbe-Grillet's works.

461 MURRAY, EDWARD. "Alain Robbe-Grillet, the New Novel, and the New Cinema," in his The Cinematic Imagination: Writers and the Motion Pictures. New York: Frederick Ungar, pp. 280-91.

Review of Robbe-Grillet's critical pronouncements from 1963, without any acknowledgment of more recent theory advanced by Robbe-Grillet. Murray is stuck on the treatment of character and seems incapable of handling structure. He sees Robbe-Grillet as a kind of trickster. He concludes that Robbe-Grillet is better suited to fiction than to film.

462 ROBBE-GRILLET, ALAIN. "Sur le choix des générateurs," in Nouveau Roman: hier, aujourd'hui (Colloque de Cerisy: II. Pratique). Paris: Editions 10/18, pp. 157-62.
Robbe-Grillet explains that he quickly renounced word-generators, since he preferred instead to work with image-generators, citing the generative operations on the color red in his novels and films to engender, for example, spilled blood, the light from a fire, and the flag of revolution in Project for a Revolution in New York.

463 SANCHEZ, ALFONSO. "Nuevas estructuras del tiempo," in his Iniciacion al cine moderno. Madrid: Magisterio Español, S. A., pp. 65-82.
Analysis of time in the films of Resnais, Robbe-Grillet, Agnes Varda and Jacques Demy.

*464 SCHULTZ, VICTORIA. "Game and Revolution. Interview. Robbe-Grillet." Changes (July 14), p. 20.
Unseen. Cited in Sturdza (See: 534).

465 SKALLER, DONALD. "Aspects of Cinematic Consciousness." Film Comment, 8, No. 3 (September-October), 41-51.
Quote by Kasimir Malevich is applied to what is called the "structural" film, defined by P. Adams Sitney as having four characteristics: (1) a fixed camera position, (2) the flicker effect, (3) loop printing (the immediate repetition of shots, exactly and without variation) and (4) re-photography off of a screen. All these tendencies are anti-illusionist. Skaller then compares Hitchcock's Vertigo with Resnais/Robbe-Grillet's Last Year at Marienbad with Michael Snow's Wavelength.

466 ST. CLAIR, IRIS. "French Professor Disconnects Cinema and Novel." New York University Alumni News (May), p. 3.
Partially an interview with Robbe-Grillet, in which he speaks of the differences between French students and American students. He defines the "new cinema" as that "whereby the film shown on the screen is always presented as fiction and not reality, as in the traditional film." He also notes his shift from scripting prior to filming toward writing as the shooting of a film progresses.

467 STURDZA, PALTIN. "Structures of the Imaginary in Robbe-Grillet's L'Immortelle." Ph.D. dissertation, Florida State University, 227 pp.
Pluralistic approach to L'Immortelle. Sturdza presents the Freudian concept of dream-work to approach the oneiric structure of L'Immortelle. Images of repression and censorship are noted. The central fantasy is oral. Sturdza notes the use of letters for names in a kind of mathematical series: L-M-N. In Part Two, he attempts an archetype

approach. Using Greimas' structuralist semantics, Sturdza presents a model, a ternary structure of movement, immobility and fixed, with its correlated contents of life, death and immortality. The correspondent archetype is then Rebirth. In Part Three, Sturdza uses Greimas' actantial model for analysis and definition of characters, noting that L'Immortelle has 97 narrative syntagms and 18 paradigmatic sequences. He points out that, although the ciné-roman for L'Immortelle does end tragically, "reintegration" or "amelioration" does take place, because N recovers his "archiactantial" status.

468 TREBBI, FERNANDO. "Robbe-Grillet o della trasparenza cinematografico." Nuova Corrente, Nos. 57-58, pp. 97-120.
On L'Immortelle. Study of structures of "transparency" (distancing devices, the comic element, the recourse to myth, the erotic elements) in Robbe-Grillet's film by the leading Italian critic on Robbe-Grillet's films.

469 YOUNG, VERNON. "Nostalgia of the Infinite: Notes on Chirico, Antonioni, Resnais," in his On Film: Unpopular Essays on a Popular Art. Chicago: Quadrangle Books, pp. 184-95.
Quoting de Chirico: "Architecture completes nature. It marks an advance of human intellect in the field of metaphysical discoveries." The quote is Young's entry to analyzing Last Year at Marienbad as an "architectural" film. "There is no absence of clues in either Alain Robbe-Grillet's scenario or in Resnais' film for an interpretation of the 'events' therein: one could well complain that there are too many for suggestiveness to be anything but hopelessly diffuse: they cancel serious curiosity." Young attacks Resnais and Robbe-Grillet as being derivative of Dali-Bunuel, of Jean Epstein and other French filmmakers of the 1920's.

*470 ZURBUCH, WERNER. "From Federico Fellini to Alexander Kluge: Film and Television Manuscripts as a New Form of Literature." Universitas, 14, No. 3, 257-62.
Unseen. Cited in French XX, 1975, #A11965 (See: Source List). On Robbe-Grillet, Godard, Renoir and Truffaut.

1973

471 APPEL, A., JR. "The Eyehole of Knowledge: Voyeuristic Games in Film and Literature." Film Comment, 9, No. 3 (May-June), 20-26.
Based heavily on Nabokov and Kubrick's film adaptation of Lolita. Examples drawn from Robbe-Grillet, Hitchcock's Rear Window and Frenzy, Chabrol's Landru, Rohmer's Claire's Knee and John Hawkes' The Lime Twig as filled with voyeurism and games of peeping.

*472 ARMES, ROY. "Cinema: Robbe-Grillet in Africa." London Magazine, No. 13 (October-November), pp. 107-13.
Unseen. Cited in Film/Literature Index, 1973, p. 118 (See: Source List). Review/article on Robbe-Grillet's L'Eden et après.

473 BETTETINI, GIANFRANCO. The Language and Technique of the Film. Translated by David Osmond-Smith. The Hague and Paris: Mouton, 202 pp.
Only passing references to Robbe-Grillet, but interesting in terms of theory and with Robbe-Grillet as symptomatic of that theory. "Thus the modern novels tends to express only the subjectivity of its author, as revealed in what Robbe-Grillet would call 'the movement of the description': no more cultural, ideological, or behavioral models, no more descriptions, but instead sensations and the communication of internal experiences."

474 BURCH, NOEL. Theory of Film Practice. Translated by Helen R. Lane. Introduction by Annette Michelson. New York and Washington: Praeger, 172 pp.
The English translation of Praxis du Cinéma, containing most of Burch's Cahiers du Cinéma articles from 1967. References throughout the book to Robbe-Grillet's films, but in particular the section entitled "Fictional Subjects" (pp. 144-48) deals with Robbe-Grillet in detail. He sees Robbe-Grillet as one of the most important stages in the functionalization of the subject with a new definition of the interaction between subject and form. The theme-and-variation principle that Robbe-Grillet introduced in literature has infinitely more possibilities in the cinema. There is a concern for organic unity in Robbe-Grillet's films. Each shot in Last Year at Marienbad refers to one other moment and usually to several others through repetition, variation and contradiction. L'Immortelle now appears to be a complete success in terms of the succession of events, scenes and even individual shots as "containers" or units of meaning. Both Marienbad and L'Immortelle are "innocent" films: nothing remains hidden. "They are not films that call for interpretation: they demand simply to be seen."

475 FRAIZER, DALE W. Alain Robbe-Grillet: An Annotated Bibliography of Critical Studies, 1953-1972. Metuchen, New Jersey: Scarecrow Press, 277 pp.
An excellent annotated bibliography of Robbe-Grillet's literary work, with some overlap into the ciné-roman and his film activity.

476 GARDIES, ANDRÉ. "Ecriture, image; texte." Etudes Littéraires, No. 6, pp. 445-55.

Discussion of the polymorphous activity of Robbe-Grillet, Michel Butor, Marguerite Duras, Claude Ollier and Robert Pinget questioning both literary and cinematographic language. Literary description fragments the object described. What's left are detours. A description of a door in Project for a Revolution in New York gives way to a woman coming through the door, at which time the door disappears. Description cannot consume the object described, since such an object never ends up duplicating its real referent in the world. Everything else belongs to the film image, which captures the object within a given moment, but once the object is seen, it no longer exists. The film text is comprised of an indefinite number of objects, while the literary text involves a finite number. And, because they are finite, they become related, one to the next. This relation is called "rhyme and echo" by Jean Ricardou. The collective nature of film work increases both the risk of the enterprise and the unforeseen, the possibilities for an on-going inventiveness. This incertitude about the process and the outcome is what has interested Robbe-Grillet the most in films like The Man Who Lies, L'Eden et après and N. a pris les dés. In a film, the spectator hears the tone of voice more than the dialogue itself, which is why voice-over narration often appears ridiculous or too literary. In a novel, any time dialogue appears, the narration is suspended, since dialogue and description struggle for the linearity of the narration. In a film both can be on-going and simultaneous. This latter situation, to be used effectively, often involves counterpoint or conflict between the sound-track and the images. Robbe-Grillet produces, not novels and films in a traditional sense, but texts, which suggests the possibility of inventing new "laws" (structures) without any reference to reality. To the preserved moment, to cinéma-vérité, to on-the-spot reportage, Robbe-Grillet would substitute instead a mythical structure involving some "popular culture" aspect of mass media (detective fiction, spy novel, exoticism, the B film). Using such materials as a point of departure, Robbe-Grillet infuses them with new discourse, thus voiding their traditional and codified (accepted) meanings. The first step in such a process is disarticulation. Such restructuring of the narrative message is often serial and associative. Thus, the theme of "prison" in L'Eden et après is "represented" in a "game of correspondence" by a dungeon, a blindfold and the labyrinth of the factory. Such multiple reverberations of the "prison" theme produce what could be called a "horizontal" reading, in opposition to the vertical reading of the more expository opening sequences (series) of the film. Five of the ten series are long and occupy much narrative time; the other five are short and like "mise-en-abime" statements. They introduce or reflect, like a mirror, a doubling of the vertical level of reading, and "doubling" is interestingly one of the twelve themes. "To causal determinism of society, Robbe-Grillet would oppose a singular point of view (thus, multiple), an aleatoric order, the principle of contradiction and the gratuity of the game. His texts force spectators to be spectators, really spectators again, readers to be readers, and both to be simultaneously critics and co-authors." The whole article is heavily based on Jean Ricardou's analyses of Robbe-Grillet. Gardies quotes Ricardou for the novels and applies Ricardou for the films.

477 GOW, GORDON. "L'Eden et après." Films and Filming, 19, No. 9 (June), 55-56.

Review of L'Eden et après. Violette finds the Stranger dead in the canal but encounters his double in Tunisia, to which land she is transported by the "unusual" method of just happening to see herself there in a film. "Quite often it resembles a comic strip which has been devoted to a certain photogenic splendour." Gow compares Violette of the film with Justine of Sade. He is less "beguiled" by this film than by L'Immortelle and finds the film less witty than Trans-Europ-Express, "but it is certainly a diverting factor in his avowed purpose of helping us to offset the extremes of profundity regarding art which have been pressed upon us from the 19th century."

*478 IOSKEVICH, I. "Za sotsiologiiata na kinozhanrovete." Kinoizkustvo, No. 28 (December), pp. 49-57.

Unseen. Cited in Film/Literature Index, 1973, p. 326 (See: Source List). A sociological reading of Robbe-Grillet's films.

479 SPIEGEL, ALAN HARVEY. "Fiction and the Camera Eye: A Study of Visual Form in the Modern Novel." Ph.D. dissertation, University of Virginia, 336 pp.

Primarily concerned with the modern novel, with James Joyce as the prototype, Spiegel does treat Robbe-Grillet in his second category ("the anatomy of motion") along with Joyce, Faulkner and Nabokov.

480 _____. "Flaubert to Joyce: Evolution of a Cinematographic Form." Novel: A Forum on Fiction, 6, No. 3 (Spring), 229-43.

The "modern" is defined in terms of the reification of narrative form. Robbe-Grillet is studied, as well as Conrad, Joyce, Faulkner, Nabokov and Flaubert.

481 SWEET, FREDERICK JOSEPH. "Narrative in the Films of Alain Resnais and Contemporary Fiction." Ph.D. dissertation, University of Michigan, 198 pp.

Many references to Last Year at Marienbad. Primarily a study of Resnais, the treatment also points out that some of the stylistic and structural constants in Resnais' films come as a result of his literary collaborations. Sweet notes the translations of literary devices into cinematic terms and compares the treatment of space, time and motion in contemporary fiction and Resnais' films.

482 TREBBI, FERNANDO. La Trasparenza Cinematografica. Saggio su Alain Robbe-Grillet. Bologna: Patron, 180 pp.

Other than the André Gardies book, this is the only book-length study of Robbe-Grillet's films. Chapter One ("La Trasparenza cinematografica") deals with L'Immortelle. Trebbi discusses the use of waking dreams in the film, the role of the imaginary, the myth of Orpheus and the use of repetition, recurrence and circularity. Chapter Two ("Il Sense con-fuso") deals with Trans-Europ-Express. Trebbi discusses metalinguistic concerns in the film: the use of quotes and quotation cinema as a stylistic device. He also analyzes accumulation and displacement, enumeration and interior duplications, the relationships between cinema and musical theater, the sado-erotic motifs and the echo of Artaud, Brecht, Bunuel and Roussel. Chapter Three ("Una visible cancellatura di se") deals with The Man Who Lies. Trebbi notes the structural use of the "incipit" section, while studying the concept of lying, the theme of usurpation, the use of autonominalism, the authorial "topos," the "partner" theme, ritual death and denigration, and the structural problems of the speaker and narration. Chapter Four ("Il Gioco dell 'io") deals with L'Eden et après. Trebbi here analyzes the process of construction, the idea of mental space, "pop" operations and a critique of pop culture, generative themes and theory based on Jean Ricardou, ludic space, the "Stranger" as being Duchemin, Dutchman and Marcel Duchamp, doubling eroticism, and the influence of Klee, Kandinsky, Delacroix and the Surrealists. Excellent filmography but no bibliography.

1974

483 ANDREU, ANNE. "Alain Robbe-Grillet, la provocation constante." La Magazine Littéraire, No. 87 (April), pp. 50-52.

Review of Glissements progressifs du plaisir.

484 ANON. "Glissements progressifs du plaisir, film d'Alain Robbe-Grillet." L'Avant-scène du Cinéma, No. 148 (June), pp. 67-68.

Synopsis of the film with quotes by Robbe-Grillet and a bio-filmography of Robbe-Grillet.

485 ANON. "On the Slipway." The Times Literary Supplement, No. 3764 (April 26), p. 433.
Review of Glissements progressifs du plaisir.

*486 ANON. Interview with Robbe-Grillet. Cinématographe, No. 7 (April-May), pp. 25-27.
Unseen. Cited in BFI Lib. Ref. (See: Source List). Interview with Robbe-Grillet on the making of Glissements progressifs du plaisir.

487 ARMES, ROY. "Film and the Modern Novel," in his Film and Reality. Baltimore: Penguin, pp. 209-14.
Faulkner noted as a sad example of the screenwriter/novelist in Hollywood. Armes notes that more freedom is possible in Europe and cites Susan Sontag and Marguerite Duras as examples. Their work, unfortunately, is very formal: "They are introspective exercises, not spectacles designed to communicate with an audience." Praises both Robbe-Grillet and Pasolini as writers-turned-filmmakers who have advanced film technique while not distancing themselves from their audiences. Robbe-Grillet plays with sound as well as images in his films. Armes calls Trans-Europ-Express the most "approachable" of Robbe-Grillet's films. Even so, the film is a constant questioning of reality. "The crossword puzzle side of Robbe-Grillet's approach is very apparent here, but it is balanced by his sense of humor and his fascination for eroticism and sexual perversion." Armes concludes that with Robbe-Grillet and Pasolini film and literature are becoming "more closely related as equal and modern forms of artistic expression."

*488 BARONCELLI, JEAN DE. "Cinéma--Glissements progressifs du plaisir, d'Alain Robbe-Grillet." Le Monde, No. 1329 (April 11-17), p. 13.
Unseen. Cited in French XX, 1975, #A10880 (See: Source List). Review of Glissements progressifs du plaisir.

*489 BASSAN, R. "Glissements progressifs du plaisir." Téléciné, No. 187 (April), p. 24.
Unseen. Cited in Film/Literature Index, 1974, p. 53 (See: Source List).

*490 BELMANS, JACQUES. "Glissements progressifs du plaisir." Amis du Film et de la Télévision, Nos. 216-217 (May-June), p. 19.
Unseen. Cited in Film/Literature Index, 1974, p. 83 (See: Source List).

491 BONNEFOY, CLAUDE. "La Dissolution du sens." Les Nouvelles Littéraires, 52, No. 2421 (February 18-24), p. 4.

Review of Glissements progressifs du plaisir as an enigmatic film in which meaning is never fixed or unchanging.

492 BORY, JEAN-LOUIS. "Au-dessous de la ceinture." Le Nouvel Observateur, No. 485 (February 25-March 3), pp. 60-61.
On Robbe-Grillet's Glissements progressifs du plaisir and Niki de Saint-Phalle.

493 BRUNN, JULIEN. "Cinéma." Raison Présente, No. 30 (April-June), pp. 111-12.
Brief reviews of Robbe-Grillet's Glissements progressifs du plaisir, Mocky's L'Ombre d'une chance, Malle's Lacombe Lucien and Blier's Les Valseuses.

494 BYRON, STUART. "Boston Journal." Film Comment, 10, No. 3 (May-June), 2, 4-5, 62-63.
Review of Glissements progressifs du plaisir, contrasting Marco Ferreri's interplay with the actors in La Grande Bouffe with Robbe-Grillet's "refusal" to do so in Glissements. Byron contrasts the "sheer mastery" of dislocation in Project for a Revolution in New York with the "unpersuasive and mechanical rhetoric" of Glissements. "The paradox is how extra-cinematic Robbe-Grillet can be when he describes something, and how literary it becomes when he shows it on a screen: what seems real on a page remains theoretical in front of a camera."

*495 CAMBER, MELINDA. "Robbe-Grillet: the 'Ironic' Treatment of eroticism." The Times, No. 59230 (October 29), p. 12.
Unseen. Cited in French XX, 1975, #A10883 (See: Source List). Interview with Robbe-Grillet about eroticism, the parody of eroticism and eroticism as a distancing device in his films.

496 CHALAIS, FRANÇOIS. "La Torture, nous voici...." Le Figaro Littéraire, No. 1454 (March 30), p. 11.
Critique of the various "punishments" and sado-erotic motifs in Glissements progressifs du plaisir.

497 CHATEAU, DOMINIQUE and FRANÇOIS JOST. "Robbe-Grillet: Le Plaisir du glissement." Ça, 3, No. 1 (January), 10-19.
Inversion of the title of Robbe-Grillet's film allows an excellent structural analysis of the game structures in Glissements progressifs du plaisir as well as the way in which elements combine and recombine to "slide" into new relationships and new meanings through the use of sound-image counterpoints.

498 CHAUVET, LOUIS. "Glissements progressifs du plaisir." Le Figaro (March 9), (n.p.).

Calls the film difficult but praises the organizational structure and notes some of the calculated shocks.

499 COBAST, C. "Glissements progressifs du plaisir." Revue du Cinéma, No. 284 (May), p. 123.
Calls the film "insupportable" in its pseudo-sophistication. Notes the awkward juxtaposition of sado-erotic motifs with a kind of quotation cinema. Cobast sees an egg as an egg and objects to seeing them tinted red and related to painting.

*500 DELFOSSE, PASCALE. "Glissements progressifs du plaisir: Robbe-Grillet et son 'nouveau langage.'" La Revue Nouvelle, 30, Nos. 7-8 (July-August), 85-94.
Unseen. Cited in French XX, 1975, #A10896 (See: Source List). Review of the film and Robbe-Grillet's evolution as a filmmaker in terms of language, erotic motifs and generative images.

501 DONIOL-VALCROZE, JACQUES. "Alice au pays de Robbe-Grillet." L'Express, No. 1183 (March 11-17), p. 40.
Review of Glissements progressifs du plaisir, its ludic structures and mythical allusions in relation to the erotic motifs.

502 FANO, MICHEL. "L'Attitude musicale dans Glissements progressifs du plaisir." Ça, No. 3, (n.p.).
Important analysis of the musical themes as generators in the film by Robbe-Grillet's collaborator in the film.

*503 FORRESTER, VIVIANE. "Robbe-Grillet. Un livre, un film." La Quinzaine Littéraire, No. 182 (March 1-15), pp. 67-68.
Unseen. Cited in French XX, 1975, #A10892 (See: Source List). Review of Glissements progressifs du plaisir.

*504 FOUGÈRES, R. "Le Jeu avec le feu." Cinéma Revue, No. 54 (August 1), pp. 16-19.
Unseen. Cited in Film/Literature Index, 1974, p. 62 (See: Source List). Discussion of Robbe-Grillet's Le Jeu avec le feu.

505 GARSAULT, A. "Glissements progressifs du plaisir." Positif, 244, No. 160 (June), 69.
Critical review of Glissements, but, based on the catalogue of hostility from the rest of the Positif staff at the end of the review, the least critical is Garsault. While suggesting that the film is banal in terms of content and sexist in its portrayal of women, Garsault points out Robbe-Grillet's technical accomplishments. The entire review is written through a series of questions which are

answered negatively. Garsault's last answer is that Robbe-Grillet is the man who lies.

506 GOW, GORDON. "Travelling Fast: the Cinema of Alain Robbe-Grillet." Films and Filming, 20, No. 4 (January), 54-56.
Discussion of the tug between sincerity and happiness in Last Year at Marienbad. Gow notes post-Marienbad techniques in Peckinpah's The Ballad of Cable Hogue and Schlesinger's Midnight Cowboy. Plot summary of L'Immortelle. The film is seen, not as a slice of life nor even as a unified subjective vision, but as a "fragmented subjective vision" of life. He sees an analogy with modern dance: look closely at the movement and let meaning take care of itself. Gow sees Trans-Europ-Express in this way and also as a comedy. He notes that this film is more accessible to audiences, proving that Robbe-Grillet is not "travelling too fast" and arriving too soon. Plot summaries of The Man Who Lies and L'Eden et après, noting that the last film is less successful than the previous three as a projection of mental time.

*507 HAAKMAN, A. "Realisme is een reglement." Skoop, No. 10 (April), pp. 13-19.
Unseen. Cited in Film/Literature Index, 1974, p. 106 (See: Source List). Interview with Robbe-Grillet, with a bio-filmography.

508 HARCOURT, PETER. "Alain Resnais: Toward the Certainty of Doubt: Part II." Film Comment, 10, No. 1 (January-February), 23-29.
Coming to grips with one's past is a theme common to all of Resnais' films, from Last Year at Marienbad to Je t'aime je t'aime. In Marienbad the acting is so stylized and the human issues so theoretical that one is invited to respond to the film as pure form. Harcourt notes three controlling images in the film: (1) the hotel where nothing grows and nothing changes, (2) the statue "frozen" in time and ambiguous in meaning and (3) the game with cards, matches or photographs. "In Last Year at Marienbad there is a neurotic dread of actual experience, of any physical contact, of the here and now." Harcourt questions to what extent the coldness of the film is due to Robbe-Grillet.

509 JOST, FRANÇOIS. "A propos de Glissements de Robbe-Grillet: Ponctuations et parataxe." Critique, No. 323 (April), pp. 326-34.
Excellent article contrasting the theory of Christian Metz and the film of Robbe-Grillet. In the traditional film, "punctuation" is self-effacing, not meant to be seen. With Robbe-Grillet, unrelated objects with apparently little significance in themselves (a kneeler, shoes, bottles, etc.)

interrupt scenes when they've just begun to hold our interest. Jost notes that Joyce broke with traditional syntax and graphics in Ulysses. Punctuation breaks syntax instead of serving it. Punctuation in Robbe-Grillet takes on the importance that shots have in other films that are more traditional narrative films. Jost sees an enumeration of images rather than a linking of images in terms of accepted rules of time, space and unity. Robbe-Grillet's punctuation doesn't fit into Metz's categories. The cutting in Glissements progressifs du plaisir does not simply re-orient the direction of narration, as Metz would have it, but rather it causes a brutal and abrupt breakdown in narration, outside of any diegetic order. Robbe-Grillet's cuttings across objects are in a metaphoric sense zero-signified's which function similarly, in terms of punctuation, to the white spaces in Mallarmé or to musical silences. Thus, there is an interplay established between narrative segments and enumerative segments, which allows punctuation to be raised to the level of the signified. Metz rightly affirms that in a traditional entertainment film punctuation can only be seen as an optical effect, often redundant. Robbe-Grillet delays his punctuation's full articulation, so that the function of each object-cut is only indirectly expressed at the time of appearance; contrary to traditional film punctuation, Robbe-Grillet's does not facilitate the linkage of two preexistent anecdotal moments; rather, it elicits an entirely new sequence. Thus, the punctuation frames propel the narrative. Alice wounds herself in the foot. The judge licks her foot to get the piece of glass out. The red spots on the piece of paper floating in the water vectorize the scene: the outcome will be fatal for the judge. The slide from punctuation to anecdotal material proper is, then, always accomplished in terms of analogy. Jost notes that the "cut" is essentially parataxic, since two "unities" are spliced together without any explicit indication of the relationship that joins them. In Glissements parataxic relationships are different, because of all the "non-story" inserts.

510 KAISER, GRANT E. "L'Amour et l'esthétique: L'Année dernière à Marienbad." South Atlantic Bulletin, 39, No. 4 (January), 113-20.

To reproach the film as being obscure is to reproach human passions for not always being clear. Form and content merge with Robbe-Grillet, contrary to Flaubert's Madame Bovary, in which Emma's obscure love affairs are shown to us with an esthetic clarity. "The doubts, darkness and fantasy-side of real love relationships are mirrored in the film by contradictory dialogue, by variable decors... and by the imaginary quality of a sound track which does not correspond to the film's images." Citing Marshall

MacLuhan and Ortega y Gasset, Kaiser proposes a psychological analysis of the film, equating the eye of the lover with the camera lens. Characteristic of both love and the camera in the film is the stripping down to essentials. Both love and the film are seen as processes of creation. Kaiser insists that the empty and geometric gardens come to life with the presence of A, thus bending the film analysis to his preconceived psychological basis for love.

511 LANGLOIS, GÉRARD. "*Glissements progressifs du plaisir*." *Ecran 74*, 206, No. 23 (March), 69-70.
Refusal of the symbolism in the film, focusing on the eggs as mere objects rather than generators. Langlois structures his review around the word *glisser* or "slide" and whether or not the images really do slide from one to another. As an exercise in semiology, the film is completely successful.

512 LATIL-LE DANTEC, MIREILLE. "Notes sur la fiction et l'imaginaire chez Resnais et Robbe-Grillet." *Etudes Cinématographiques* (Alain Resnais et Alain Robbe-Grillet: Evolution d'une écriture), Nos. 100-103, pp. 117-45.
Summary of the work of Resnais and Robbe-Grillet since *Last Year at Marienbad*, with the thesis that the two were at a crossroads with that film and have taken radically divergent paths since then. She notes that the critical confusion surrounding *Last Year at Marienbad* was in part due to a view of Resnais as a "literary" filmmaker and Robbe-Grillet as a "cinematic" novelist. Since *Marienbad*, Resnais has continued concerns that date back to *Hiroshima mon amour*, whereas, since *Marienbad*, Robbe-Grillet has made films that continued his concerns in the novel. She notes their film work after *Marienbad* as proof: Resnais in *Muriel* returns to the claustrophobia of the concrete and the verisimilitude of the dream, whereas Robbe-Grillet in *L'Immortelle* distances himself from verisimilitude even further than in *Marienbad*. Robbe-Grillet's films become increasingly self-conscious "fictions," while Resnais' films give real body to the "imaginary": thus, the two poles of the article's title. Latil-Le Dantec notes that Robbe-Grillet is questioning the very act of narration in his later films, and, when point of view becomes ambiguous, it is lost. Her "ambiguity" toward Robbe-Grillet's later films derives in part from her forced symbolism, seeing, for example, the symbol of the "father" in Duchemin in *L'Eden et après*. Whereas Godard and Agnes Varda are questioning the cinema itself for "serious" moral and political reasons, Latil-Le Dantec sees Resnais and Robbe-Grillet as being outside of any of these categories, but still at opposite poles from each other. She notes that Robbe-Grillet's films as games

of construction are a kind of tyranny on the spectator, who is now dispensable, accessory to the internal creation.

*513 LEFEVRE, RAYMOND. "Glissements progressifs du plaisir." Revue du Cinéma, Nos. 288-289 (October), pp. 143-44.

Unseen. Cited in Film/Literature Index, 1974, p. 83 (See: Source List). Review of the film with credits.

514 ______. "L'Eden et après." Revue du Cinéma, No. 286 (August), pp. 80-84.

Excellent analysis of the film. Because the film breaks completely with traditional narrative structure and is achronological, Lefevre chooses to follow Robbe-Grillet's example, which means the format of his article includes (1) quotes from Robbe-Grillet, (2) "plot" summary and (3) analysis of the film based on the scenario and the quotes. He breaks the film down into thematic segments: (1) the reality of the Cafe Eden, at which the bored students play games until the arrival of the "Stranger"; (2) the factory and the meeting between reality and the imaginary. Violette finds the Stranger dead. Her friends come. The body disappears. (3) Tunisia: a walk in the imaginary. Violette dreams about a post-card of Djerba which she found on the body of the Stranger. She goes to see a film on Tunisia and is transported there. Her friends are there, suddenly becoming her persecutors. (4) Return to the Cafe Eden and reality-imaginary mixed. Lefevre notes that Robbe-Grillet thus questions traditional cinematic forms by refusing "realism": the world exists only inside each one of us. Any chronology is a personal prejudice. The spectator can no longer look for plot or intrigue. There are only structures. Robbe-Grillet is quoted as looking for structures, but structures which question themselves, which destroy themselves in their formulation and construction. The "pretext" for a story in the film is a stolen painting. Behind the pretext is a questioning of film's way of telling a story, especially in the discontinuous opening credits and titles, which present an "inventory" of all the "themes" which come into play in this film-game. The characters play games in the film, but the spectator never learns the rules. Robbe-Grillet juggles appearances, surfaces, false doubles. He plays with time and space, with reality and the imaginary, with eroticism and allusions to art, with colors (the blue and white of the painting and of the Tunisian landscape, the red of blood and of the Cafe Eden). Robbe-Grillet is quoted as saying that he would like to replace the notions of "profundity" and "depth" in the work of art with the notion of the game. Thus, Robbe-Grillet has built his film on a serial arrangement of twelve themes in series of ten, all themes coming into play in each series. The series are: (1) credits; (2) the Cafe Eden before the Stranger comes; (3) the fear potion and the hallucinations; (4) the cafe after the Stranger's arrival; (5) the factory; (6) the projected film on Tunisia; (7) the Tunisian village; (8) the house of Dutchman; (9) the prison; (10) the various mirages of Violette lost in the desert. The twelve themes are: (1) the painting, which is also a post-card and a Tunisian village; (2) blood: the game at the Cafe Eden, the suicide of Sonia, the wounds; (3) the double: double poisoning of Boris, double drowning of Duchemin, double dance of Violette and the meeting with Violette's double; (4) the dance; (5) light; (6) the labyrinth; (7) the prison; (8) images and symbols of sperm; (9) eroticism; (10) death, simulated or imagined; (11) water; and (12) doors. Lefevre concludes by praising André Gardies book on Robbe-Grillet and noting the influence of Mondrian and Marcel Duchamp in L'Eden et après.

515 _____. "Trans-Europ-Express." Revue du Cinéma, No. 286 (August), pp. 118-21.

Telegraphic style for a structural analysis of Trans-Europ-Express, with a discussion of the film's setting as a basis for "generating" the narrative structure, for presenting a critique of the traditional film plot in detective thrillers, and for fusing the various mental (real/imaginary/simulated) planes. Lefevre focuses on the deconstruction of the role of "actor" in the film. Trintignant plays three roles: (1) Elias, (2) Trintignant the actor and (3) Trintignant the actor who caricatures the fictional character.

*516 LENNE, G. "Glissements progressifs du plaisir." Ecran, No. 23 (March), pp. 69-70.

Unseen. Cited in Film/Literature Index, 1974, p. 48 (See: Source List).

517 MAAKAROUN, ELIE. "Expériences et stylistiques du manque chez Resnais et Robbe-Grillet." Etudes Cinématographiques (Alain Resnais et Alain Robbe-Grillet: Evolution d'une écriture), Nos. 100-103, pp. 105-16.

Analysis of the "lack" or "void" or "hole" in the films of both Resnais and Robbe-Grillet from the perspective of sociology, politics and style. Forced but interesting comparisons between their films: the irony and humor of Claude Ridder in Resnais' Je t'aime je t'aime (1968) with the irony and humor of Boris Varissa in Robbe-Grillet's The Man Who Lies (1968). Maakaroun compares the real and imaginary Algeria of Resnais' Muriel with the real and imaginary Turkey of Robbe-Grillet's L'Immortelle. The Man Who Lies is seen as a critique of religious faith, because it doesn't fill the void. Resnais' Je t'aime je t'aime is a critique of science, because it doesn't fill the void. Robbe-

Grillet's L'Immortelle and Resnais' La Guerre est finie explore the sexual incompleteness or void. All of their films are haunted with the idea of death, the ultimate hole, void and incompletion. There are no longer any heroes, any subjects: the lack becomes the lack of existence, and ultimately both Resnais and Robbe-Grillet proclaim their lack of anything to say. In different ways, both filmmakers are undertaking the ideological deconstruction of contemporary society and its forms.

518 MAGNY, JOEL. "De Resnais à Robbe-Grillet: instauration d'une écriture." Etudes Cinématographiques (Alain Resnais et Alain Robbe-Grillet: Evolution d'une écriture), Nos. 100-103, pp. 146-58.

The focus of this article is to note that Resnais, despite the political themes in many of his films, is a traditional content-oriented director, while Robbe-Grillet, attacked for his formalism, is a radically innovative and political film director, in that his films emphasize their own production, their own status as artifacts, their own interior involvement as a material production in a materialist society. Magny suggests that much of the negative criticism of Robbe-Grillet as a filmmaker stems from the spectator having lost the "privileged" position of being the center of the work, a position engendered by nineteenth-century industrial and capitalist society. The work of art then becomes opaque, a material and formal product, a signifying system to be deciphered. Magny notes that in a bourgeois society the "value" of a work of art is in its material worth or in the "meaning" that it gives. Robbe-Grillet has substituted structure (product) for meaning. Meaning is no longer given; it is produced, and film then is seen in its historical perspective as a production machine for meaning. For Robbe-Grillet, the image, whatever meaning it gives or whatever real-life referents it reveals, is still just an image and meant to be manipulated as such. To see films like Last Year at Marienbad in terms of binary oppositions like real-imaginary is to ignore the concrete organization of images and sounds in the film. To impose such oppositions on a Robbe-Grillet film is to emphasize the anecdotal nature of such a film, which is clearly counter to Robbe-Grillet's intentions and which renders the film absurd. Magny notes that Robbe-Grillet's use of flattening devices (post-cards, billboards, etc.) and his appropriation of "pop" culture elements is a critique of the dominant ideology of the society at the same time that it is an admission of the art work existing within that society.

519 MAILLET, DOMINIQUE. "Glissements progressifs du plaisir." Cinématographe, No. 8 (April), pp. 25-27.

Describes the film as a mixture of detective fiction, science fiction, eroticism, and, thus, a refusal of all three in their traditional format.

520 MOELLER, HANS-BERNHARD. "Literature in the Vicinity of the Film: on German and nouveau roman authors." Symposium, 28, No. 4 (Winter), 315-35.

Focus on the financial benefits for young writers to sell "properties" to film or to write film scripts, with Brecht cited as the first example. Mentions the Literarisches Colloquium series entitled "Veranderungen im Film," which presented Robbe-Grillet, Jean Cayrol, Gunter Herburger and other author-filmmakers. Moeller notes the publication of film scripts by Peter Handke, Thomas Bernhard, Alexander Kluge, Norman Mailer, Truman Capote and Robbe-Grillet, suggesting that such publications "insure" against the possible failure of the film project. Moeller studies cinematic devices in La Jalousie and traces the "hedonism" of the later Robbe-Grillet since La Maison de rendez-vous.

*521 MONTFORT, J. "Glissements progressifs du plaisir." Cinéma Revue, No. 54 (March 7), p. 11.

Unseen. Cited in Film/Literature Index, 1974, p. 48 (See: Source List).

522 MOSCOWITZ, GENE. "Glissements progressifs du plaisir." Variety, No. 274 (March 27), p. 14.

Finds the technique acceptable but objects to the "highbrow" treatment of the theme and the "tame porno under the guise of art."

523 PASSEK, JEAN-LOUP. "Glissements progressifs du plaisir." Cinéma 74, No. 185 (March), pp. 126-27.

Comparison between Robbe-Grillet and Killy (the King of Ski), Elvis Presley (the God of Rock) and Castel (the Emperor of Nights of Paris). Robbe-Grillet is the head of the "modern style circus": "He dreams up his theories. Great. Makes films. Very good. Shows them. Unfortunately."

524 PETRIE, GRAHAM. "Theater Film Life." Film Comment, 10, No. 3 (May-June), 38-43.

Notes that in Last Year at Marienbad Resnais and Robbe-Grillet "demonstrated conclusively that images of fact, dream, hallucination, memory, desire, fear and foreboding all possessed the same degree of physical validity on the screen; and that deprived of the normal clues to separate one from the other, audiences could be persuaded to accept them all as being equally 'real.'" Before Resnais and Robbe-Grillet the major alternative was the theater as an "intermediary" between real life and the reflected illusion of real life on film. Petrie sets up a dialectic between theater and life, between theater and film and between film and life. He sees Lubitsch's To Be or Not to Be (1942), Renoir's The Golden Coach (1952) and Bergman's The Magician (1958) as the forerunners of Last Year at Marienbad in terms of their theatrical devices.

525 PIATIER, JACQUELINE. "Alain Robbe-Grillet: Appel à l'intelligence du lecteur." Monde (des Livres), No. 9083 (March 29), pp. 15-16.
Review of Glissements progressifs du plaisir, emphasizing Robbe-Grillet's invitation to the intelligence of the spectator in order to perceive structures and, thus, derive meaning.

526 QUAREGNA, P. "Robbe-Grillet e le allegorie dell' impotenza." Cinema Nuovo, No. 23 (November-December), pp. 409-10.
Loose analysis of the image of women in Glissements progressifs du plaisir, specifically that of the "prisoner" protagonist and her power to render men impotent. A thematic and awkwardly Freudian treatment, in this Letter to the Editor.

527 ROBBE-GRILLET, ALAIN. Glissements progressifs du plaisir. Paris: Minuit, 220 pp., 56 photos.
The ciné-roman for the film. Robbe-Grillet notes that nothing can replace the images and sounds of the film, not even the detailed descriptions of the ciné-roman. Yet these descriptions allow the reader to spend time on individual shots or sequences and to follow with a critical eye the generative evolution of a film. He indicates marginal notes in italics as details and precisions added after filming and explains the three parts of this film-novel as (1) the synopsis, (2) the dialogue continuity and (3) the montage record. He signals that the synopsis provides "meaning," but that the synopsis alone least provides the reader with the structural organization of the film. He also notes that the montage record seems void of such "meanings" as a structural record which refuses to be seen as such. For Levi-Strauss "structure" was synonymous with "meaning," whereas for him, "structure" is synonymous with "non-sense" or non-meaning.

*528 _____. "Le Droit au jeu et à la volupté." Point, No. 75 (February 25), p. 76.
Unseen. Cited in French XX, 1975, #A10907 (See: Source List).

*529 _____. "Livre-film: La cover-girl du diable." Nouvel Observateur, No. 484 (February 18-24), pp. 54-55.
Unseen. Cited in French XX, 1975, #A10908 (See: Source List).

530 ROCHER, DANIEL. "Le Symbolisme du noir et blanc dans L'Année dernière à Marienbad." Etudes Cinématographiques (Alain Resnais et Alain Robbe-Grillet: Evolution d'une écriture), Nos. 100-103, pp. 5-86.

Over-written "literary" criticism of Last Year at Marienbad, based on binary oppositions: "white" duration versus "black" chance; action in the reality of memory versus inaction in the prison of chance. Divided into three sections, only the third section escapes these easy oppositions and provides some useful analysis: specifically, on the spoken narration, the use of sounds with or without their corresponding visual counterparts, and the structures of memory and "absence" in the musical sound-track.

531 ROSENBAUM, JONATHAN. "Paris." Film Comment, 10 (May-June), p. 2.

Brief mention of Glissements progressifs du plaisir.

*532 SICLIER, JACQUES. "Deux cinéastes et l'érotique: Les Glissements progressifs d'Alain Robbe-Grillet." Monde (des Arts et des Spectacles), No. 9040 (February 7), p. 17.

Unseen. Cited in French XX, 1975, #A10909 (See: Source List). Treatment of eroticism in the film.

533 STOLTZFUS, BEN. "D'un langage à l'autre: les deux Robbe-Grillet." Etudes Cinématographiques (Alain Resnais et Alain Robbe-Grillet: Evolution d'une écriture), Nos. 100-103, pp. 87-104.

The novels and films of Robbe-Grillet are both the vision of a closed world and that of an open world where liberty invents itself. Characters are both submitted to a rigorous determinism and left free to play with reality. In both instances, there is the ultimate goal of creating a mental time, with its passions, obsessions, strangeness, holes and obscure regions. Progression in the analysis between film and novel, from La Jalousie and Last Year at Marienbad to Le Voyeur and L'Immortelle, noting similar processes at work in both media, without much concern about the distinct properties of the medium in question. Stoltzfus notes that Robbe-Grillet may have suppressed the kind of symbolic metaphors that a Proust used, but his "neutral" images, nevertheless, carry symbolic weight. He also notes the dialectic between creation and erasure at work in La Maison de rendez-vous and Trans-Europ-Express. About the latter film, Stoltzfus suggests that it may be Trintignant's dream to occupy the time, while a young woman (the real Marie-France Pisier) awaits him at the train station. From the protagonists enclosed in labyrinths in the earlier films and novels, Robbe-Grillet has evolved toward protagonists who are entirely free to create their own reality. Such protagonists are no longer passive dreamers like the professor in L'Immortelle; instead, like Boris of The Man Who Lies, they are aggressive in their constant fabrications of reality. Stoltzfus quotes Robbe-Grillet: "The most beautiful contemporary works leave us empty, abashed. Not only do they lay claim only to the reality of the reading or the viewing, but also they seem to be always contradicting themselves, questioning themselves as they are being constructed." Stoltzfus concludes that Robbe-Grillet's concerns in the novels and the films are the same.

534 STURDZA, PALTIN. "The Structures of Actants in Robbe-Grillet's L'Immortelle." Language Quarterly, 12, Nos. 3-4 (Spring-Summer), 26-28.

Somewhat derivative of his dissertation, this is a structural analysis of L'Immortelle. Sturdza relates Robbe-Grillet with the linguist Tesnière, who replaces the notions of subject and predicate with those of "actant" and "process"; thus, character is an actant and the narration is a process. Sturdza uses the Greimas model to interpret Le Voyeur. According to Greimas, the initial sequence of the narrative structure of a récit has its counterpart in the final sequence where the alienation of the hero is replaced by his reintegration. Thus, shot #354 (next to last one) in L'Immortelle is the same as shot #2. The "reintegration phase" explains the "resurrection" of L at the end of the film. There is also a negative transformation of the quest into "wait," as Sturdza calls it.

535 TERMINE, L. "Spostamenti progressivi del piacere." Cinema Nuovo, No. 23 (July-August), pp. 288-89.

Termine accuses Robbe-Grillet in Glissements progressifs du plaisir of nominalism and of structuralism with the "rigidity" of a manifesto.

536 VAN WERT, WILLIAM and WALTER MIGNOLO. "Julia Kristeva/Cinematographic Semiotic Practice." Sub-Stance, No. 9, pp. 97-114.

Semiology, in both senses of the term given by Metz. The first section deals with theory, that proposed by Kristeva governing relational models for anaphora. The second section involves pratice, an application of Kristeva in the principle of cross-reference, as a means of "reading" the films of Resnais, Robbe-Grillet and other members of what is loosely called the "literary" New Wave.

537 VAN WERT, WILLIAM. "Structures of Mobility and Immobility in the Cinema of Alain Robbe-Grillet." Sub-Stance, No. 9, pp. 79-96.

Excellent article on the use of freeze-frames, cutting within frames and the use of mobile camera in Robbe-Grillet's films, but limited to his black-and-white films, from L'Immortelle to The Man Who Lies. Van Wert notes that the techniques used by Robbe-Grillet are not new to the cinema: the use of freeze-frames is analyzed in Citizen Kane and Robbe-Grillet's treatment of objects, his use of mobile camera to create doubling effects within the frame is seen in the films and theory of Maya Deren. What is important is that Robbe-Grillet bridges the gap between Deren's experimental cinema and Welles' Hollywood narrative film, extending film's boundaries in terms of subjective camera and its relation to both point of view and time. With Citizen Kane the freeze-frame is the device by which the film skirts all of the different levels of reality without calling too much attention to itself (camera as functional instrument). In Robbe-Grillet's films the freeze-frame accomplishes just the reverse: characters are deliberately and artificially caught in mid-action, frozen in geometric or architectural poses, immobilized in the "mind's eye" of the camera-protagonist. Thus, N in L'Immortelle is the projection of N, the unseen camera-narrator, which allows for the doubling of N, shots in which N is seen in several stages of a mobile pan or in which N is seen by N, both clearly visible in the frame at the same time. Robbe-Grillet's structures of immobility question the very nature of cinema as moving picture; that apparent contradiction is what allows Robbe-Grillet to explore time and point of view in such radically new ways. Motion by definition implies sequential and spatial relationships. It is in terms of motion that film has been saddled with the "responsibility" of "capturing" reality. Robbe-Grillet asserts that to see (for the camera-protagonist) is to immobilize, to fixate, to desire a cessation of movement. That fixation reinforces the voyeurism of the unseen camera-narrator, as do the relational looks between characters (they seldom look at each other directly and instead assume theatrical poses of looking "off") and between characters and the camera (when characters within the film are about to face the camera, there is usually a cut, as indicated in the scenario for L'Immortelle), since the camera-narrator as voyeur cannot bear to be looked at. Van Wert also analyzes counterpoint between a "leading" sound-track and an "accompanying" image-track, noting that Robbe-Grillet's films are "games" of construction, largely unsuccessful because they demand new habits of perception from the spectator.

538 ZIMMER, CHRISTIAN. Cinéma et politique. Paris: Seghers, 354 pp.

Analysis of Allio, Barthes, Boisset, Comolli, Duras, Godard, Renoir, Resnais and Sartre, as well as Robbe-Grillet. Robbe-Grillet's films are "political" in terms of their questioning of bourgeois society's discourse, in terms of their subversion of nineteenth-century notions of the work of "art" as privileged and not as determined and of the privileged spectator or reader. Robbe-Grillet's films, then, serve a political purpose in terms of the "ideological deconstruction" allowed by Robbe-Grillet's use of "pop" culture, mass media and game structures, drawing attention again upon the work itself as product.

539 _____. "La Paille dans le discours de l'ordre." Les Temps Modernes, 29, No. 336 (July), 2492-2505.
Review of Malle's Lacombe Lucien and Duras' La Femme du Gange from the standpoint of Robbe-Grillet's Glissements progressifs du plaisir, in terms of which Robbe-Grillet stated that the moral order was not far from the narrative order, that both were of social origins, not "natural" origins.

540 _____. "Riche Reich." Les Temps Modernes, 30, No. 339 (October), 170-82.
Discussion of the critical problems in dealing with Robbe-Grillet as brought up by the special Etudes Cinématographiques (Nos. 100-103) issue on Resnais and Robbe-Grillet. Zimmer notes that Joel Magny sees Robbe-Grillet's films as didactic and Robbe-Grillet himself as political. Magny contends that Robbe-Grillet achieves an ideological deconstruction of bourgeois ideas about art, while noting that Robbe-Grillet is, nevertheless, not a Marxist and not committed politically to any program or point of view. On the other hand, Mireille Latil-Le Dantec sees him rather as one who alienates the spectator. Zimmer sides with Magny.

1975

*541 ALFREDSON, H. "Eget ljud-och andras: Chaplinredaktionen har gjort en enkaet om ljudets betydelse och 35 regissoerer och ljudmaen fraan naer och fjaerran svarar."
Unseen. Cited in Chaplin, 17, No. 4, 180-206 (See: Film/Literature Index, 1975). Questionnaire for 35 film directors, Robbe-Grillet included, about games, games structures and the role of the ludic in their work.

*542 ANON. "Alain Robbe-Grillet inaugure les décades de Cerisy." Monde (des Livres), No. 9461 (June 20), p. 14.
Unseen. Cited in French XX, 1975, #A17307 (See: Source List). Concerning the very important critical debates on the relationships between the new novel and the new cinema, focusing on the work of Robbe-Grillet, and including as participants the leading critics of his work.

*543 ARMES, ROY. "Cinema: Playing with fire." London Magazine, 15, No. 2 (June-July), 87-90.
Unseen. Cited in Film/Literature Index, 1975, p. 298; French XX, 1976, #A17308 (See: Source List). Review of Robbe-Grillet's Le Jeu avec le feu.

*544 BECHTOLD, C. "Le Jeu avec le feu." Cinématographe, No. 12 (March-April), p. 9.
Unseen. Cited in Film/Literature Index, 1975, p. 298 (See: Source List). Review of Le Jeu avec le feu.

545 BEYLIE, CLAUDE. "L'Année dernière à Chamonix." L'Avant-scène du Cinéma, No. 156 (March), pp. 5-10.
Marginally pertinent as an analysis of Resnais' Stavisky with references to Last Year at Marienbad.

546 BILLOTTE, LOUISE. "Last Night at Alain Robbe-Grillet's." Villager (October 30), p. 20.
Discussion of Robbe-Grillet's French film class at New York University and a critique of his assertions on pornography.

*547 BOLDUC, A. "Le Jeu avec le feu." Positif, No. 167 (March), pp. 83-84.
Unseen. Cited in Film/Literature Index, 1975, p. 298 (See: Source List). Review of Le Jeu avec le feu.

*548 BORY, JEAN-LOUIS. "Le Jeu avec le feu." Nouvel Observateur, No. 535 (February 17), (n.p.).
Unseen. Cited in Robbe-Grillet (See: Source List).

*549 FORRESTER, VIVIANE. "Le Jeu avec le feu." La Quinzaine Littéraire, No. 208 (April 16), (n.p.).
Unseen. Cited in Robbe-Grillet (See: Source List). Review of Le Jeu avec le feu.

550 FRENKEL, LISE. "Alain Robbe-Grillet: Glissements progressifs du plaisir." La Revue des Sciences Humaines (Le Cinéma en savoir), No. 159, pp. 448-50.
Psychoanalytical reading of Glissements progressifs du plaisir.

*551 GODARD, COLETTE. "Robbe-Grillet et le mythe de la cover-girl." Le Monde, No. 9367 (February 26), p. 23.
Unseen. Cited in French XX, 1976, #A17312 (See: Source List). On the use of certain types of women in Robbe-Grillet's color films, with their emphasis on eroticism.

552 HAYMAN, DAVID. "An Interview with Alain Robbe-Grillet." Contemporary Literature, 16, No. 3 (Summer), 273-85.

Interview with Robbe-Grillet. Typically, Robbe-Grillet seldom answers questions directly, but his answers are helpful in unexpected directions. Most of Hayman's questions have to do with literature, while Robbe-Grillet includes his films in his answers. On the modern work: "One could say that the reader of one of my novels or the spectator at one of my films is not really in front of but within. The work does not exist except through his presence. That is, unless there is someone within it who can reproduce the creative process. The relationship between author, work, and public is no longer the relationship between someone who creates a finished work and another who receives it. We now have a work which can exist only in a creative motion, which has its primary existence when the author writes or makes a film and exists a second time when the reader, the spectator, or in music the listener, is again within the work as if he were himself creating it." Robbe-Grillet notes the place of the erotic in his present novels and films as having become increasingly distanced from the traditional notion of what is erotic. Love relationships and sexual relationships are practically absent. "What we find is not bodies but images of bodies. They are quite often not even images but images of images...." There is discussion of how a scene from Project for a Revolution in New York engendered or "generated" a scene in Glissements progressifs du plaisir. Robbe-Grillet speaks of his collaborative work with Robert Rauschenberg and with Paul Delvaux, both painters, as well as with David Hamilton, the photographer. He notes that the "little girl" in his books and films is a composite of Nabokov's Lolita, Lewis Carroll's Alice, Sade's Justine and Queneau's Zazie. He explains that there is intertextuality between his novels and films on a thematic level more than on any technical level: "What is remarkable is that thematic aspect. You know I really enjoy not so much adapting my novels to the film as employing identical thematic materials in both, like, for example, the tortured mannequin we were speaking of earlier, or a broken glass, or blood." He calls a "literary" cinema the films of Truffaut and Chabrol, a novelistic cinema that continues the literary forms of the nineteenth century.

553 JOST, FRANÇOIS. "Notes: Le Film-Opéra." Critique, 31, No. 336 (May), 544-51.

Article on Le Jeu avec le feu. Fortunately, Jost writes short articles, for the reading is dense and almost too thought-provoking. He's one of the few post-structuralist critics who relies on analysis over footnotes, who perceives structures in terms of their "global" meaning, whose analyses of Robbe-Grillet's films, often limited to studying three or four sequences, are both unique and accessible. Jost notes that a syntagmatic analysis of a film usually implies a study of the image-track in order to understand narration. He points out that there are elements smaller than the sequence which can play an important role in a film and which must be studied by the critic. His interest is in such elements, in their role as extra-narrative generators. He notes that Le Jeu avec le feu has more sequences than any other Robbe-Grillet film. He separates the message that constitutes the narrative structure proper and seemingly identical messages, still filmic, that co-exist with the narrative message, but which either contradict it or go beyond it. Thus, the scene of "kidnapping" in the film includes an inscription on the suitcase that reads: "Live Animal." The words of Trintignant in that sequence reinforce the "animal" aspect, mixed with train sounds for aural support. Jost perceives in those train sounds a psychoanalytical symbol, the rolling of the train announcing the rape to come. At the same time, the train serves as intertextual symbol, since Trintignant as Elias in Trans-Europ-Express "raped" Eva in a similar position and on a similar bed. Thus, the scene "sends" us to the level of the soundtrack (train sounds) as well as to the diegetic level (rape). He compares the musical text of the film with Berg's Wozzeck. In L'Immortelle and L'Eden et après there was a musical treatment of the anecdote, but its function was quite different from Le Jeu avec le feu, since those two earlier films began with an enumeration of all the films' themes; thus, the initial sequences of both films were "outside" of the usual narrative code. In Le Jeu avec le feu there is one shot of soldiers, which is also outside of the narrative code, since no other shots of soldiers appear in the film. But such a shot serves as a visual representation of a sound, reversing the traditional relationship in film between image and sound. Robbe-Grillet's film is an attempt at film-opera.

*554 LEFEVRE, RAYMOND. "Le Jeu avec le feu." Revue du Cinéma, No. 294 (March), pp. 105-107; No. 299 (October), pp. 199-200.

Unseen. Cited in Film/Literature Index, 1975, p. 298 (See: Source List).

555 MORRISSETTE, BRUCE. "Post-Modern Generative Fiction: Novel and Film." Critical Inquiry, 2, No. 2 (Winter), 253-63.

A fascinating article, the only equivalent I know if in English to Jean Ricardou's equally important "Esquisse d'une théorie des générateurs." The key word of the title is "generative": "...fiction in print and on film lie to a great extent in a unified field not only of diegesis but also of structure. In fact, any sort of artistic intentionality constitutes a kind of 'generator.'" He notes two kinds of generators: (1) linguistic generators and (2) situational generators. The latter produces fictional structures, while the former may be limited to poetry or to texts of non-fictional prose. The most evolved generative texts have both. Morrissette treats the work of Queneau, Perec, Enard and Le Lionnais in terms of their generative texts, founded on the anagram principle in Saussure. Such texts lead to concepts of intertextuality, to creating through rewriting and to quotation literature. He cites L'Eden et après becoming the unshown N a pris les dés as an example of syllabic reversal or anaphonics. Robbe-Grillet gave Morrissette his working table of generative themes and series for L'Eden et après, and the table is reproduced at the end of the article. Morrissette concludes by noting that the neo-Marxists still believe in the possibilities of this kind of formal revolutionary work breaking down bourgeois acceptance of established codes of art.

556 _____. The Novels of Robbe-Grillet. Ithaca and London: Cornell University Press, 318 pp.

Finally translated from the French (Les Romans de Robbe-Grillet), the last two chapters (added for this edition) are of special interest. Chapter 9: "The Narrator and His Doubles: Project for a Revolution in New York" (262-87) deals mostly with that novel, but there are interesting parallels drawn with L'Eden et après. Morrissette is the only critic working in English who has dealt with Robbe-Grillet's film and literature activity from the perspective of intertextuality rather than from the more traditional format of "false" comparisons between the two media or from the viewpoint of one medium crying injustice against the other. He points out the emergence of present-day realities in Robbe-Grillet's novels and films, then notes that such contemporary realities are immediately reshaped and falsified by Robbe-Grillet. "L'Eden et après (1970) presents for the first time what may properly be termed a thematic use of socio-political reality." He analyzes the film as being "superficial," in the sense that Robbe-Grillet uses that term. Even more important for our concerns is Chapter 10: "Modes and Levels of the Cinematic Novel: Glissements progressifs du plaisir (1974)" (288-309). This last chapter is especially interesting, speculative and insightful. Morrissette quotes Noel Burch to the effect that Robbe-Grillet's true importance will be found in the cinema: "arising in literature, these procedures run the risk of monotony.... Whereas in the cinema they can resonate throughout a gamut of materials at all levels." Morrissette studies the lack of publication in ciné-roman form of the three films after Last Year at Marienbad and L'Immortelle. The reason for no publication seems to be in the fragmentary preliminary texts, the notes for those intervening films, which depend more upon improvisations during the shooting and editing than the earlier scripted films. He then analyzes the book of Glissements progressifs du plaisir. "What is merely 'given' in the film is described in the text; the revolutionary or 'scandalous' nature of the film's subversive structures is thus identified and recuperated into a logical coherence by the act of conscious recognition." He points out contradictions in the montage record between the supposed "absence of structural clues" and the revealing headings given by Robbe-Grillet for the sequences. The non-cinematic texts make linkings in an implicit way; the ciné-roman texts make linkings in an explicit way. The text of Glissements is a kind of barrier against all other interpretations or explanations. And while Ricardou, Ollier and Simon use separate essays as texts for their structural designs, Robbe-Grillet inserts them in the work itself. Increasingly, Robbe-Grillet uses the word "archetype" to describe "popular" or paraliterary models. The plot to Glissements is seen as a perpetuum mobile. Morrissette points out that the inspector asks a series of insane and unrelated questions, which later in the film are given a context and become pertinent. In the film no attempt is made to justify unexplained sequences as "subjective" sequences. The use of myriad "punctuations" marks a radical change in Robbe-Grillet's former notion of the cinema as the realm of pure mental content. "The cinematic field thus expands to engulf its own thematic abstracts, its metaphors, its non-anecdotal structures, its punctuations. Instead of seeking to reduce all its images and sounds to a 'justified' subjectivity, a work like Glissements converts even its justified scenes, such as those analyzed above, into elements of more or less 'pure' structure." Process becomes plot.

557 MOSCOWITZ, GENE. "Le Jeu avec le feu (Playing With Fire)." Variety, No. 277 (February 5), p. 22.

Calls the voyeurism of Le Jeu avec le feu "puerile" and notes that it adds little to Robbe-Grillet's already convoluted films. Baffled in his abbreviated plot summary, Moscowitz sees the film as simulated soft porn.

558 ORASKY, V. "Lustans gradvisa glidningar." Chaplin, 17, No. 3, 144-46.

Review of Glissements progressifs du plaisir.

559 OSTER, JERRY. "Material is the Message." New York Daily News (October 29), p. 94.

Quotes Robbe-Grillet on the differences between American distributors, who think there is only one film-viewing public, and French distributors, who recognize several film-viewing publics. Robbe-Grillet quotes Nabokov: "No I don't have a message. I am not a telegrapher." He admires Orson Welles and Michael Snow as filmmakers.

560 PRIGOGINE, HÉLÈNE. "Alain Robbe-Grillet. Les Glissements progressifs du plaisir," in Théorie et pratique du code. Edited by André Helbo. Brussels: Degrès, pp. h, 3-h, 5.
Analysis of Glissements progressifs du plaisir.

561 RENAUD, TRISTAN. "Le Jeu avec le feu." Cinéma 75, No. 197 (April), pp. 155-56.
Contends that Robbe-Grillet's films have become more and more the "echo" of his literary work, the paradox being that, the more Robbe-Grillet becomes the master of a cinematographic language, and Le Jeu avec le feu is technically masterful, the closer he gets to his novels: the camera becomes the extension or repetition of words, phrases, plots and especially of looks for which Robbe-Grillet was already well-known in the novels. His earlier films were mediocre in quality, but they were necessary steps in Robbe-Grillet's cinematic treatment of the imaginary. While his literary output suffers in comparison with his earlier novels, his films have become technically accomplished and sophisticated. Especially masterful in this film is the distance kept between Robbe-Grillet and the "game" he gives the spectator. This distance is crucial for the full exposition of the film's humor. Renaud concludes that the game is not so much with "fire" as it is with "narrative structures," and in that sense Robbe-Grillet is playing dangerously, figuratively playing with fire.

*562 ROBBE-GRILLET, ALAIN. "L'Immortelle." Revue du Cinéma, No. 301 (December), p. 17.
Unseen. Cited in Film/Literature Index, 1975, p. 67 (See: Source List).

563 _____. L'Immortelle. Paris: Editions 10/18, 312 pp.
Reissue of the ciné-roman.

*564 RYBALKA, MICHEL. "Théorie? Antithéorie? Robbe-Grillet à Cerisy." Monde (des Livres), No. 9484 (July 18), p. 12.
Unseen. Cited in French XX, 1976, #A17319 (See: Source List). Review of Robbe-Grillet's role and pronouncements at the critical debates on film and literature at Cerisy.

*565 SICLIER, JACQUES. "Le Jeu avec le feu." Le Monde, No. 9366 (February 25), (n.p.).
Unseen. Cited in Robbe-Grillet (See: Source List). Review of Le Jeu avec le feu.

566 STURDZA, PALTIN. "The Rebirth Archetype in Robbe-Grillet's L'Immortelle." French Review, 48, No. 6 (May), 990-95.
Robbe-Grillet's generative themes come from the collective unconscious of modern man, close to the definition of

archetype. The Jungian distinctions between archetypal situations and archetypal figures become in Robbe-Grillet the distinctions between dynamic and static. The first is dominant, and Robbe-Grillet characterizes his ciné-roman for L'Immortelle as pure movement. Sturdza analyzes the Rebirth archetype in the film. Its forms are either as resurrection or renovation, with its antithetical counterparts being death and decay or destruction. Objects in the ciné-roman belong to both categories: boats are shown to be repaired and later to be sinking or sunk. Sturdza notes that the Rebirth archetype fails as renovation; "Rebirth can be achieved only as reconstruction, resurrection in the imaginary world." That same archetype succeeds as resurrection, in that, after her death, L remains in N's hallucinations, and after N's death L is again resurrected by the author. "The failure of renovatio and the success of resurrectio reflects the preponderance of repetition over continuity: time is not an arrow oriented from the past to the future, but circular and repetitive and the end of L'Immortelle repeats the beginning."

*567 TESSARI, R. "Giochi di fuoco." Cinema Nuovo, No. 24 (September-December), pp. 445-47.
Unseen. Cited in Film/Literature Index, 1975, p. 298 (See: Source List). Review of Le Jeu avec le feu.

568 VAN WERT, WILLIAM. "The Theory and Practice of the Ciné-Roman." Ph.D. dissertation, Indiana University, 396 pp.
Chapter Two: "The Theory and Practice of the Ciné-Roman" (22-59) emphasizes the parallel publication of the film scenario in conjunction with the film as (1) a memory-aid for those who have seen the film; as (2) a form of meditation, reflection or close critical analysis for those for whom the images and sounds of the film have gone by too quickly to assimilate; as (3) a means of approaching the film for those who have not seen the film or for those who will have no reasonable chance to see the film; as (4) preparation for those about to see the film, in the same way that the libretto, in Robbe-Grillet's terms, serves the opera; as (5) compensation for the peculiarities of distribution; as (6) a means for the screenwriter to approach the public directly and in print, as opposed to indirectly through the film in images; and (7) as a means of directing critics and audiences alike as to possible interpretations and authorial intentionality. Robbe-Grillet, Agnes Varda, Jean Cayrol, Alain Resnais and Henri Colpi are studied in terms of their statements on the ciné-roman. Differences between the ciné-romans and the films are noted, culminating in either Robbe-Grillet's intertextual approach to complementing film and literary activity or Marguerite Duras' variable-work-of-art approach, by which the work can be

simultaneously written, staged or filmed. Chapter Three: "The Nouveau Roman and the Cinéma des Auteurs" (60-95) studies Robbe-Grillet, Duras and Cayrol in terms of their literary activity, their apprenticeship with Resnais on collaborative films and their own films. Chapter Four: "The Structural Limits of the Cinematographic Novel: Alain Robbe-Grillet's Dans le labyrinthe" (96-138) analyzes the novel in terms of its cinematic structures, proposing a "reading" method based on cross-reference. Chapter Five: "Explorations and Innovations of the Cinéma des Auteurs" (139-297) treats the films of Resnais, Marker, Varda, Cayrol, Duras, Colpi and Robbe-Grillet in terms of (1) their use of "subjective" documentary techniques; (2) their stylized use of color; (3) their innovative use of music; and (4) their treatment of time. Extended examples for Robbe-Grillet are taken from L'Immortelle and L'Homme qui ment, but references to Last Year at Marienbad, Trans-Europ-Express and L'Eden et après are made as well. There is a questionnaire at the end, to which Robbe-Grillet, Marker, Cayrol and Colpi responded.

*569 WARNOD, JEANINE. "Rencontres--Paul Delvaux et Alain Robbe-Grillet." Le Figaro Littéraire, No. 1507 (April 5), pp. 1, 15.

Unseen. Cited in French XX, 1976, #A17310 (See: Source List). Interview with Delvaux and Robbe-Grillet, who are working on a collaborative text.

*570 WEEMAES, G. "Le Jeu avec le feu." Film & TV, Nos. 218-219 (July-August), pp. 35-36.

Unseen. Cited in Film/Literature Index, 1975, p. 298 (See: Source List). Review of Le Jeu avec le feu.

1976

571 ANON. "Robbe-Grillet à la question," in Robbe-Grillet: Analyse, Théorie (Colloques de Cerisy. II: Cinéma/Roman). Paris: Editions 10/18, pp. 410-35.

Questions asked of Robbe-Grillet at the end of the 1975 Cerisy debates and presentations. He notes that each novel that he wrote "saved" the preceding novel, and that the gap between when he made a film and when the public and the critics accepted that film was even worse than that for the novels. He states that his role as editor at Minuit is the reverse of the traditional editor. His role is not to look for texts which would be well received by an already existent public, but rather to invent a public for texts that already exist. He relates his experiences with French television, noting that much freedom is possible in literature, less in the cinema, and none at all in television.

He made N a pris les dés for Albert Ollivier and French television. The film was an anagram-transfer of L'Eden et après, employing out-takes from that latter film and inserting an "ending" to the anecdotal plot in which Violette would discover that all her adventures had been due to her being the center of a televised game, thus making TV a central concern in the film. The film was never shown. Robbe-Grillet notes that his concerns with painting have become foregrounded with his color films: allusions to Mondrian and Marcel Duchamp in L'Eden et après, to Yves Klein in Glissements progressifs du plaisir. He has come to treat the film screen as a canvas for colors, and he notes the use of colors in L'Eden et après as an example. When asked about his religious training, he points out that he was baptized, that he never set foot in a church after that, that he is fascinated with the New and Old Testaments, even to the point of declaring them the first "new novel" and that the four Evangelists appear in Trans-Europ-Express (Jean, the filmmaker; Lucette, the script-person; Marc, the producer; and Mathieu, the young boy at the end of the film). References are made to Judas and Veronique in The Man Who Lies.

572 ARMES, ROY. "Alain Robbe-Grillet: The Reality of Imagination," in his The Ambiguous Image: Narrative Style in Modern European Cinema. Bloomington and London: Indiana University Press, pp. 131-40.

Contrasts the novel and the film for Robbe-Grillet. Novel-writing is a private and solitary endeavor, while filmmaking is public and collective. Armes traces Robbe-Grillet's development as a critic of both the novel and the cinema. Robbe-Grillet's characters are rooted in a new sense of time, choosing simultaneously all paths at once. Armes analyzes the "eternal present" in Robbe-Grillet's films. He suggests that Robbe-Grillet's stylistic devices--the "statuesque gestures, theatrical diction and remote baroque setting"--are only used as alienation devices or distancing devices. Robbe-Grillet's films are less polished and less sophisticated than Resnais'; at the same time, they are more direct, more realistic and more erotic than Resnais' films. He quotes Robbe-Grillet on Raymond Roussel as indicative of Robbe-Grillet's fictions as well: "Everything is shown in movement and yet immobilised in the very middle of this movement by the description that leaves all the gestures...in suspense, perpetuates the immanence of their end and deprives them of their meaning. Empty enigmas, time standing still, signs that refuse to be significant, gigantic enlargements of minute details, tales that turn in on themselves." There is a long analysis of Trans-Europ-Express, almost at the expense of Robbe-Grillet's other films. Armes concludes that Robbe-Grillet's method of constructing films is similar to that of Pierre Boulez in music.

573 BISHOP, TOM. "Géographie de Robbe-Grillet," in Robbe-Grillet: Analyse, Théorie (Colloques de Cerisy. II. Cinéma/Roman). Paris: Editions 10/18, pp. 52-68.

Primarily focuses on the novels and the treatment of real and imaginary locales, the real ones being as imaginary as the imaginary ones. With Last Year at Marienbad, there is a shift from the geography of the novels that preceded it, in that geography in the film becomes a reflection of ambiguous wavering. The physical space of the film is a closed world: abstract, fictional, dream-like and frozen. It takes on all the characteristics of the labyrinth. With L'Immortelle the portrayed world is one of myth and deceiving appearances. The Turkey presented is that of myth and that of tourists, of post-cards and illusions. The Istanbul of L'Immortelle anticipates the Hong Kong of La Maison de rendez-vous, the New York of Project for a Revolution in New York and the central Europe of The Man Who Lies, as well as the Western Europe and Tunisia of L'Eden et après. In both Trans-Europ-Express and The Man Who Lies the geography has a kind of cartoon-strip look and treatment. Bishop notes that the train in Trans-Europ-Express has become, since Hitchcock, the stereotyped locale for all kinds of intrigues, with spy implications. Robbe-Grillet accentuates this aspect with his emphasis on mystery, drugs, prostitution and false identities in the film. Yet all this falsification is within the context of a real train, real people (like Robbe-Grillet within the film), real streets. The imaginary begins from, and builds upon, the real. Bishop notes that L'Eden et après is Robbe-Grillet's most structurally complex film, noting that the passage from a real European city to a real Tunisia implies neither time nor trajectory, since it is effected within a film that Violette is watching and then, suddenly, is within. All of these landscapes and all this "geography" is both false and oneiric, while based on the real; thus, Robbe-Grillet reverses the traditional reasons behind location shooting.

574 CHATEAU, DOMINIQUE. "La Question du sens dans l'oeuvre d'Alain Robbe-Grillet," in Robbe-Grillet: Analyse, Théorie (Colloques de Cerisy. II. Cinéma/Roman). Paris: Editions 10/18, pp. 320-36.

Ostensibly a study of the ciné-roman for Glissements progressifs du plaisir. Chateau notes that the ciné-roman is a half-way stage between the novel and the film. She alludes to the published film-novels for Last Year at Marienbad and L'Immortelle and notes that the ciné-roman for Glissements is more complex, more sophisticated, more detailed. She relies heavily on generative semantics (MacCawley, Lakoff, Bach) in her treatment of "sense" in Robbe-Grillet. With Glissements Robbe-Grillet has taken a standpoint of some distance on his own mental universe, and the ciné-roman gives "sense" to what the film had left ambiguous. Thus, Chateau accuses Robbe-Grillet of interpreting his own film. The published ciné-roman shows that all the narrative propositions have a defined meaning, but that their composition within the film has no narrative meaning.

575 DUMONT, LILLIAN and SANDI SILVERBERG. "An Interview with Alain Robbe-Grillet." Filmmakers Newsletter, 9, No. 9 (July), 22-25.

Interesting interview with Robbe-Grillet during the time he was teaching at New York University in the fall of 1975. He acknowledges the influence of Godard on him. He uses what he calls "contamination shots" where seemingly disjointed objects and events are rapidly intercut. He suggests that his themes are culturally bound: the television commercial, tabloids, the B movie, pop magazines. He intercuts explicitly sexual scenes with shots of seemingly unrelated objects which serve no function in terms of pornography. In Glissements progressifs du plaisir Alice is about to take a man to bed that she has picked up on the street. Cut to a blue shoe. In the next shot, the man is lying dead on the floor. Asked about similarities between the novel and film, Robbe-Grillet speaks of punctuation: the use of devices that denote transitions within the linear, "discursive" structure. He notes that there are cinematic counterparts to commas, periods and paragraphs in literature. The many types of cuts that link shots such as dissolves and jump cuts are examples of film punctuation. He says punctuation is content as well as form. In Glissements the blue shoe, the broken bottle, the sea, the iron bed, the wedding crown and the bouquet in the bell jar are used as punctuation, cutting up content shots. "They recur, out of context, throughout the film, and they connect, by inference and by their associative, conotative power, one shot to the next." Objects are used as cutting devices rather than a straight cutting in a more traditional sense, so that a man digging a grave "means" digging into memory as well. He notes that blood as an image has appeared only since his color films. Glissements is based on Jules Michlet's "The Sorceress," with allusions to Cinderella (the blue shoe) and to Alice in Wonderland (the protagonist's name is Alice). He discusses the use of three interlocking musical themes in Le Jeu avec le feu. He notes that sound can be used as "decoration," the sound of the sea in Glissements suggesting memory. The most interesting color in color films for him is white. He notes that his characters, who occupy apparently unlimited space, are really prisoners of time, and he emphasizes this point by having them look often at their watches. He concludes by praising the cinematography of Yves Lafaye.

576 FANO, MICHEL. "L'Ordre musical chez Alain Robbe-Grillet. Le Discours sonore dans ses films," in Robbe-Grillet: Analyse, Théorie (Colloques de Cerisy. I.). Paris: Editions 10/18, (n.p.).
Extremely important document by the composer and musical director of all of Robbe-Grillet's films. Fano speaks of the "language" of the sound-track, the use of sounds structurally and generatively, and the continuum sonore in all of Robbe-Grillet's films.

577 FRENKEL, LISE. "Lecture psychanalytique du Jeu avec le feu," in Robbe-Grillet: Analyse, Théorie (Colloques de Cerisy. II. Cinéma/Roman). Paris: Editions 10/18, pp. 392-400.
Psychoanalytical reading of Le Jeu avec le feu. Frenkel notes that the narrator, the "old pensive prince," is related in Freudian terms to seduction and power. Combining Saussure with Freud and Lacan, Frenkel analyzes the opening credits and their displacement, engendering relationships between scenes and events later in the film, including the duplication of character: Carolina becomes the "false Carolina," Christa, whose crucifixion is "announced" in the opening credits by the word "crucified," Virginia and Lisa. The scene from Othello is a projection of paternal jealousy, a condensation of the incest and infanticide themes. Carolina in disguise is a symbol for homosexuality through an identification with the father and as protection against incest. Frenkel analyzes the dream of the burning child, both in Freud and in the film, and relates it to the music of Verdi, an opera in which a child is burned by mistake. The film is a pornographic opera, beginning with Sleeping Beauty and ending with the sadism of Bluebeard. Frenkel notes that Metz's grande syntagmatique is insufficient for the study of dreams and symbols in a film like Le Jeu avec le feu. What is necessary for a close study of such a film is the formulation of a grande fantasmatique, to deal with the structures of the imaginary.

578 GARDIES, ANDRÉ. "Récit et matériau filmique," in Robbe-Grillet: Analyse, Théorie (Colloques de Cerisy. II. Cinéma/Roman). Paris: Editions 10/18, pp. 85-111.
An analysis of The Man Who Lies based on the theories of Jean Ricardou. Gardies emphasizes the use of sound in the film and breaks "sound" into words, sounds and music, citing Michel Fano as having noted that the three "slide" (glisser) in and out of each other for meaning. In the opening scene of the film, in conjunction with visuals of the protagonist in the pine forest, there are sounds of boots marching on

a pavement. Such sounds not only reinforce the possibility of another space (boots wouldn't sound like that in a forest) but also of another time. When Boris and Sylvia are talking in the park, there is on the sound-track the song of a bird, without the bird ever being visible. Such a sound would seem "natural" in this setting, but the sound of the bird disappears and reappears with such a regularity that the sound loses its "natural" quality and comes to serve as a punctuation in the dialogue, an ironic commentary on the stereotyped love-words between Boris and Sylvia. The sound of the goat in the cemetery is an intertextual sound, relating to the sound of a goat in the cemetery in L'Immortelle. Thus, sounds are also used as intertextual quotations in Robbe-Grillet's films. Gardies cites Jean Ricardou for having attempted to join film and novel in terms of the use of mise-en-abime structures in Last Year at Marienbad. Such structures not only relate to the new novel but also to medieval painting. Gardies points out that the Codex in the pharmacy in The Man Who Lies is really a photograph album, in which are photos of Jean Robin's childhood (giving him a "past" that Boris Varissa doesn't have), photos of the on-going present, and foreshadowing photos, photos which will "animate" and circulate within the film later. Gardies sees the false Codex as photo album in terms of the character of the druggist, a confirmation of Lisa's accusation that the druggist had an affair with Jean Robin. Another photo of Jean Robin with Maria is seen as proof of an earlier liaison between them, especially given the ease with which Boris begins an affair with Maria. From Ricardou, Gardies defines the sequence as a series of events proposed without a break or hiatus, and a transition would be any change between sequences. Gardies studies such changes or "transitions" in The Man Who Lies. He notes one point in the film in which a gesture is begun by Boris and completed by Jean Robin. The "transition" is smooth, since the gesture is completed, but the continuity in terms of content is broken. Gardies notes as well the sequences in Robbe-Grillet's films in which spoken language stops before the power of the images: the cabaret in L'Immortelle, the chained slave-dancer in Trans-Europ-Express, the dance of Violette around the fire in L'Eden et aprés and the scene of "Maria punished" in The Man Who Lies. In such sequences, the narrative line of the film is suspended and a "deflation" of meaning occurs. Gardies points out that sounds employed in the film have extra-cinematic meanings as well. The use of scissors in The Man Who Lies, especially given the content of the film, is a reminder of the punishment for women (cutting the hair) for having loved an enemy soldier. Scenes such as that of "Maria punished" prove that Robbe-Grillet is not a novelist dabbling in film, but rather a filmmaker fully conscious of the plurality and heterogeneity of the basic material of film.

579 JOST, FRANÇOIS. "Les Télèstructures dans l'oeuvre d'Alain Robbe-Grillet," in _Robbe-Grillet: Analyse, Théorie (Colloques de Cerisy. II. Cinéma/Roman)_. Paris: Editions 10/18, pp. 223-47.

Analysis of _The Man Who Lies_, using the Markov model. In Robbe-Grillet's novels and films linkage between sequences is usually affected by structures of analogy: similarities or oppositions, which, in the films, is related with the repetition of gestures, camera angles or framing. For example, Boris jumps on the counter in _The Man Who Lies_, but it is the jump of Jean Robin on a false floor which completes the jump of Boris through a cut. Jost notes that there are few "subordination" cuts in Robbe-Grillet. That lack of traditional subordination has given rise in some critics to a comparison of Robbe-Grillet's "writing" with automatic writing. Jost points out that Robbe-Grillet's calculated structures and linkages couldn't be more removed from automatic writing. He notes games of "echo" in the dialogue of _Le Jeu avec le feu_, specifically in the words and imagery of Trintignant, which relate otherwise unrelated scenes. Jost calls "télèstructure" structures in the films which have long-distance or cross-referential impact.

580 ROBBE-GRILLET, ALAIN. "_Piège à fourrure_: Début d'un projet de film." _Minuit_, No. 18 (March), pp. 2-15.

Extremely important "explanation" of the film Robbe-Grillet is about to make. This is perhaps his most detailed pre-scripting for the public, and it reflects his overriding concerns with structures over plot or story. Briefly, the "story" concerns an investigator in charge of an important mission, who, because of an accident, is sidetracked from his mission. Only too late does he understand the relationship between his mission and the side issue which surrounds him. What he wished to put aside as a distraction turns out to be the mission itself. There are nine generative signs to be used in the film, relating each to the others in a serial arrangement: footsteps, fur, opening, knife, scream, penetration, fall, dripping, viscous spot or stain. Some of these generative signs are related to sounds by their definition, while others carry referential sounds (the falling of a human body with a broken glass). But for every generative sign there will be a corresponding sound, yet to be determined. What interests him at the moment is the process of transformation, from an objective sound to a musical sound. The inverse is also true: choosing musical sounds for those generative themes which have no given referential sound (fur or the viscuous spot), which will gradually generate objective sounds, natural sounds with definite referents. Robbe-Grillet explains his use of certain erotic objects and scenes as making full use of one's already explored storehouse. If the above-mentioned series is shown in alphabetical order, there is in that order a metaphor for sexual aggression which culminates in a deflowering or an assassination. He notes that the use of the word metaphor can be applied to all his previous works, in terms of the use of metaphor-objects where the formal characteristics are displaced from one object to the next. The nine generative themes or signs are what constitute the investigator's mission. He will consider them as pieces in a puzzle. But they function quite differently from the causal relationships of the traditional detective novel. They are related associatively, not logically, and in a serial, not causal, arrangement. The film is divided into nine episodes, which are each begun by the succession of the nine generative signs in a different order. Each episode will last around ten minutes or so. Each episode will be preceded by a brief "summary" of the nine generative signs in a rhythmic pattern, emphasized by the use of a metronome. Thus, each of the nine signs will begin one episode and will end one episode. Some means of "naturalizing" the various episodes will be found: for example, the projection of slides on a screen with the accompanying sounds of the projector. Robbe-Grillet reflects on the use of serial arrangements, noting that Hollis Frampton in Zorns Lemma and a certain sector of the American "underground" cinema use serialism as a total refusal of the anecdotal subject. In the "dys-narrative" cinema, Robbe-Grillet is attempting to incorporate structures which are seemingly incompatible with narrative cinema. His L'Eden et après is the only fiction film in which the story itself is produced by the organization of themes in successive series, according to a system somewhat comparable to that of Schönberg in music. In Piège the attempt will be to conserve the cadence of the serial arrangement, while employing it as the initiator of diegesis and not as a function within the diegesis. There will be a masculine narrating voice, which will give indications to the actors and crew and will comment on the action from time to time. The film begins on a close-up of the protagonist Néro (his full name is Néroby) watching the series of generative signs in a cinema: mens' shoes and the tip of a cane advancing in a corridor, fur coat that moves on a bed, bedroom door that opens slowly, hand holding a hunting knife, head of a young woman who turns toward the camera and begins a scream of terror. A young woman named Ava L. comes to get Néro on a motor-bike. She gives him a fur coat that Néro must transport for a certain Van de Reeves. En route Néro will come across the body of Christa on the road. She seems to have been deflowered and she is mute. He tells her that he is on an important mission and that he will let her off at the first house, which turns out to be the "Villa Seconde," where nobody understands either French or English but where no questions are asked about Christa's condition or about the reasons for her staying there."

581 VEILLON, OLIVIER-RENÉ. "Le Jeu avec le feu critique de L'Année dernière à Marienbad - de l'épure aux faseiements de l'idéologique," in Robbe-Grillet: Analyse, Théorie (Colloques de Cerisy. II. Cinéma/Roman). Paris: Editions 10/18, pp. 139-58.

The latter film (Le Jeu avec le feu) is used as a standard with which to measure Last Year at Marienbad in terms of ideology. Robbe-Grillet's films are a cinema of "formal" invention: Le Jeu avec le feu seems to be more "narrative" than Marienbad, and yet it cannot be retold or paraphrased. Veillon uses Metz and the actantial model of Greimas to study both films. He analyzes Marienbad as "diegesis stripped bare by its metaphor, even," an obvious reference to Duchamp. He studies the exchange between the narrative voice of X and the actors in the play within the film. The entire film is a metaphor for the Orpheus myth. He notes that the diegesis is obscured in Le Jeu avec le feu, so that there are at least two contradictory versions of the "story" that are possible in the film, both centering on the relationship between de Saxe and his daughter and which one is duping the other. He analyzes both versions according to the Greimas model.

582 WESTERBECK, C. L. "Intrastructures: the Films of Alain Robbe-Grillet." Artforum, No. 14 (March), pp. 54-57.

Return to World War Two to situate Robbe-Grillet in the line of Astruc's caméra-stylo, as one who merged writing and filming. Westerbeck insists on Robbe-Grillet's complete scenario for Last Year at Marienbad, with camera indications that Resnais followed for the most part. In all his films, the opening sequences establish a confusion between art and life. Secondary people in the films appear to be "statuary candelabra rather than flesh and blood." Like the print of the hotel garden in Marienbad, an Abstract-Expressionist painting in L'Eden et après becomes, when turned on its side, the house Violette visits in North Africa. Snapshots are used in The Man Who Lies to anticipate future events, themselves presented in freeze-frame photography. Despite his innovations and importance, Robbe-Grillet's films are relatively unknown and largely unseen. He is still thought of as a writer. To demonstrate that Robbe-Grillet's approach to the scenario is not too "literary," Westerbeck compares Robbe-Grillet's methods with those of Hitchcock. The two deal with similar worlds but from opposite perspectives. The dilemmas that Hitchcock's characters face are moral dilemmas; those that Robbe-Grillet's characters face are metaphysical. The only relationship between scenes in Robbe-Grillet's films is an imagistic one. Contrary to traditional film, Robbe-Grillet's films allow the imagery to become apparent, while the narrative remains hidden or vanishes altogether. His approach to literature and film has always been one of emphasizing description over narration. Westerbeck sees the central image of _The Man Who Lies_ as the lesbian kiss between Maria and Sylvia, which extends to Violette and her double in _L'Eden et après_ and to the lesbian love affair that leads to murder in _Glissements progressifs du plaisir_. Before _The Man Who Lies_, recurrences in the films were temporal; with _The Man Who Lies_ they become spatial. Robbe-Grillet's films are not surrealistic, but "intra-realistic": they document realities that exist only within the artist's own perceptions.

Performances and Other Film Related Activity

Writings: Fiction

1953

583 Les Gommes. Paris: Minuit, 226 pp. Translated by Richard Howard as The Erasers (New York: Grove Press, 1962), 256 pp.

1955

584 Le Voyeur. Paris: Minuit, 255 pp. Translated by Richard Howard as The Voyeur (New York: Grove Press, 1958), 219 pp.

1957

585 La Jalousie. Paris: Minuit, 218 pp. Translated by Richard Howard as Jealousy (New York: Grove Press, 1959), 149 pp. Also translated by Richard Howard in Two Novels by Robbe-Grillet (New York: Grove Press, 1965), 272 pp. (Includes Jealousy and In the Labyrinth).

1959

586 Dans le labyrinthe. Paris: Minuit, 221 pp. Translated by Richard Howard as In the Labyrinth (New York: Grove Press, 1960), 207 pp. Also translated by Richard Howard in Two Novels by Robbe-Grillet (New York: Grove Press, 1965), 272 pp. (Includes Jealousy and In the Labyrinth). Also translated by Christine Brooks-Rose as In the Labyrinth (London: Calder and Boyars, 1967), 189 pp.

1962

587 Instantanés. Paris: Minuit, 109 pp. Translated by Barbara Wright in Snapshots and Towards a New Novel (London: Calder and Boyars, 1965), 161 pp. Also translated by Bruce Morrissette as Snapshots (New York: Grove Press, 1968), 72 pp.

1965

588 La Maison de rendez-vous. Paris: Minuit, 216 pp. Translated by Richard Howard as La Maison de rendez-vous (New York: Grove Press, 1966), 154 pp.

1970

589 Projet pour une révolution à New York. Paris: Minuit, 213 pp. Translated by Richard Howard as Project for a Revolution in New York (New York: Grove Press, 1972), 183 pp.

1976

590 La Belle Captive. Paris: La Bibliothèque des Arts.

591 Topologie d'une cité fantôme. Paris: Minuit, 201 pp.

Criticism

1963

592 Pour un nouveau roman. Paris: Gallimard, 183 pp. Translated by Richard Howard as For a New Novel: Essays on Fiction (New York: Grove Press, 1965), 175 pp. Also translated by Barbara Wright in Snapshots and Towards a New Novel (London: Calder and Boyars, 1965), 161 pp.

Robbe-Grillet was supposed to have published Avant L'Eden: Théorie des images génératrices with Skira in 1973-1974. It was to have been a collection of articles on the cinema, a companion piece to Pour un nouveau roman. To date, Robbe-Grillet has never finished it.

Ciné-Romans

1961

593 L'Année dernière à Marienbad. Paris: Minuit, 172 pp., 48 photos. Translated by Richard Howard as Last Year at Marienbad (New York: Grove Press, 1962), 165 pp.

1963

594 L'Immortelle. Paris: Minuit, 210 pp., 40 photos. Translated by A. M. Sheridan Smith as The Immortal One (London: Calder and Boyars, 1971), 173 pp., 20 photos.

1974

595 Glissements progressifs du plaisir. Paris: Minuit, 220 pp., 56 photos.

Unpublished Screenplays

1961

596 La Japonaise.
Robbe-Grillet was invited to Japan to write the screenplay for a film. After several revisions, Robbe-Grillet left Japan. The producer was imprisoned shortly thereafter, and the film was never made.

1965

597 Le Retour de Franck (Frankie's Return).
Robbe-Grillet wrote the script for Grove Press/Evergreen. No film was ever made.

Collaborative Works

1973

598 Les Demoiselles. Paris: Minuit, 140 pp. Text by Robbe-Grillet, photographs by David Hamilton. Translated by Martha Egan as Sisters (New York: Morrow, 1973), 135 pp.

1976

599 La Belle Captive. Paris: La Bibliothèque des Arts.
Novel by Robbe-Grillet, with illustrations by René Magritte.

600 Traces suspectes en surfaces.
Text by Robbe-Grillet, original lithographs by Robert Rauschenberg. Specifications: text from four chapters of Robbe-Grillet's Topologie d'une cité fantôme, sometimes accompanying the lithographs, sometimes within the lithographs; 29 X 41, folded in two, 35-40 numbered and autographed copies. To be on exhibit in selected American museums in 1977. For more information, contact:
Ms. Tatyana Grosman
Universal Limited Art Edition
5 Skidmore Place
West Islip, Long Island, New York 11795
(516-669-6571).
Note: Robbe-Grillet is also at work on a text with Paul Delvaux. Still unfinished.

Articles and Interviews

See the Index for a complete list of articles by Robbe-Grillet and interviews with Robbe-Grillet. The numbers in the Index correspond to annotated entries in Section IV: the Annotated Guide to Writings By and About Robbe-Grillet.

Performances: Acting

1966

601 Trans-Europ-Express. Directed by Alain Robbe-Grillet.
Robbe-Grillet plays the part of Jean, the filmmaker within the film.

1968

602 Je t'aime je t'aime. Directed by Alain Resnais.
Robbe-Grillet plays the part of an editor in the office where the protagonist works.

1974

603 Glissements progressifs du plaisir. Directed by Alain Robbe-Grillet.
Robbe-Grillet is a passer-by in the film.

Film Adaptations of Robbe-Grillet's Fiction

1962

604 In the Labyrinth. Directed by Robert Liikala. 12 minutes.
"This short film of 12 minutes was done in response to Alain Robbe-Grillet's In the Labyrinth in 1962. I first encountered Alain Robbe-Grillet through Le Voyeur, which I read in 1960. As a painter I admired his descriptive draftsmanship--the elegance of the continuous flowing line--time-event-object merged into the ever-present moment. Prior to the film I produced a series of woodblock prints reflecting this way of seeing and sent a print to Alain Robbe-Grillet which particularly caught a passage from Le Voyeur, a description of a row of trees seen from a column-enclosed porch. He responded with a friendly thank-you and an invitation to visit." --Robert Liikala.
Film distributed by
Film-Makers Cooperative
175 Lexington Avenue
New York, New York 10016
(212-889-3820).

1969

605 Les Gommes. Franco-Belgian co-production. 90 minutes. Black and white, with English or Spanish subtitles. Directed by Lucien Deroisy. Adaptation and scenario by René Michard. Photography by Frédérick Geilfus.
Robbe-Grillet saw the film and disliked it.

1972

606 La Jalousie. TV film, supposedly based on a scenario by Robbe-Grillet. (Moeller, see 520).

Archival Sources

607 Donald Velde, Inc. 311 W. 43rd Street, New York, New York 10036 (212-581-6040)
Stills for Last Year at Marienbad, L'Immortelle and The Man Who Lies.

608 New York Public Library at Lincoln Center. Lincoln Center for the Performing Arts, Third Floor, 111 Amsterdam Avenue, New York, New York 10036 (212-799-2200)
Some stills, clippings files for all the films, collection of reviews of the films by the New York newspapers. No scripts or correspondence.

609 Alain Robbe-Grillet c/o Editions de Minuit, 7, rue Bernard-Palissy, 75006 Paris, France

Film Distributors

1961

610 L'Année dernière à Marienbad (Last Year at Marienbad)
Macmillan (Formerly Audio-Brandon). Rental E ($85).

34 MacQuesten Parkway So.
Mount Vernon, N.Y. 10550
(914-664-5051)

8400 Brookfield Ave.
Brookfield, Illinois 60513
(312-485-3925)

3868 Piedmont
Oakland, Calif. 94611
(415-658-9890)

1619 N. Cherokee
Los Angeles, Calif. 90028
(213-463-0357)

2512 Program Drive
Dallas, Texas 75229
(214-357-6494)

1963

611 L'Immortelle
Films Incorporated ($75)

5589 Peachtree Road
Atlanta, Georgia 30341
(404-451-7445)

161 Massachusetts Ave.
Boston, Mass. 02115
(212-889-7910)

5625 Hollywood Blvd.
Hollywood, Calif. 90028
(213-466-5481)

440 Park Ave. South
New York, New York 10016
(212-889-7910)

Deseret Book Co.
Film Division
60 East South Temple
Salt Lake City, Utah 84110
(801-328-8191)

Knight's Film Library
Marine Division
3911 Normal Avenue
San Diego, Calif. 92103
(714-298-6163)

4420 Oakton Street
Skokie, Illinois 60076
(312-676-1088)

1966

612 Trans-Europ-Express

(1) Kit Parker Films ($65)
Box 227
Carmel Valley, Calif. 93924
(408-659-4131)

(2) Macmillan. Rental C ($60)
For addresses, *see* 610.

(3) United Films ($75)
1425 South Main
Tulsa, Oklahoma 74119
(918-583-2681)

(4) Westcoast Films ($50)
25 Lusk St.
San Francisco, Calif. 94107
(415-362-4700)

1968

613 L'Homme qui ment (The Man Who Lies)
Films Incorporated ($150)

For addresses, *see* 611.

1971

614 L'Eden et après (Eden and After)
Mundial Films (Apply)

856 Devon Avenue
Los Angeles, Calif. 90024
(213-273-9310)

615 N a pris les dés

(no distribution)

1974

616 Glissements progressifs du plaisir (Slow Slide into Pleasure)
Mundial Films (Apply)

856 Devon Avenue
Los Angeles, Calif. 90024
(213-273-9310)

1975

617 Le Jeu avec le feu (Playing with Fire)
International Film Exchange (Apply)

Jerry Rappaport
159 W. 53rd St.
New York, New York
(212-582-4318)

1977

618 Piège à fourrure (Fur Trap)

(no distribution)

Index